THIRD AN

RECOLLEC M

A LIFE

To David

one of the very best

Ram

30 January 2016

THIRD MAN

RECOLLECTIONS FROM A LIFE IN CRICKET

V RAMNARAYAN

w

westland ltd

61, II Floor, Silverline Building, Alapakkam Main Road, Maduravoyal, Chennai 600 095
93, I Floor, Sham Lal Road, Daryaganj, New Delhi 110 002

First published by westland ltd, 2014

ISBN: 978-93-84030-82-7

10 9 8 7 6 5 4 3

Typeset by PrePSol Enterprises Pvt. Ltd.
Printed at Thomson Press (India) Ltd.

To my parents

CONTENTS

FOREWORD

A search for himself

I must admit to being a bit biased in writing about this book. Ramnarayan takes me back to a wonderful world of cricket in Hyderabad; listening to it and reading about it as a child and playing it as a young adult. As I read it, the names sprang from my computer screen and started playing in front of my eyes. Not just the Pataudis, the Jaisimhas and the Abid Alis but so many others who made Hyderabad cricket such a treasure of tales.

He writes of those formidable SBI and SBH teams and the class of Jaisimha's MCC. And names like the many Ramprasads (B, N and H) come alive along with John Tarachand, the friendly B Mahendra Kumar, the wayward genius of Mumtaz Hussain and the frittered talents of Abdul Hai and Sultan Saleem. And Nagesh Hammand, I can see him in front of my eyes, a fine University player I watched more than any other and against whom I had the opportunity to play for Osmania against SBI. And that lovely story of 'Sam' Swaminathan with his acquired English accent. I relate to it easily. In an inter-college game when a difficult pick-and-throw had produced a run out at the bowler's end he turned to me and said, *"Now that.....(pause for accent!) was brilliant."*

I relate too, to the frailties of Hyderabad cricket, as I do to its many charms. And of the many intrigues that occasionally beset it. Ramnarayan tells the stories simply, occasionally with pain but we are one in our affection for the lovely Fateh Maidan.

Ironically I disliked Ramnarayan when he first came over from Chennai. I had no reason to. I hadn't seen him bowl, I had no appreciation of his high quality off-spin. But he took the place of one of our players, Noshir Mehta whose father too had been a fine Hyderabad player and finds mention in the book. Then slowly word spread that he was, in fact, a better bowler and I began warming to him. All this, remember, is the irrationality of a child fan!

He writes with equal, if not greater, feeling about Madras cricket. You always remember the people you played with first with most fondness and though I don't know all the names (Belliappa and Ramesh and Venkataraghavan and VV Kumar were of course known beyond Madras), their stories are worth a read. For this is not only the story of Madras cricket, it is a snapshot of one of the most cricket loving cultures of India. I use the world 'culture' carefully because there is more to cricket than just playing it.

The word sits comfortably on Ramnarayan for not only does he have interests in the arts (quite distinct from the art of off-spin!) but he married well too. His wife Gowri is a familiar by-line and of robust lineage and I know of no other cricketer who, in his later years, became editor of a magazine on the performing arts. I fear that the generation of cricketers who might have managed that path is long gone.

In a world before liberalisation, and where a public sector job was an insurance for life, Ramnarayan was a probationary officer in the State Bank of India. If you do not understand the significance of that in the India he grew up in find someone who will tell you about it. Essentially, all of India applied to be a PO in a nationalised bank. SBI was the icing on the cake. I point this out because there was an era in our cricket when you had to be otherwise qualified because cricket gave you respect and memories but not the wherewithal to run a household. I wonder sometimes if mine is the last generation that even knows of this phase in Indian cricket.

There is another reason this story needs to be told. Indian cricket is rich in stories and dire at story-telling. And with the television induced urge to follow the stars, life just underneath is a tale untold. What chance do characters from club cricket have! But they too are part of Indian cricket, they build the base on which the players and spectators give Indian cricket its power and riches.

The amateur is the true cricket lover for he gives to the game generously. His stories are innocent and there is charm in the small achievements of a man not cut out for bigger things. You will find many of those in this book and if you have time to pause from the incessant coverage of international cricket (and I am part of that story!), spend some time relating these anecdotes to some of your own.

But my favourite part of the book is reserved for the nuggets on off-spin bowling. In an era where the easiest way to impart nip and turn is to bend the elbow, these lines are a beacon in the darkening world of finger spin. His friend and mentor Rajamani tells Ram *"....you whip the ball as if you were spinning a top, the arm comes down fast but the ball travels in a parabolic loop".* There is much discussion on length and the adherence to it amidst variations in flight and pace.

I sense this book, and its acceptance, will bring Ram peace. His life has been a search for himself within a game he adored. Now he has given back to it in a manner few do. Writing it has been time well spent.

Harsha Bhogle

A proper reverence for tradition

In Ramnarayan's essay for Wisden India Almanack on players who were good enough to represent India but didn't, two things struck me. First, he recognised, "We are dealing with cricketers unproven at the highest level no matter how distinguished their record in first class cricket." Sportsmen too can rise to their level of incompetence.

More interesting was his choice of off spinner. He picked Hyderabad's Kanwaljit Singh. Did Ramnarayan think he himself was not good enough? Did he place modesty above cricketing judgement? Or did he assume that it just wasn't cricket to pick himself? Perhaps he went by record (Kanwaljit had 369 wickets to his own 96)?

It intrigued me, and I recalled conversations with the great spinners who were Ramnarayan's contemporaries. Erapalli Prasanna felt that Ramnarayan didn't get enough opportunities. Bishan Bedi considered Ramnarayan an 'intelligent' spinner who made the transition from performer to writer smoothly. Venkatraghavan thought Ramnarayan superior to the Hyderabad off spinners of the time. Some 'alleged' off spinners have played for India, which must make Ramnarayan's disappointment at missing the bus acute. But he can also take some consolation from the fact that it took two of the best – Prasanna and Venkatraghavan - to keep him out of the Indian team.

In an era when cricket was not the paying profession it is now, Ramnarayan switched from Tamil Nadu, where had learnt his game, to Hyderabad where he saw better opportunities. Perhaps it needed not a shift from a state where Venkatraghavan was well established, but to another zone where Ramnarayan might have played more first class matches than the 25 he eventually did after making his debut at 28.

For South Zone were richly served. There was Prasanna himself, Venkatraghavan, V V Kumar, Bhagwat Chandrasekhar, Shivlal Yadav, Narasimha Rao, all of whom played Test cricket, and the likes of Noshir Mehta, Mumtaz Hussain, B Vijaykrishna who might have, in another age and time.

This book, however, is not so much about the frustration of not having played at the highest level as the joy of having played with some of the biggest names in Indian cricket. In Hyderabad there were Tiger Pataudi, M L Jaisimha, Abbas Ali Baig, Abid Ali, Krishnamurti, Jayantilal, Govindraj. A team of stars which, however, never won the Ranji Trophy. It was Ramnarayan's 7 for 68 against Mumbai in a quarterfinal that seemed to open the door. Hyderabad took the first innings lead in the three-day match, but their star-studded batting let them down after Mumbai set them a target of 217.

Ramnarayan describes the match and its aftermath here with a warmth and self-deprecatory touch that is a feature of the writing overall. Perhaps not surprisingly, Ramnarayan wrote on music and cricket with the deep understanding that is given only to those who have the passion and take the trouble to broaden their grasp of the subject with wide reading and endless conversation. Ramnarayan is of the old school, with a proper reverence for the traditions of the game and a gratitude for its many blessings.

Third Man – the almost-Graham Greene title – might suggest that this is the story of cricket as told by an outsider, but while it is Ramnarayan's story, it is equally an insider's look at the game as played at the league and first class level, with vignettes of the characters who lit up the maidans in Chennai, Hyderabad, Kolkata and around the country.

Ramnarayan comes from a cricket-obsessed family. Younger brother Sivaramakrishnan was Tamil Nadu's highest run-getter for a while. An uncle, P N Sundaresan was a cricket writer and Wisden's India correspondent for over two decades. The two strains – player and writer – come together nicely in Third Man, a charming book of what was, with an occasional wistful what-might-have-been thrown in.

Suresh Menon

Bangalore

August 2014

INTRODUCTION

I long postponed this book because I believed no one would be interested in the story of a cricketer who did not play for India. My friends assure me otherwise. Every cricketer has a story to tell, they believe. The stories I tell are, according to them, stories they can relate to, the average cricket lover can enjoy. So here I go.

Until I was 28, it seemed I would never play first class cricket, thanks mainly to the timing of my birth—a few years after that of India's greatest off spinner EAS Prasanna and just two behind his own rival for a spot in the Indian team Venkataraghavan. When Prasanna and Venkat were leading Karnataka and Tamil Nadu respectively, and both already India veterans, I came into the Hyderabad team. While my entry into my native Tamil Nadu side had been blocked by Venkat's presence there, my move to Hyderabad in mid 1971 hadn't helped at all, as off spinner Noshir Mehta was firmly entrenched in the Hyderabad team. Worse, it took me a couple of years to even establish myself as a regular in the strong State Bank of India team, one of the champion sides there. It meant that I could hardly catch the state selectors' eyes until the 1973-74 season.

Just when I was ready to give up all hope of playing first class cricket, I made my Ranji Trophy debut in the 1975-76 season, and straightaway started to perform consistently. Within a year I was selected to represent the Rest of India versus the Ranji Trophy champion Bombay in the Irani Cup, and named as a Test probable to attend the conditioning camp preparatory to India's 1977-78 tour of Australia, the only specialist off spinner other than the two world class spinners Prasanna and Venkataraghavan. No prizes therefore, for guessing the logic behind the title of this book. The one obstacle to my further progress was my inability to break into the South Zone team, whose three-pronged spin attack consisted of Chandrasekhar, Prasanna and Venkataraghavan.

I was sixteen by the time I discovered my talent for off spin, having tried medium pace and leg spin before that. An early fascination with Dattu Phadkar's bowling action had attracted me to pace bowling. I had been reasonably quick and had a natural outswinger even as a kid, but switched to slow bowling following my father's advice. "In India, with the heat and slow wickets, you will burn out very quickly," he warned me, and I was an obedient son. I switched my allegiance from Phadkar to Subhash Gupte and tried to imitate the great leg spinner. I soon discovered that my leg breaks and googlies lacked bite, though I hugely enjoyed fooling batsmen with the variations. First Ghulam Ahmed and later Jim Laker provided the inspiration for me to try my hand at off spin. It was in my final year at school, during the feverish session of cricket during the daily 40-minute lunch break in the school compound, that I realized I could bowl quite a vicious off break, aided considerably by the uneven, hard surface of the school's forecourt, where a couple of hours later the whole school would gather for the daily drill. Though I did make allowances for the undue advantage the so-called pitch at school gave my bowling and the poor quality of batsmanship I encountered there, I felt encouraged to try out my new action and grip in good cricket conditions. Bowling in the nets organized by a friend at Vivekananda College during the following summer, I realized that I was actually on to something good.

More later about all that, and the amazing turnaround in my fortunes in 1975 which almost, but not quite, led to a fairytale ending to my cricket story, but I must confess that during my years in the wilderness, I often thought of writing a book I would call *Autobiography of an Unknown Cricketer* in imitation of the title of Nirad C Chaudhuri's memoirs, because I always immodestly believed I belonged as an off spinner at the highest level—a view some loyal cricket mates shared and nurtured—with a story to tell. (That was indeed the title of the late Sujit Mukherjee's book on cricket in India).

My story would also include in its sweep some of the best cricketers not to have played for India, though its bias would ever so subtly tilt towards the best South Zone cricketers I have had the privilege to partner or oppose on the field of play.

In the evening years of my cricket career, I discovered I had excellent recall of the many experiences and personalities good, bad and mostly funny, which had enriched my days under the sun. That was when some of my friends began to urge me to write those stories for public consumption. The result was a column I called *Curdrice Cricket*, largely a light-hearted tribute to cricket in Tamil Nadu. Mostly about the players and unique flavour of cricket in my home state, but including very little about my own cricket, it later formed an important part of my first book, *Mosquitos and Other Jolly Rovers: The Story of Tamil Nadu Cricket.*

My sojourn in Chennai was only one part of the story of my cricket. The decade I spent in Hyderabad was the more fruitful, rewarding part of my career and I had not touched on it in *Curdrice Cricket* or *Mosquitos*. I moved to Andhra Pradesh in December 1970, joining State Bank of India as a 'probationary officer' and spending most of the first year of my tenure there at rural Anakapalle, before the glorious uncertainties of life took me to Hyderabad and a fresh opportunity to play cricket in July 1971. I was four months short of my 24th birthday.

The struggle to make a mark was long and hard. It took me well nigh two years to even gain a regular place in the bank's star-studded team in the local league and two more to be selected to represent Hyderabad in the Ranji Trophy. What followed was a minor miracle and I was an official Test probable within a year!

ML Jaisimha. Mansur Ali Khan Pataudi. Abbas Ali Baig. Syed Abid Ali. What a constellation of stars!

My peers and I were privileged to rub shoulders with these outstanding cricketers in the Hyderabad line-up of the 1970s. It was perhaps the most glamorous outfit in Indian cricket then, comparable with the Test team. People queued up, at least in the major centres, to buy tickets to watch our team in action. I remember the 30,000 strong crowd that watched Tiger Pataudi score 198 at Chepauk and the cricket mad fans at smaller centres. I remember the train journeys in which the team was closeted together sometimes for longer than 24 hours, and the relaxed atmosphere of those trips. I remember how knowledgeable and wise was our skipper Jai, the most stylish cricketer to walk on our grounds. I remember how dashing and handsome was our Abbas, serious competition to the youngest team member in the department of sex appeal even in his thirties! I remember the brilliant all rounder Abid (who can ever forget him?), my brother, mentor and critic, without whom our dressing room would have been a dull place. I remember Tiger Pataudi, who blended so quietly into the middle class background of our team, even if he was the most charismatic cricketer India ever produced. Noshir, Mumtaz, Nagesh, Sultan Salim, Vijay Paul, Jayantilal, Krishnamurti, Prahalad, Narasimha Rao, Jyoti Prasad, Abdul Hai, a powerhouse of talent welcomed me into the Hyderabad dressing room when I made my Ranji Trophy debut at the ripe old age of 28 in the 1975-76 season.

While I savoured every moment I spent in the exalted company of my illustrious teammates and being recognized as someone with an outside chance of replacing Prasanna or Venkataraghavan in the Indian team, my swift dismissal from all forms of first class cricket five years later left me bewildered, hurt and angry.

For a few years after my inglorious exit, I could not bear to watch cricket—except the street variety, which always stopped me in my tracks, striking an instant chord with childhood memories. Distance, or the passage of time, rather, lends enchantment and I turned to cricket writing once I was sure I could do so without bitterness, and that is how, aided by the devastating effects of a couple of poor career moves I made, I became a freelance journalist around 1994, starting with contributions to the Saturday Sports page of *The Hindu.* The demands from my family and close friends to write my cricket memoirs have continued over the decades—and, thanks to the encouragement I have received from some better known authors—I have finally decided to inflict them on the reading public.

If the foregoing has given the impression of one long sob story, let me correct it. I enjoyed my cricket, recognition or none. Most cricketers will understand me when I say I played cricket because I could not help it, playing the game was its own reward. After more than 40 years in the game and now decades after my last game, I have no regrets, only gratitude that the sheer chance or blessing of some talent for the game made my life so meaningful, so exciting.

BEGINNINGS

CRICKET IN THE AIR

Looking back, it had to be divine intervention—a completely benign arrangement of the stars in my favour—that helped my cricket along, when there was no conscious effort to make a career of it, on the part of my parents or myself. The first time I held a bat was around 1952, in the backyard of our Quilon (now Kollam) home, in the company of my brother Nagan, a left handed, more talented and stylish novitiate into the game at which so many in the family were good. I was barely five and for the next three years, the only cricket action we saw was provided by my father's exploits in the game.

PN Venkatraman, Ramani to his siblings, cousins, and cricket mates, was Appa to us, his children—by then four of us, with the latest addition Krishnan arriving on 13 May 1952. *Appa* had been a stalwart of Mylapore Recreation Club, albeit a reclusive, even reluctant one, mainly because he was a bit of a hypochondriac and feared he would collapse on the cricket field, thanks to an imaginary heart condition a mischievous uncle or elder cousin had led him to believe afflicted him. (When I saw the Adoor Gopalakrishnan film *Anantaram* in the 1980s, a scene in it reminded me of my father's unhappy experiences with elders in the extended family, who casually planted in him fears and anxieties with far reaching consequences, preventing the full flowering of this gentle, shy, unusually talented young lad).

We must have come back to Madras during 1955 or 1956, for I clearly remember listening to the radio commentary in our first floor house on Murrays Gate Road when Jim Laker took 19 for 137 against the Australians at Old Trafford, the second time the off spinner claimed all ten wickets in an innings that season, having performed the feat for Surrey against the visitors. I remember twiddling the knobs of our old Murphy valve radio to find the exact spot where the BBC commentary was at least half way audible. I was not yet ten and went to a Tamil medium school, so, much of the commentary must have gone way above my head, even if I did manage to hear the voices of probably Swanton and Co. amidst all the static. I don't think John Arlott was as yet a member of the team, nor Brian Johnston or Christopher Martin Jenkins. It was much later that I began to recognize these much beloved voices as I did Rex Alston, Norman Yardley and Trevor Bailey. Still, there wasn't a single cricketing point that I—or my teeming army of brothers and cousins—missed. The explanation is simple: we belonged to a completely cricket-crazy extended family.

We lived on Murrays Gate Road, a quiet enough street then, extending east west from Alwarpet Corner to Teynampet, the whole stretch a long straight line from the Santhome Church, via Kutcheri Road and Luz Church Road, almost all the way to Mount Road. 'Suprabha' was our home, a two-storeyed bungalow facing north. We lived on the first floor, my father now the agent of the Mylapore branch of Indian Overseas Bank, and downstairs lived my father's elder brother PN Sundaresan, Raja to family and friends, at the time a struggling reporter in *The Indian Express*, but soon to join *The Hindu.*

Raja was an attacking batsman who opened the innings for Mylapore Recreation Club 'A', one of the top sides in the Madras cricket league, whose clashes with arch rival Triplicane Cricket Club starring MJ Gopalan, CR Rangachari and the like, were known as the War of the Roses. MRC had many of its own stars, with most of Buchi Babu Nayudu's sons, nephews and grandsons turning out for the club at one time or another. The well known diplomat G Parthasarathi or GP, an aggressive leg spinner-batsman, CR Pattabhiraman, son of Sir CP Ramaswami Ayyar and the founder of the club, and opening batsman M Swaminathan were some of the MRC regulars.

My father's uncle PS Ramachandran or 'Pattu', the tall, wiry fast bowler who took 10 for 18 for MRC vs. TCC, was overlooked by the selectors who met the same evening to pick the 'Indians' for that season's Presidency Match. Pattu, like quite a few other cricketers of his time, was an orthodox brahmin, whose hairstyle consisted of a shaven head with a tuft of hair tied in a *kudumi* or chignon at the back. As he ran up to bowl his fast medium seamers, his knotted hair came off and fluttered in the breeze, and he almost instinctively reached for it to tie it back in place even as he was completing his follow through. In group photographs, he is seen wearing a black cap more like a Gandhi *topi* than a cricket cap.

Though he missed out on the Pongal match after that splendid burst in the Roses battle, he managed to impress the selectors enough to be included in a tour game for Madras against the visiting MCC team under the captaincy of Douglas Jardine. Pattu bowled well in both innings, picking up a couple of wickets. He was probably in his late forties when I first heard him describe the cricket he played in his youth. "Jardine said, 'Well bowled!' to me at the end of the match. He even patted me on my back." When Pattu came home that evening, his mother, whose word was law in family circles, must have told him to wash even harder than usual, as he had made physical contact with an outcaste!

Pattu lived and practised law in a gracious old bungalow in a sprawling compound on Eldams Road, parallel to and behind Murrays Gate Road, and his elder brother PS Venkatraman, a building contractor and leading tennis player of his time, was his next door neighbour. Their two houses were named Sundar (after my great grandfather Justice PR Sundara Iyer) and Parvati (after my great grandmother). Pattu's three sons Kalyanam, Dorai and Thambi (Sundaram, Venkatachalam and Viswanathan, to give their official names) took after their father and became more than useful medium pace bowlers, two of them making it to the Ranji

Trophy team and Dorai almost getting there. My uncle Raja's sons Narayanan and Ramachandran were both fine all rounders. While Narayanan played Ranji Trophy cricket, Ramachandran just failed to make it. Add to these five, my brothers Nagan, Krishnan (V Sivaramakrishnan) and yours truly and we needed just three more for a complete eleven, though Kalyanam was far too senior to play with all of us.

Two uncles, UNDP official and founder of *Sruti* magazine N Pattabhi Raman (despite being a polio victim) and PV Sundaram, a leading molecular biologist, were enthusiastic cricketers, both leg spinners. Venkatakrishnan was a cousin twice removed who played competitive cricket in the Chennai first division league. My brother Nagarajan (Nagan), a year younger than me, showed early talent as a left handed batsman, but gave up cricket once he joined IIT Madras and later migrated to the United States. All of us played for Mylapore Recreation Club at one time or another.

FIRST STEPS

Unlike most kids of my generation, I did not graduate from tennis ball cricket to playing with the real stuff—the hard cricket ball—perhaps because I belonged to a family of cricketers who would have considered the softer option infra dig. It helped that the family had a club competing in the Madras league and therefore enjoyed a constant supply of used cricket balls for the boys.

At home, we had plenty of open space, with no compound wall separating the two houses *Sundar* and *Parvati* on Eldams Road and *Suprabha* on Murrays Gate Road. We energetic youngsters were constantly running from one house to another and playing a whole range of outdoor games, in which the girl children of the family were also included—in all the games except cricket. And as if all this were not enough to spoil us silly by way of sporting facilities, bang opposite *Suprabha* was a vast open field where we played the more organised cricket everyday after school. The Ground, as we called it, is untraceable today, as it has been completely built over—a residential area called *Venus Colony*.

Narayanan was the most talented all round sportsman of the family, if a bit laid back. Everything he did, he did with style. It came naturally to him. He was of medium height, very slightly built, supple and agile. He was a smart ball game player who used the angles to advantage whatever game he played. In cricket, he was all wrists and timing, a very good eye and quick reflexes. I do not remember his exploits as a schoolboy cricketer. In fact, not until he completed his undergraduate studies from Vivekananda College and joined the Madras Law College did he blossom into a consistent opening batsman and an off spinner with an uncanny ability to break partnerships. In the 1960s, he became a mainstay of *Jolly Rovers*, the team that dominated Madras cricket for the next four decades, sometimes outperforming his more glamorous teammates, and often giving the side a scintillating start, matching his partner KR Rajagopal stroke for stroke. Those who watched Raja in his prime would know what a huge compliment that is. The wicket keeper batsman narrowly missed selection to the Indian team that toured Australia in 1968.

At the school level, it was Narayanan's younger brother Raman (PS Ramachandran) who came into prominence in representative cricket. He bowled vicious leg breaks and played attacking shots from the word go as an opening batsman. Of the three fast bowling brothers who were my father's cousins, Kalyanam or PR Sundaram (by now the reader would have guessed that each of us has two names) was a genuine quickie, who should surely have played more matches at the first class level than the solitary Ranji Trophy appearance he was allowed to make. His two brothers were good bowlers too, and all three were rated highly by the West Indies fast bowler Roy Gilchrist when he coached Madras's promising young pace bowlers handpicked by the selectors in the 1960s.

My brother Nagan was a stylish left-handed batsman who later played for Vivekananda College and IIT Madras. He never fulfilled his early promise, because he simply did not have the patience or temperament to build innings and he chose to focus more on academics than cricket. Capable of attacking any bowling successfully, he was on his day a delight to watch. My youngest brother Sivaramakrishnan, Krishnan to all of us at home, was the opposite of Nagan in terms of temperament. Five years younger than me, he was a thorn in the flesh from the time we let him join us older brothers and cousins, showing an annoying tendency to score double hundreds even at the age of ten. He went on to score more than 5,000 first class runs, coming close to selection as India's opener during the Gavaskar-Chauhan era.

The family team across generations would read like this:

1. PN Sundaresan
2. PS Narayanan
3. PS Ramachandran jr.
4. V Nagarajan
5. V Sivaramakrishnan
6. V Ramnarayan
7. PS Ramachandran sr.
8. PN Venkatraman
9. PR Sundaram

10. PR Venkatachalam
11. PR Viswanathan
12. GR Venkatakrishnan
13. N Pattabhi Raman
14. PV Sundaram

The team of 14 is somewhat overloaded with bowlers, especially medium pacers (seven in all).

Only those who lived on Murrays Gate Road or Eldams Road qualified for selection. Other cousins and uncles who played serious cricket included PB Venkatraman *(Mambalam Mosquitos)*, PS Ashok (MRC) and G Balachandran (Tirunelveli District). Ashok was a useful medium pacer who was overshadowed by the PR brothers.

All of us honed our cricket skills on the Venus Colony ground in the 1950s and 1960s. We were barefoot cricketers who wore no protective equipment, sometimes played on uneven, even dangerous wickets and always used a cricket ball and not a tennis ball. I am convinced that some of us would have been better batsmen had we played on good wickets during our formative years with a semblance of protection.

Much later in life, we had a few more additions to the cricketers' list of my family: my sister Sarada's husband S Nataraj, a brilliant all-rounder who played for Karnataka and Tamil Nadu without quite fulfilling his potential, his sons Naveen and Harish, again very talented cricketers who sought careers abroad far removed from cricket after their father's untimely death at 48, and my brother Sivaramakrishnan's son Vidyut, an all-rounder who started as a left-arm spinner, and actually scored a Ranji Trophy hundred batting at no.11. Vidyut promised greater things in first class cricket before selectorial indifference and resultant loss of confidence cut short his ascent.

My most vivid memory of the Ground is of being hit on the forehead fielding at short leg ridiculously close to the batsman who pulled a short ball from my leg spinner cousin Raman, and the world around me going black. Once I came to, I was reluctant to miss the action that followed, but my mother who had been watching from home dragged me away, bleeding and concussed. Another time, I got a tooth knocked out while bending to stop a powerful drive when the ball got deflected by a pebble. These two incidents probably decided my batting technique in the years to come, with my forward strokes characterised by an unconscious reluctance to smell the ball. And though I could stoutly defend and occasionally play some authentic drives, my discovery around age 16 that I could spin a cricket ball rather well made bowling a much more attractive proposition than batting.

I batted well enough in inter-collegiate cricket to earn selection into the university and under-25 teams as an all rounder. Unfortunately, I only flattered to deceive as a batsman at that level, but the real decline in my batting began when I became a member of strong batting line-ups at Hyderabad and was rarely called on to contribute with the bat. In first class cricket, my batting record easily rivalled BS Chandrasekhar's.

SCHOOL CRICKET COACHES

Organised cricket began for me when no doubt owing to my cousin Raman's clout, I was inducted into the junior team of PS High School, Mylapore, a formidable combination of State Schools level cricketers and other representatives of the finest Mylapore talent of the day. Before we were picked for the school team, of course, we had to prove our mettle in inter-class competition. First Form 'D' to which I belonged was captained by R Prabhakar, later to become a bit of a legend in Madras cricket, thanks to his ability to hit the ball long, hard and frequently and his six-hitting prowess. From First Form 'B' was PK Venkatachalam, Babu to close friends, a talented medium-pacer all rounder, who appeared even at that early age to be Test cricket material on the evidence of his technique, elegance and temperament. Cousin Raman was already a star of the school's senior team, which boasted the likes of SVS Mani and S Veeraraghavan, elder brother of Venkataraghavan.

Venkat was still in PS Secondary School off Kutcheri Road, to move to PS High only next year. Other sensational PS High school cricketers of the time included 'Suspense' Srinivasan, a medium pacer whose windmill action kept the batsman guessing, hence the prefix to his name, gentle Kadir or A Srinivasan, an elegant batsman, Kaattu Govindan, a brilliant fielder, NA 'Kulla' Sivaraman, wicketkeeper and wit who kept us all in splits with his jokes and mimicry, and Sashikant—later famously known as Seth—a medium pacer who decades later took all ten wickets in a league match innings bowling off breaks.

Our physical director Ganesamurthy and his assistant Mohanakrishnan watched me and 'Babu' PK Venkatachalam with amused tolerance, calling us 'tiffin players' much to our discomfiture. We were the babies of the team, and never really stood a chance of making it to the playing eleven in inter-school matches, on account of our extreme youth, ten or eleven at the most, while our seniors were already teenagers. We made our presence felt only at lunch or tiffin time, tucking in enthusiastically without having worked for it by way of chasing balls on the ground.

Babu was one of the most gifted young cricketers of my time, tall, strapping and athletic. He bowled sharp medium pace and batted in an erect, free-stroking style with a penchant for the cover drive and punched backfoot on-drive. At school, he was way more successful than the rest of us, though another natural, R Prabhakar, was an exciting talent not yet fully revealed. Babu unfortunately fell into bad company and drifted into alcoholism and worse. He never did fulfil his great promise and died in the prime of his life. Prabhakar went on to represent the state in the Ranji Trophy in which he played some brilliant innings and bowled well on occasion without quite reaching the heights he was believed capable of by his legion of admirers. He has a fan club that still believes he never received the breaks he deserved. On my part, I went unnoticed at the school level, especially as my father's job took us from city to town to city, and schools without too many sporting facilities.

The bright spot of my school years at Chennai was my school sending me to attend coaching camps at the Madras Cricket Association's BS Nets. I was lucky enough to come under the benevolent gaze of AG Ram Singh and TS Worthington, two wonderful coaches. Both knew when to coach and when to leave well alone. KS Kannan, who assisted them, was another marvellous coach with great empathy for the diffident among the boys.

Before and after Ram Singh

The hiring of foreign coaches by India and other cricket playing countries has been the subject of much debate in the last decade or so, but English and other coaches from abroad have done duty in India, South Africa, New Zealand and West Indies at the first class and other levels of domestic cricket for well over fifty years.

Albert Frederick Wensley (1898-1970), a veteran Sussex all-rounder, was among the earliest to coach in India, after he came to assist Nawanagar in the Ranji Trophy in the 1936-37 season. He played a stellar role in Nawanagar's title triumph that season, with eight wickets in the final against Bengal. He also played an equally crucial role scoring 67 in the second innings of the final against Hyderabad next year, which Nawanagar lost by one wicket, with Hyderabad succeeding in a thrilling 310-run chase. Amar Singh and Vinoo Mankad were among his Nawanagar teammates in what were perhaps the sunrise years of professional cricket in India.

Organised coaching in Madras was first arranged in the BS Nets, a facility the Madras Cricket Association established in 1944 in memory of B Subramaniam (BS), Buchi Babu's faithful lieutenant. The much loved 'Pattu', V. Pattabhiraman, and the respected cricket writer SK Gurunathan were the two-member committee entrusted with the task.

Very soon, BS Nets, which opened at the northeastern corner of Chepauk, and later expanded to include such branches as the Bhat Nets at MUC, became the hub of official coaching activity in the city. Wensley was imported by the Madras Cricket Association largely through the efforts of Pattu, and he was instrumental in the development along proper lines of many a promising Madras cricketer.

Wensley made quite a few trips to Madras, even into the 1950s, when many young cricketers enjoyed his benevolent guidance.

A direct beneficiary of Wensley's coaching skills was AG Ram Singh, who, first assisted him and, in time, became a much-respected coach himself. In turn, Ram Singh was assisted by such devoted coaches as KS Kannan and NJ Venkatesan, who served Tamil Nadu cricket very well for years.

Another veteran coach to distinguish himself was SE Audhi Chetty, while the much younger PK Dharmalingam was a fixture in official TNCA coaching efforts for many years. Dharma, in addition to coaching State teams at various levels, also had the distinction of assisting in coaching camps for the Indian team, besides being a pioneer in coaching women cricketers.

To go back to 'MCA' days, the BCCI-constituted Raj Kumari Amrit Kaur scheme enabled the association to avail itself of the services of many coaches under the scheme. Some of them were Ram Singh, Hemu Adhikari, CK Nayudu, and M Rehmat Baig. There were a few English coaches as well, coming to India during their winter to run short camps. Frank Tyson, Eddie Paynter and Mike Goodwin were some of the more prominent imports. Goodwin and TS Worthington coached in Madras.

An unforgettable foreign coach was the West Indies fast bowler Roy Gilchrist who was in Madras in the 1960s under a special dispensation of the Board, coaching our young fast bowling prospects and also playing for South Zone in the Duleep Trophy. Known for his unorthodox, even eccentric ways, Gilchrist was a tough taskmaster, and sure enough some of the fast bowlers in his camp started playing truant after the first few days of his camp. Some of us were witness to the spectacular sight of Gilchrist (who was watching a cricket match at the Government Arts College) chasing a recalcitrant young paceman on Mount Road when he caught him trying to slip away.

Syed Mushtaq Ali, the most exciting Indian batsman of the pre-War era, Ramnath Kenny and Joe Kamath were some of the coaches from other States to do duty in Tamil Nadu.

The MRF Pace Foundation was started by the tyre major MRF Limited two decades ago. The Foundation's coaching programme to unearth and train fast bowlers was spearheaded by Australian fast bowling guru Dennis Lillee, assisted by Tamil Nadu and India fast bowler TA Sekar. Today, Glen McGrath and M Senthilnathan have taken Lillee's and Sekar's places.

Another premier coaching establishment of Madras has been the MAC Foundation's Spin Academy, supported by the AC Muthiah-led MAC group of companies. The first spin bowler of calibre to head the academy was VV Kumar.

BOTTOM OF THE LEAGUE

"Do you remember who got dropped by the MRC 'B' captain in a league match back in the sixties after his team entered the field and a quick headcount revealed twelve on the ground?" the young man asked me. Though taken aback by these opening remarks of the bridegroom at a wedding I attended at Coimbatore, even as I greeted him, I knew the answer in no uncertain terms. "It was me," I informed Krishna, but he was not so sure, so he asked his father, N Murali, who bowled left-arm medium pace for the club after I left it. "It was either your brother Sivaramakrishnan or 'Vaalberi'," he confidently asserted, referring to Thyagarajan of that unfortunate nickname.

I maintained my stand and confronted 'Bobjee' Rangaswami—who had led the side in 1962 and pointed the offending finger that signalled my exit from Teachers College 'B'. Bobjee smiled vaguely but seemed to have no recollection of the episode. Soon enough, in came Vaalberi, who too stoutly denied being given the marching orders after entering the ground all those years ago, but admitted to carrying a grudge still about being unfairly excluded on some other occasions, mainly on account of a rival's superior resources that enabled him to foot the lunch bill at matches.

Murali was still not convinced I had been the victim of Bobjee's belated success at counting up to twelve, so two days later, he asked my brother at the reception held at Chennai, if it had been he who had suffered the indignity of being found supernumerary at such a late hour. Sivaramakrishnan assured him that he had never played for MRC 'B' and that the child prodigy he had in mind had indeed been his brilliant and deserving elder brother.

Murali should not have bothered to ask so many people, because I could never be wrong about an incident that had had me close to tears. Ask any fifteen year old who has been dropped from the eleven—before or after the toss—and he will tell you that he is not likely to forget the experience in a hurry. To be dropped after actually crossing the ropes to take the field was much worse than my friend Balu's experience of being run out first ball of the match off a ricochet from the bowler's hand, after he had sat up all night brushing up on Don Bradman's coaching tips for batsmen.

Though that first year in league cricket was forgettable in terms of personal achievement, the lunches courtesy *The Hindu* family were excellent, and I learnt to swear like a Madras rickshaw wallah from the good doctor Bala who opened our innings.

My second season was memorable. Playing for Jai Hind CC under the adventurous captaincy of the inimitable S Raman, I blossomed as an off spinner. He had complete faith in my bowling ability and gave me some superbly attacking fields. He was our best—and often only—batsman, and my bowling efforts were wasted as my team invariably crashed to two-digit totals, losing ten matches and barely managing to draw one.

Years later, Raman—a good TT player in his youth like his younger brothers Lakshmanan and Bharathan, and a *vaastu* expert in his senior years—stopped me at a petrol station and extolled my bowling virtues, much to my embarrassment, moved as I was by his warmth and generosity. "You are good enough to play for India; next time I meet Venkataraghavan, I'll ask him why you could not play alongside him for the state, so that the national selectors might consider you," he threatened. This was at the end of my career, but Raman felt I was still fit enough to bowl off spin for Tamil Nadu and India!

My embarrassment that morning was nothing compared to what I was to experience soon afterwards. He accosted Venkat and me at the *upanayanam* ceremony of a young cricketer, and actually proceeded to ask him why he had done nothing to promote my cricket career. He gave him a detailed account of my many sterling qualities of head and heart, and described the glory of my flight and the viciousness of my spin in such glowing terms that a passerby would have been pardoned for mistaking the object of his admiration to be Jim Laker or Erapalli Prasanna.

THE DON OF MADRAS CRICKET

My idyll with Jai Hind CC was too good to last, though it was courtesy my success with that club that I was selected to tour Bombay with the Colts. Jai Hind at the time was run by 'Don' Rangan, whose first eleven in the league was Nungambakkam Sports Club 'A', to which I was promoted the next season, while Jai Hind was relegated to a lower division.

Don Rangan was an imposing personality in the 1960s, when he ran NSC 'A'. He was monarch of all he surveyed at the Pithapuram ground at Nandanam, Madras, which he leased and maintained single-handedly, no doubt running through his family's finances in the process. He ran a sports-goods business as well, which meant that his club always owed his firm substantial sums of money! In his heyday, he lived in style, dressed smartly, drove a Volkswagen Beetle, and offered net practice facilities round the year, insisting on his players attending these sessions without fail. The number of new cricket balls he made available at practice would be considered extravagant by any standards.

All this helped create a larger than life image of Rangan, and he took full advantage of that while putting the fear of God into his boys and demanding great performances from them. And he miraculously got the best out of them match after match. The Rangan influence over a whole bunch of young cricketers of the period was quite considerable. For years and years, they would rise to his defence against his numerous critics.

D Ranganathan—for that was his full name—was a cocky little fellow, all muscle and sinew, very fit, a fiercely competitive cricketer quite unlike the gentle Madras stereotype of his time. A competent, workmanlike but always positive opening batsman, he was aggression personified as a wicket keeper, not afraid to stand up to fast bowlers, and capable of the most convincing histrionics while appealing to the umpire. He was also a more than useful medium pacer, a facet of his cricket he never let us forget, resorting as he invariably did to the discarding in mid-innings of his gloves and pads to have a go at the batsman. His supreme confidence usually resulted in the breaking up of a troublesome partnership, enabling Rangan to crow over his success where others had failed. He always had a chip on his shoulder about being ignored as a player by officialdom; and running his own club like a prince was his way of challenging the establishment. He not only scored tons of runs and won most of his matches, but also made sure these victories were made possible by stellar contributions from other players the official selectors had overlooked. He was an original, not an imitation of some Test cricketer he admired. If there was anyone he hero-worshipped, it had to be Rangan himself. Virtually unbeatable in the lower divisions of the TNCA league, his team was a dark horse capable of toppling the best in the senior division, once it was promoted to that level of combat.

I played under Rangan's captaincy for exactly one season, at the end of which my uncles hijacked me to Mylapore Recreation Club 'A', the family club, brainwashing me into believing Rangan was a bad influence on me. At any rate I was not ready, according to them, for the first division, where NSC 'A' was now. The season I did spend with NSC had been an exciting phase in my cricket, with some of the best practice facilities in Madras at my disposal at our superb home ground with a pacy matting wicket and a lightning fast outfield. If Rangan's captaincy was eccentric, imaginative and defiant of convention and reputations, his loyal band of talented players were equally iconoclastic, partly out of fear and respect for Rangan, but also acquiring by osmosis the skipper's in-the-face contempt for the opposition.

Rangan loved a fight and made it a point to get under the skin of opposing players. He taunted and teased them before, during and after matches. The bigger the reputation of the visitors to Pithapuram, the more hostile was the reception. He was notorious for his gamesmanship and his strenuous efforts to win at any cost. He was even credited with cheating at the toss, picking the coin up and announcing, 'We bat,' before the rival captain saw which way it fell.

We played matches every Saturday and Sunday, including so-called friendlies in the absence of official fixtures. On these occasions, Rangan enjoyed inviting strong opposition and defeating them with his young team. One such practice match was against the star-studded Jolly Rovers, who among others included Salim Durrani and S Venkataraghavan. The visitors ended our giant killing spree but not before we had put up a bit of a fight. Batting first, we were bundled out for 99, with Durrani, Venkat and the medium pacers doing the damage on a lively wicket. Going in at number 9, I made an unbeaten 15 or so, inspired by the occasion to defy Jolly Rovers' top class spin attack. I was raring to go when it was our turn to field, wanting to do well against the stars, in particular, Salim Durrani, whom a largish crowd had come to watch. Our medium pacer KV Mahadevan, 'Maka' to all of us, was in full flow and brought on early, I too, was all charged up, desperately wanting Durrani's wicket. (I was barely 18 then and Rangan revelled in throwing his young ones in at the deep end, and cocking a snook at established reputations. My growth as an off spin bowler was accelerated by the supreme confidence Rangan showed in my ability).

Soon Jolly Rovers were some 40 for 4, Maka and I sharing the spoils equally. Durrani and Venkat came together and Rangan gave me an extraordinarily attacking field, with close catchers breathing down the batsmen's necks. The wicket assisted Maka as well as me, and we were both transported to another, exalted zone by the excitement of the moment. We gave the batsmen hell and they had to bat out of their skins to survive, but survive they did, until they won the game without further loss—thanks to their skill, determination and experience, not to mention some dropped catches. At the end of the match, Durrani, offered to coach me at the nets the Jolly Rovers captain S Rangarajan had organized at Farm House, *The Hindu's* family estate. I was mighty thrilled by the offer, but being the idiot I was, did not follow up, succumbing to my uncles' advice—the same uncles who would remove me from NSC 'A' at the end of the season.

That was NSC's and Rangan's golden age. Even people who did not like him—and there were many such people, thanks to Rangan's constant aggression on and off the field—admired and respected him for the enormous contribution he made to the development of the game in the city. Almost every league, state and national cricketer of Madras came to practise at the Pithapuram nets and play in the hundreds of games he organized there. Rangan met the needs of a whole generation of cricketers better than formal institutions.

Unfortunately, Rangan's fortunes nosedived in the 1970s and steadily grew worse through the decades. As professionalism crept into cricket, it was no longer possible for individuals or clubs not sponsored by corporates to continue to support the game. Rangan who had been a non-smoker, teetotaller and an awe-inspiring figure for his wards, started adopting a more laidback lifestyle, eventually running into financial difficulties. Used to lording it over the many people whose cricket he touched, he proved incapable of holding a steady job into his forties and later. Nobody took his stories of the past and his grandiose plans for the future seriously, though nothing could stop him from weaving those tales. Young cricketers could not see why the old timers still humoured him, but any cricketer who came across Rangan in his prime was prepared to forgive him a great deal. He died a lonely man in his seventies.

COLLEGE AND THE BIG LEAGUE

I share one distinction with former India captain S Venkataraghavan. We were both found not good enough to bowl off spin for Vivekananda College. He and I both did our Pre-University course there before he moved on to Engineering College, Guindy and I to Presidency College. He was two years my senior in college. I did not even make it to Viveka's 15-member squad. The same physical director, Mr. TV Venkataraman, an eccentric but dedicated man who served the college with distinction for decades, declared us both unfit for the job—in my case, with a categorical No. I was of course disappointed, but had the philosophical detachment even then to move on. Ram Ramesh, a tall, lanky opening batsman who simply murdered college attacks, captained the Vivekananda team, scoring hundreds at will.

During the summer vacation before that academic year, I had been among many young cricketers in the Mylapore-Alwarpet belt who practised in the nets Ramesh had organised on the college ground. He had been very encouraging, impressed with the turn and bounce I was getting on the matting wicket with the new action and grip I had discovered at Vidya Mandir in my final year at school. When it came to the selection of the college team, Ramesh must have been vetoed by the PD, and my inexperience held against me. Also, joining Viveka that year was K Ganapathi, a reputed opening batsman-off spinner from Coimbatore, and that might have ensured my omission. Ganapathi, left-handed opener Ramji and Ramesh were the prolific scorers of the season, with 'Ganpa' getting a few wickets too, with his impressive flight and control. Soon, my exclusion was forgotten if it was at all an issue to begin with.

Ramesh was a cousin's cousin who died in the prime of his life more than a decade ago, collapsing at home after a round of golf with Sir Garry Sobers on a Chennai visit. The summer vacation had brought us close together, though I was still a shy 16 going on 17, to whom net practice was the major event of the day, after sleepy afternoons listening to Vividh Bharati's Hindi film music programmes. Ramesh was very much the elder statesman at the ripe old age of 20 or 21, in the second and final year of his MA Philosophy, most of which he spent under the large neem tree near the college gate regaling his crowd of admirers. My better known cricketing cousins were also regulars at the nets, as was 'Alley' Sridhar, a left handed batsman and leg spinner who lived in nearby Royapettah. I didn't know it then, but Ramesh and Alley were to soon play a crucial role in my cricket career; in fact, there would have been no cricket career for me but for their intervention.

I did reasonably well academically, obtaining a first class in the PUC exams. I had above average grades without scoring a distinction in any of the subjects. This proved beneficial in the long run as my grades in Natural Science though very good were not good enough to get me into medical college. I would have probably made a lousy doctor and would have had to say goodbye to serious cricket. I joined Presidency College, the only college to offer a BSc Chemistry combination with botany as one of the ancillary subjects, in order to keep alive my chances of finding admission in medical college later. It turned out a good decision in unexpected ways—one of them my selection to the college cricket team, something that might have been more difficult in a college with a stronger team.

I nearly did not get selected to play for Presidency, for the simple reason that I nearly did not attend the selection trials. It was my friend from the summer nets, Alley Sridhar, now my collegemate, who forced me to take part. I had not taken my cricket gear to college the day of the trials, and lived too far for me to rush home and bring it in time for the selection. Alley went to his Royapettah residence and brought me a set of whites and a pair of keds and virtually pushed me into the cricket ground, despite my protests that after my Vivekananda experience I no longer fancied my chances of getting into any college team.

It was a conspiracy of sorts. Ram Ramesh, a close friend of VV Rajamani, a charismatic cricketer and *de facto* Presidency captain—U Bhaskar Rao was the official nominee—was there at the nets to ensure along with Alley and Rajamani that I was selected. But for this miraculous piece of luck and generosity of heart of my friends, I would probably never have played any competitive cricket.

To my pleasant surprise, not only was I picked in the college squad of some 15 cricketers, I was also straightaway inducted into the playing eleven, and very soon treated as one of the main bowlers of the team. If I am not mistaken, the first match we played in the Pennycuick league was against lowly placed Government Arts College, captained by S Gopal Rao, one of at least two brothers prominent in Madras's league and college cricket in the 1960s. His elder brother S Venkat Rao was already out of college, while a third brother, S Satyadev, was to play a crucial role in guiding my cricket fortunes years later. Gopal Rao was an all rounder, who batted in the middle order and bowled military medium pace. I don't remember doing anything of note as a spinner in the match, but I was involved in a last wicket partnership of some length of time if not runs, with my spin bowling partner PS Ramesh, whom the description pencil-thin fit like a glove, to mix a few metaphors. We both stuck around for some 30 minutes or so before I was adjudged leg before off Gopal Rao's bowling—for the only time in my life without the ball striking any part of my body. The umpire must have grown tired of our obdurate but boringly defensive batting. I think Ramesh had a decent match as a bowler, the main damage being done by medium pacer Rajamani.

Ramesh was one of the more interesting spinners around, very similar to Ajantha Mendis of Sri

Lanka, but more perhaps like Sunil Narine of the West Indies. He gripped the ball between his index and middle fingers and turned it just a teeny-weeny bit either way, keeping the batsman guessing. Very accurate and persistent, he proved quite a handful for college batsmen, though he never managed to impress the selectors at the university level. He had a nice film actor's hairstyle with his frontal hair rising in an impressive 'puff' and the rest of it neatly slicked back with Brylcreem. He liked to dress well and was quite the matinee idol of the team. His batting was useful at no.11 and his running in the field dignified and measured if not downright slow. His throws from the deep were something our teammate Suri liked to describe as well flighted.

It was in the Presidency College nets that I really learnt the craft of off-spin bowling. There was a very pleasant atmosphere in the side, with no unhealthy competition marring it. It was quite a strong combination, with the inclusion that year of a number of good cricketers who had known success in other colleges. Rajamani took a keen interest in my bowling and often watched me bowl from behind the nets to be able to shout out an occasional piece of advice. One evening, as I was concentrating on giving the ball air, he cried out, "Faster." When I pushed a few down quicker, he said, "No, I didn't mean the ball, I meant the arm. Bring it down quicker and spin the ball hard in the same trajectory." I understood what he was saying, as I already knew that the faster I brought my arm down, the harder I could tweak the ball, get more spin and loop out of it, always keeping the batsman guessing as to where it would land length-wise. I just needed a reminder and Rajamani gave it to me. It was he who decided I should be the college's strike bowler.

By the time our league fixture against Vivekananda College came round, I was well settled in the team and a confident bowler. Vivekananda opened confidently through Ganapathi and Ramji, but Ramesh and I, brought on early, troubled all the batsmen, and dismissed Vivekananda for 121. (Ramji still remembers being clean bowled the first ball he faced me). Ramesh took six wickets and I four, though I bowled at least as well as he did. Because of my sharp spin and the extra bounce that my high arm action caused on the matting surface, many a catch went a-begging, with the wicketkeeper and close-in fielders not quite equal to the task of holding on to those blinders. To rub salt into the wound, those missed chances often sped away to the boundary.

We seemed to be cruising to victory when it was our turn to bat, but a spectacular running catch by KG Appaji near the midwicket boundary, with the ball swirling in the strong sea breeze, ended a brisk little innings by Rajamani in the middle order, and soon panic set in against the accurate off-spin of Ganapathi and sharp left-arm spin of tall Ashok Dave. We lost the match by one run.

At the end of the match, Mr Venkataraman, the Vivekananda PD, sought me out and said: "You bowled very well. I owe you an apology for misjudging your talent last year." It was an unexpected gesture.

That year, N Ram, an opening batsman and wicket keeper, who had a good record in college cricket turning out for Loyola College, with his big hitting and smart work behind the stumps, joined Presidency to do his masters in history. He eventually went to journalism school at Columbia University in the USA, before returning to India to join *The Hindu*, of which his father G Narasimhan was then the editor.

Alley Sridhar had moved from New College. He was an aggressive left-hand batsman without the usual grace we associate with southpaws. He was also a more than useful fastish leg break and googly bowler, besides being a good, if eccentric fielder, who would think nothing of running from mid-off to mid-on to stop a ball or attempt a catch.

Over the next couple of seasons, a number of competitive cricketers migrated to Presidency from other colleges, making us one of the better teams in the city. JS Gupta, perhaps in his mid-twenties, must have joined Presidency just for the love of cricket, because in his restaurant business (Ratna Café, Shanti Vihar) I don't think he needed an additional degree, nor did he ever attend any of his classes. He was a useful opening batsman who among other things had developed a little dinky chip over slip's head.

Gentle, ever smiling R Premkumar was another excellent addition in the batting department. He could always be relied on to score 40 to 50 runs in an unhurried fashion. He later became an IAS officer and moved to Maharashtra.

SV Suryanarayanan was more than a bits and pieces cricketer, though neither his bowling nor his batting was of the exciting type. He swung the ball at medium pace and nudged it around to good effect at no.4. He was a confident cricketer of great self-belief and a successful motivator of his teammates, with his mischievous humour and tendency to burst into song without provocation. He spoke a particularly plebeian kind of Tamil, rather unusual in a man of his social class, and addressed everyone as *Vadyare*, a typically working class usage that literally meant 'Teacher', somewhat in the manner of 'Boss' in English.

John Alexander was the character of the team. Stockily built, he batted with excellent technique and steely determination. Never one to run away from a good fight, he was at his best against the strongest opposition, particularly against Engineering College, the reigning champions. Of Ken Barrington and David Steele, it was said that the Union Jack fluttered in the breeze in front of them when they went into bat. When John crossed the boundary line, it was easy to imagine the Presidency College flag proudly preceding him. He would have scored many more runs than he actually did, if only he would play more attacking shots. Like Vijay Manjrekar, the great Indian batsman of the 1950s and 60s, on whose batting I suspect John modelled his, he curbed his strokeplay in the interests of the team. Though he reserved his best for our matches against the senior Engineering team, he played his most memorable innings against Engineering 'B', the college's second eleven, when he scored an unbeaten half-century and won the match for our college in the company of No.11 SP Balachandran, adding more than 50 for the last wicket. The duo returned to the pavilion to thunderous applause from all of us players and the small crowd that had stopped to watch the thrilling finale. John and Bala often recalled with great pride long afterwards that Venkataraghavan, the captain of the senior Engineering team, and already a Test cricketer, who happened to be watching, shook their hands at the end of the match.

Balachandran, 'Bala' to all of us, was a superb athlete, on the tall side and wirily built. He bowled a very decent pace with a rather square-chested action off a smooth run-up in which he accelerated nicely and jumped at the right time to generate pace and bounce. His action was sometimes questioned, though I always believed it was clean. Bala was the most dapper, well-dressed member of the team, with military manners, always dreaming of joining the army. Sure enough, he was recruited by the army and rose to be a brigadier before he put in his papers prematurely. He played some cricket in the Services where he was converted into an off-spinner, along with the late 'Kuttu' Krishna Rao or KK, a genuine tearaway in his Chennai days. Bala enjoyed some success as an off spinner, but not as much as KK, who played for Services in the Ranji Trophy. Suri and John (as well as KK) are no more with us.

CS Dayakar, a pugnacious left-handed all-rounder was to join us next season. He had been my classmate at Vivekananda College the previous year, but had missed a year by flunking his Sanskrit paper at the university exams. One of five cricketing brothers—the others were Ekambaram, Kothandaraman, Padmanabhan and Kadiresan—Dayakar was an accurate spinner and obdurate batsman with very aggressive instincts. Even more than Alexander, he was at his best against our strongest opposition and on the biggest occasions. In this he was different from some of our star batsmen who loved easy pickings against weak teams but were dismissed by the big names in the league even before they reached the crease. (I was invariably the sacrificial lamb who opened the innings against good pace attacks, promoted from my normal position at no.9 to no.1 for these special occasions).

Alley, Alexander and Dayakar were our most consistent batsmen over the next couple of years, while the spinners dominated the bowling, with Dayakar and I forming a successful pair. Alley bowled in a Jimmy Adams type of action, all legs and arms—and all aggression. He was not infrequently successful, especially against batsmen not of the highest class. He was also a brilliant fielder and thrower anywhere.

In my mature years, I fancied myself as a reasonable strategist and good leader of men, a view unfortunately not shared by the selectors at any level. Captaincy, however, came very early to me, when I, the vice-captain of the Presidency

College team, had to lead it in the absence of the regular skipper N Ram, who decided to miss the second half of the 1965-66 season in order to focus on his studies. He was in the second year of his MA in History and after achieving distinction in the university examination, he would soon be off to Columbia University for higher studies there. I was very raw and not very assertive when I actually led the side, and my job was made tougher by non-cooperation on the part of at least one senior player. Alley Sridhar obviously resented my elevation—and I don't blame him, as he was my senior in every respect and had actually been my virtual godfather for a while now.

In typical Indian fashion not much was said to me to my face by way of criticism, but plenty apparently was, behind my back, as I soon discovered, when I met Test off-spinner Venkataraghavan at a wedding reception. "I hear you jockeyed to become captain ahead of Alley. I didn't expect it from you," he said in a forbidding tone of disapproval. Extremely upset by this unjust accusation—for I have never canvassed for anything—I did not say anything in my defence. For one thing, I was too stunned to react, and secondly, I believed I did not have to explain my actions or non-actions to anyone, a nonchalance that was to be eroded with advancing years.

One of the high points of my nascent cricket career was my first wicket against the all-conquering Engineering College team, which in my first year of inter-collegiate cricket, starred Venkat and AG Satvinder Singh, one of the finest batting prospects from Madras, and other cricketers of merit like skipper Cherian, N Rajendran, NS Manohar, and the twins S Ramachandran and S Lakshmanan. I clean bowled Satvinder Singh with a faster ball. He was someone I had admired from afar for years. As a schoolboy I had closely followed his exploits via the sports page of *The Hindu* just as I had the fortunes of his elder brothers Kripal and Milkha. Kripal scored a hundred on his Test debut at Hyderabad against New Zealand, while Milkha's performances on the Indian Starlets' tour of Pakistan had been nothing short of spectacular. By waving to me from his scooter on his way to college while I awaited my bus to my college at the Adyar bus stop Satvinder made my day almost every morning.

Unfortunately, after we had dismissed half the Engineering side for about 50, Cherian, with a half century, and Manohar, with a hundred, led a brilliant recovery. Their 250 plus was too stiff a target for us, though Alexander made a fighting half century and I a useful 37 late in the batting order.

Though we were outplayed by Engineering in the Jain College tournament in the final that year, we did not disgrace ourselves. We had a few very creditable wins in the run-up to the final. Though I don't remember the details, I do recall that Ramesh and I did reasonably well in the slow bowling department and Bala with the new ball. Left arm medium pacer Sashi it was, I think, off whose bowling I took a blinder off a hard slash towards third man, running in towards the ball from the boundary, holding the shiny ball chest-high. The memory of this catch has remained with me, as it was something that did me proud at that stage of my career. Most of our batsmen batted consistently until the final, when the occasion seemed to overwhelm them.

I think we lost again to Engineering next year, when N Ram led our side. Again the details elude my memory, except for a single conversation I had with the captain. Coming on first change in one of the games, perhaps the final, I was proving a handful to the batsmen, with my disconcerting turn and bounce on the matting surface, when Ram said, "Is the wicket taking turn?" I was quite puzzled. This was the first time someone had put it to me that the pitch, not I, was doing the turning. I really believed it was all my doing, so I innocently answered in the negative. I was some 19 years old then, and had read in the newspapers and heard through radio commentary about the role of the playing surface in cricket, but it had never occurred to me that such stuff applied to the cricket I was playing—especially on a mat. Imagine today's youngster being so naïve!

It was in my final year of college that we eventually won the Gold Cup, under Alley Sridhar's captaincy. We beat Engineering in the final, a feat we at last achieved, no doubt mainly due to the absence of Venkataraghavan, who had graduated. Still they were a strong team, and we did have to dismiss Satvinder Singh twice in the match. He was out cheaply to me in the first innings, for the third time, if I remember right, and made a fifty or thereabouts in the second. Alley and John were our best batsmen, and I contributed stolidly with the bat, more by way of time spent at the crease than runs scored, in both innings, before I was foxed by Satvinder's donkey drops in the second innings. In a nerve-wracking finish, we narrowly managed to prevail, thanks to a catch Satvinder missed in the closing moments. It must have been a case of nerves, because it was the sort of chance he would have normally snaffled in his sleep.

These few failures against us take nothing away from how good Satvinder was. He was a class act, as he had proved with a magnificent hundred in the Tarapore Trophy in the previous season, when I led Presidency in the second half of the season. I think I troubled him early in the innings, but once he settled down, he played some imperious drives off every bowler, including me, once easily carting me out of the Pachaiyappa's ground for the ball to land on top of a moving bus. At one stage, we had a reasonable chance of restricting Engineering within our first innings score, but with Satvinder in top form, we were fast losing control, when Alley walked up to me and asked to bowl his fast leg breaks. I very stupidly said I did not want to experiment at the stage—which was an entirely wrong assessment of the situation besides being totally tactless. Satvinder took the game away from us. By not exploiting all my resources I really blew any chance I had of overcoming Engineering under my captaincy. I also deeply offended Alley in the process. We had to wait till next year as we saw above, with Alley leading the side, to beat Engineering.

UNIVERSITY TRIALS

For four consecutive seasons, Dayakar and I were among the most successful spinners in the collegiate circuit, certainly the most consistent pair. The university selectors, however, did not seem to think much of us, judging by our lack of success in the selection trials, year after year. In the selection format in vogue then, with trials held over three days, hundreds of us were watched in the elimination round on the first day in the nets, and a more manageable number on the second. On the third and final day some 30 players were made to play a selection match, in which, after a brief look at them, certainties were made to retire in favour of those under trial. After the trial match, the City Colleges team to play Districts Colleges in a two-day match was announced. The University team was selected based on performances in the City vs. Districts match.

In my first two seasons, I, like Dayakar, was ruthlessly eliminated on the first day, with my performances during the season counting for nothing. My omission was understandable, as Test bowler Venkataraghavan was the off spinner in the City Colleges XI, but I don't remember the bowler or all-rounder who kept Dayakar out year after year.

When I entered my final year of college, Venkat had completed his engineering degree and I was almost assured of a place in the City Colleges XI, as I had enjoyed another good season with both bat and ball. An unfortunate development was my poor performance in the half-yearly examinations in college. With the final university examination looming barely months ahead of me, I promised my parents I would give cricket the miss until I prepared well for the exams. This meant that I did not even attend the City College trials.

Ironically, I missed my final exams through illness, which meant I graduated only in September 1967 instead of March 1967. I joined the MA programme in the college only in the 1968-69 academic year. That year, I did not play an active role in the season, but attended the selection trials at the University Union ground on Spurtank Road, Egmore. Though the other selectors continued to be unimpressed by my bowling, chief selector MJ Gopalan, the former India double international, saw merit in it and insisted on my inclusion, I was to learn later.

We played the City vs. Districts match at Salem, a district headquarters town, famous for The Little Flower High School, where we were lodged in a dormitory accommodation. The match was played at the school ground.

Salem was the hometown of RT Parthasarathi, former Ranji Trophy cricketer, Member of Parliament, radio commentator, and chairman that year of the university selection committee. His son Vijayaraghavan was an off spinner who had already played for the university and was now more or less a certainty. I had to do something special to displace him. In fact, it needed an extraordinary performance on my part, as he had been doing well.

The arrangements at the school were rather spartan. It was pleasantly cool, and we enjoyed bathing in the morning in water heated in huge boilers on a coal stove. Breakfast was at a nearby thatched shed cafeteria, with the players receiving a daily allowance of Rs. 7 and having to fend for themselves. Lunch was of course provided at the ground, while we had to pay for breakfast and dinner. The food was ridiculously cheap and hot, hygienic and delicious. The idli-dosai and sambar-chutney at breakfast not only kept hunger away till lunch, but also lifted our spirits before the start of the match.

The match went very well for me. The matting wicket suited my bowling to a T and I really struck mid-season form, troubling all the batsmen and taking five wickets for less than fifty runs. When it was our turn to bat, I scored a brisk 39 not out, striking the ball so well that my delighted captain Vikram Thambuswami—expected to lead the university team—told me he expected a hundred from me on the morrow. "That will ensure a place in the university eleven for you. You are in such good form I expect you to go on to play for South Zone Universities."

I disappointed Vikram by getting out for 47 next morning, but it was generally agreed that I had done enough to merit inclusion in the playing eleven of the university team.

Unfortunately that was not to be. Vijayaraghavan, not I, was picked in the side that played Osmania University at the Marina ground next week. From the reserve bench, I watched Osmania beat us by a huge margin. As it was a knockout tournament, it was the end of the road for me. I had to wait one more season. And if my memory serves me right, Dayakar did not figure in the playing eleven at Salem.

In an interesting interlude, I discontinued my studies, as I had to go to Calcutta to look after my ailing father. While there, I got to play for Rajasthan Club—as VR Narayanan, I think, as the rules would not allow me to play in two states—in the local league. Playing under the captaincy of the completely unpredictable, eccentric Swaranjit Singh, it was a roller-coaster ride of a half season, but I loved it.

Swaranjit Singh, a Cambridge Blue, was a left-handed all rounder—a swing bowler and powerful batsman—who once incurred the wrath of the West Indies fast bowler Roy Gilchrist by hitting him for a boundary and asking him, “How did you like that one? A beauty, wasn’t it?” The sardar had already been beamed at by Gilchrist, and this was rather foolhardy of him, as he was soon to realise, as the next of the beamers de-turbanned him. To the West Indies skipper Gerry Alexander, a Cambridge mate of Swaranjit Singh, this was the last straw, as Gilchrist’s wild behaviour on the tour had already created great problems for him. Gilchrist was sent back home and never played for the West Indies again.

I had my father to thank for my joining Rajasthan Club, as he spoke to AR Sridhar, a former Madras state player who was now working for Parry Calcutta and turning out occasionally for Rajasthan Club. Sridhar was kind enough to recommend my name to Swaranjit Singh. The big man welcomed me heartily and straightaway made me feel at home. I bowled very well in the few matches we played before the season ended, and learnt a few important lessons, bowling regularly on turf for the first time in my life as I did. Wickets were not covered those days, and my first spell on a drying wicket was a huge learning curve, as I beat the bat continuously for over an hour, only to be frustrated by two experienced Eastern Railway batsmen, one of them left handed, see me off through extremely watchful cricket, and go on to put on nearly 200 once the wicket dried out into a beauty. It took me a few more years to learn to force a batsman to play when the ball was turning enormously.

Rajasthan Club was not the strongest team in the Calcutta league but no pushover either. Swaranjit Singh was a very accomplished batsman, as was Ravi Kichlu, the elder of the two Kichlu Brothers of Hindustani vocal music fame. We had a few other good batsmen in the side, with Tapas Roy perhaps the most dependable. All rounder Pradeep Ganguly was a volatile young man with a heart of gold, better known for his soccer skills. Prakash Poddar was known to be a member of the club, but I did not see him in action that season. Veteran off-spinner Deepak Dasgupta was a prodigious turner of the ball, perhaps past his best when I played with him (I met him a few years ago, and found that he had no recollection of my stint with Rajasthan). A former schoolmate from Madras, Premchand was a stylish middle-order batsman who was going through a horrendous lean trot. Opener CB Singh, an orthodox UP Brahmin with a handlebar moustache, who wound his sacred thread around his right ear everytime he went to the toilet in order not to defile it by accident. Ravi Kichlu, my partner in the slips, often burst into *alap* during the game to my utter delight.

Happily for me, we won more matches than we lost, and we were a cheerful lot, and I had earned my spurs with some consistent bowling. I remember a game at the Kalighat ground when fastish leg spinner Dipankar Sarkar, for a while a Test prospect, bowled a good spell against us. My most memorable match was at the picturesque Calcutta Cricket and Football Club at Ballygunge. The host team CC&FC, not yet recovered from its colonial hangover, had a good half of the side made up of British expatriates. It was a practice match, and buoyed by the surroundings and my own good form, I enjoyed a very good spell, thanks also to the captain's confidence in me. I took four wickets including the scalp of their best batsman David Moller, who had played county cricket. I am sure he did not realise how much he lifted my spirits when he told me during lunch that I should flight the ball more for me to do well in England.

I realised this was his way of saying I belonged at that level of cricket.

That was the first time I had a *shandy*—and that too during lunch. The high I experienced after that was quite pleasant and actually helped make a brisk unbeaten 30 or so batting at no.6, along with my captain. The high point of the match was reached when Swaranjit Singh declared himself not out after the umpire (an off-duty bearer of the club) declared him lbw. His reputation was so overwhelming that our opponents did not dare to raise even a whimper of protest. He made 70 or so as we romped home winner by six wickets, once shouting at the top of his voice to me: "What do you mean 'No'? I'll show you how we can run three for this!" running furiously all the while.

One of the pleasant experiences of my Calcutta sojourn was the opportunity to watch a Duleep Trophy match at Eden Gardens. To collect my pass from Satvinder Singh and Venkataraghavan, the Madras players in the South Zone team, I had to go to Great Eastern Hotel, an imposing landmark of the city. In a low-scoring match, I watched my future batting idol GR Viswanath bat beautifully on a torrid surface on which young left-arm spinner Dilip Doshi was quite a handful. I caught a glimpse of the South Zone skipper ML Jaisimha, too, as he was leading his team off the nets after pre-match practice. "Why can't they fuckin' roll the wicket?" I heard him mutter

Invited by Sporting Union for the new season, the leading team in the city, thanks to my good showing for Rajasthan and my friend Tapas Roy's recommendation, I seemed to have a bright future in Bengal cricket, as the state team did not have a frontline off-spinner, but, with my father much better, I decided to go back to Madras where the college—particularly my spin twin Dayakar—was rolling out the red carpet for me. The decision was to cost me six more years in the wilderness, before I played Ranji Trophy cricket for Hyderabad.

Captaining Presidency

To return to inter-collegiate cricket, playing for Presidency was one of the happiest experiences of my cricketing life. While we were a positive, confident unit, rarely given to doubt or insecurities, we were also quite relaxed about the outcome of matches. There was no pressure from college authorities to win trophies, but we received every legitimate support we needed. Our kit was of a good standard, the college ground facing the Marina beachfront was immaculately maintained and the matting wicket was a beauty, swept and rolled meticulously by our staff Munuswami, Raji and Perumal. (Decades earlier, the Marina ground briefly sported a turf wicket, the handiwork of the iconic physical director PR Subramaniam. That was the time a couple of Ranji Trophy matches took place there. PRS could be seen on the roads of Madras well into the 1980s riding a two-wheeler and wearing a solar *topi* that dominated his very slight frame).

Our pavilion was a true heritage structure with a tiled roof and its walls painted green. It looked dilapidated, but we were comfortable in it. To our right was a gallery with steel girders, which filled up during important matches but always had a few locals seated or sleeping there. The trees around the ground—except on the far side close to the Beach Road—shaded spectators who lolled around the whole day and offered unsolicited advice to the fielders closest to them.

Our assistant physical director Mr Subramanian was a small, lovable man, soft-spoken and endowed with an abundance of native wit. He was quietly supportive of the team but could be outspoken on occasion, especially if he felt we had not applied ourselves diligently enough. He showed admirable courage and character when he resisted pressure from minister Satyavani Muthu to appoint KG Arul Prakash—armed with a certificate to the effect he belonged to a Scheduled Caste—as the captain of the team in his very first year in the team. Arul Prakash—a younger brother of our former vice-captain Vidyasagar and Appaji of Vivekananda College—eventually led the side when I came back to college after a brief stint as a sub-editor at the Indian Express. He was a nice guy, and had improved as a batsman, but never comfortable with that kind of politics, I tried to play as few matches as I could, citing academic reasons. That was the year I had to leave mid-season for Calcutta to be with my father. I came back only in the new academic year.

When I did, I was made captain of the college side, this time for the whole season, unlike my first partial stint three years earlier. We did not win any trophies but we did win many good victories, some hard-fought, some comprehensive, against some of the best sides in the city. My strongest ally in the team was Dayakar, by now arguably the best all rounder in the collegiate circuit. He was also a man of very firm, almost unyielding views, and managed to exert a powerful influence on my own thinking as a captain. One of the strategies he came up with rather early in the season was for us both to do all the bowling in every important match of the season—which meant that in a 50-over game, we delivered 25 overs apiece while the other bowlers in the side simply fielded. It was a preposterous idea, and I cannot believe that I actually carried out the plan, but I did, and it seemed to work. We won several good matches, but I don't think the resultant heartburn among our young teammates was worth it at all, nor could it have been the only way to accomplish our ends. Who knows, we might actually have done better had I utilised the services of medium pacers Osman Ali Khan and Kasi Viswanathan or leg spinner PS Venkatesh, who was indeed a promising young bowler.

To be fair to the Dayakar theory, neither he nor I batted or bowled in matches against weak sides—not even once during the season. While other prominent players in the circuit used these occasions to boost their tallies of runs and wickets, we scrupulously let our teammates corner all the glory in all but the toughest matches.

In one unforgettable match against Central Polytechnic at the home team's ground, I had the unusual experience of being continuously booed and barracked by one spectator just beyond the boundary line. It was my former league captain

Don Rangan, who had landed at the ground to promote his boy Osman Ali Khan's cause. Osman, a tall, shy giant, who had never shown any signs of dissent at my unfair tactics, was then playing for NSC 'A' under Rangan's captaincy. I ignored Rangan's shouts nonchalantly and refused to bring on Osman at any stage of the match. The match was a personal triumph for me as I took six wickets and made 67 runs (with opener MS Rajagopal remaining unbeaten on 85), but Dayakar who opened the batting and bowling that day, failed with both bat and ball. Most of Rangan's ire was directed at Dayakar (whom he had identified as the arch villain of the whole scheme). At the end of the match, I offered Rangan a ride home in my father's Standard Herald car, which I had borrowed for the day, and it was a relief to know that we were friends still, though he totally disapproved of my tactics (and rightly so).

Despite this unfair practice I adopted, it was a most enjoyable season, with the team rallying around me wholeheartedly. Besides the bowlers I mentioned, we had only a couple of batsmen capable of playing substantial innings, but everyone chipped in with useful, often fighting contributions. We had a few brilliant fielders and the others worked hard at improving their standards. Besides Dayakar, we had two outstanding batsmen in Rajagopal (Raju) and Swaminathan (Chama), who never let us down when we needed sizable innings from them. Leg spinner Venkatesh was the best of the other bowlers, while Kasi Viswanathan (Congress leader

P Kakkan's son, Kasi joined the police force after college, but died young) was a spirited medium pacer and excellent fielder. Osman could be quick on his day, but lacked consistency. He was a useful wielder of the long handle. Venkatesh could also resist stubbornly in the lower middle order, besides striking a few lusty blows. There was also the tall opener Krishnan, whose batting we could count on, but not so his temperamental wicket keeping. Middle order batsman PN Vijay promised much in the nets and did come up with a few bright innings, though he was not as consistent as his knowledge of the game and decent technique suggested. He was the most brilliant scholar of the team, an all rounder who swept all the prizes in the university circuit in debates, quiz competitions and the like. (An avowed Marxist in his student days, he became a much respected, successful finance professional in his adult life, changing his political affiliation drastically, even becoming the BJP's financial adviser at one time).

Chama was the character of the team. A stylish left-hand batsman and easily the team's best fielder who prowled in the covers, Chama cycled everywhere, singing all the while. He refused to travel any other way even to far-flung destinations. Amazingly, his long bicycle rides to reach the ground never affected his performance. He was a walking compendium of Subramania Bharati's poetic works, and in fact knew his long verses like *Panchali Sapatham* and *Kannan Paattu* by heart. He sang Bharati while cycling from place to place besides entertaining his teammates on the rare occasions when he felt inspired enough to do so.

Chama and I started off on entirely the wrong note, when he tried to behave like a *prima donna*, used as he had been to star status at Government Arts College, his earlier stop in college cricket. In his first match for Presidency—at the Marina against an unfancied opponent—he demanded that I promote him from No.3 to the opening slot. When I demurred, he refused to go in at no.3 (or the whole story could have been the other way around, as my memory is rather vague about the incident). I took a tough stand and demoted him straightway to no.11. The message had a salutary effect, not only on Chama, but on the whole team, as that turned out to be the only instance of any kind of indiscipline for the whole season.

Neither Chama nor I referred to this episode later, and he became an integral part of the batting line-up and patrolled the covers superbly throughout the season. He was easily our most successful batsman, partly because of hundreds against the weaker teams, but also through vital contributions in the important matches. He and Raju struck a very good partnership at the top of the order. Raju was a basketball ace at the state level and was blessed with lovely wrists, a straight bat and an excellent temperament. He too was one of our better fielders.

Two matches against Vivekananda College, arguably the strongest outfit in the city, stand out in my memory. The first of them was a great disappointment because we fought hard and looked like snatching victory from the jaws of defeat after a poor start, but Vivekananda prevailed over us by 17 runs or so. Batting first on the University Union matting wicket on Spurtank Road, Egmore, Vivekananda were 170 all out and we had to overtake them in the allotted overs, easy by today's standards, but formidable then, especially with a particularly lush, slow outfield. If TE Srinivasan starred for our opponents, Raju and Chama batted superbly to give us a decent chance of winning, before I joined Dayakar at the fall of the third wicket at around 75. Scoring boundaries was not easy, so Dayakar and I ran like never before. Some of the singles and twos we stole were suicidal and we repeatedly escaped by the skin of our teeth before the inevitable happened, and I was run out for 28 with the score at 140 or so. A collapse followed and we were all out for 153, with Dayakar unbeaten with a half century.

That match was one of the last times MDS Murthy, our official umpire, stood in one of our games. He was a chain smoker, pencil thin, dark in complexion and a gem of a man. To see him steal a smoke during drinks intervals, with the cigarette held between his middle and ring fingers, and him dragging the smoke through his cupped hand, was quite a sight. Early in my career, he frequently turned down my appeals if he felt I was not bowling well. "I won't give you a single decision today if you don't flight the ball," he would warn me. Of course, in all the years he umpired our matches, he never once said, "Well bowled" to me, but I knew he approved of my bowling. He was an eminently honest umpire and never favoured the home team, but in this particular game, he earned the wrath of the Vivekananda players by declaring their wicket keeper Sabu run out, when they felt he had reached home. Not exactly known for their sporting spirit, they immediately denounced his umpiring as partisan. The allegation hurt him deeply.

Murthy had been a racing correspondent at *The Indian Express*, but he now seemed to depend entirely on his earnings as an umpire. He was apparently a bachelor and could not afford a house, so he stayed at our cricket pavilion. He is believed to have died there (I had left Madras by then), the first of at least two cricket personalities to pass away there. The second was the khadi-clad, bald, stocky YMA Kannan, who retired as a demonstrator in the chemistry laboratory of Vivekananda College. Kannan was one of the founders of Young Men's Association, a prominent club of Madras those days, but he too must have fallen on hard times, for he too came to stay at our pavilion like Murthy. Unknown assailants allegedly murdered him in what was believed to be a case of mistaken identity.

We tasted sweet revenge towards the end of the season, when we beat Vivekananda by ten wickets in an early round of a knockout tournament for the Tarapore Cup. I had the personal satisfaction of picking up six Vivekananda wickets with one of my better bowling spells. Naturally, the only other successful bowler was Dayakar, as we were still following the two-bowler formula. We had to get some 140 runs to win the match, but Chama and Raju made it all look so easy in a lovely unbeaten opening partnership.

There were several sterling performances by my colleagues but no match could equal our first round encounter with Jain College in the Tarapore tournament in that last season of mine in college. Playing at Pachaiyappa's 'A', we won the toss and elected to bat. We ran into some fine seam and swing bowling by Ghouse Khan, an idiosyncratic, extremely effective all rounder, and AK Subramaniam, who had toured England with the Indian Schoolboys a couple of years earlier. I was bowled for a first ball duck by a beauty by AKS, and all our frontline batsmen failed.

When we went in to defend this paltry total, we were all determined to do the impossible, though I had no idea how to go about it. That is when Dayakar came up with the idea that I bowl packing the onside with seven fielders and giving no air, thereby restricting the batsman's scoring opportunities. He too bowled quicker than usual. I remember that I was trying to imitate Venkataraghavan's action and bowling in an arc similar to his, which had a slightly lower trajectory than my normal style. It really worked, and after a few overs, I went round the wicket, making it even more difficult for the batsmen to play attacking shots. Jain had a good batting line-up in which PC Doshi, AKS and Ghouse were prominent, and at one stage they were 92 for 4, needing only 24 to win. It was a 35 eight-ball over affair, but they had plenty of overs to spare. This is when our persistence began to pay and wickets fell in a heap all of a sudden. With the score at 112 for 8, the batsman played a full-blooded sweep, which would normally have gone for four, but forward short leg Vijay brought off a spectacular catch, because he had never taken his eye off the ball. 112 for 9. The last man in took a cheeky second run off a push to extra cover and Chama's careful throw knocked one bail off, but the batsman was just in, and the pair were now attempting a difficult third run, with our short fine leg Shantaram, perhaps the slowest fielder in the side ambling after it, amidst wild shouts from all of us. The third run would level the scores, but Shantaram seemed to be unfazed by the prospect as he underarmed a gentle lob towards the stumps. The batsman was still clearly short of the crease, when the ball hit the off stump and dislodged the bail. Amidst much shouting and celebrations, Chama ran to me, hugged me and actually kissed my cheek! I have never been more embarrassed in a cricket match, but I did not mind. It was the sweetest of victories and a few excesses were forgivable after such an extraordinary match. Umpire Chittbabu, who stood at my end, was uncharacteristically emotional. "Your bowling was special today," he said, "something to cherish." (*Un bowling innikki kannule othhikkaraappale irunthathu*).

The win started a chain of good performances by us—including the ten-wicket victory over

Viveka—taking us all the way to the final. In a shoddy performance, inexplicable with our morale so high, we lost by a big margin to Pachaiyappa's in the final. Thus ended my campaign as captain. We had several good performances, enjoyed great camaraderie and developed quite a few young players, but in the end had only a bare cupboard to show for our efforts.

Intercollegiate cricket threw up some excellent talent. Among the many fine batsmen in the circuit, TE Srinivasan of Vivekananda College looked a very good prospect, with his positive attitude and ability to drive on the up. V Krishnaswamy, of the same college, was another very promising batsman. At the college level, he was a difficult batsman to dislodge, and he proved himself in inter-university cricket with several mature innings, but his first class career did not exactly take off, even though he received early recognition by way of a place in the Irani Cup competition and the South Zone team. His opening partner Suresh—succeeded the year after I left college by my brother Sivaramakrishnan—was nicknamed Milburn for his physical resemblance to the rotund England opening batsman of the same name. Just as aggressive a strokemaker as Milburn, Suresh was involved in several exciting opening partnerships with Krishnaswamy. He made one particular assault on a stiff target set by Pachaiyappa's College at the Marina ground memorable with some of the most audacious shotmaking I had seen until then. Sivaramakrishnan who was in the reserves of the college team that year went on to partner Krishnaswamy for both the college and Madras University next season, when Madras won the all India Rohinton Baria trophy with great contributions from them both, as well as P Mukund, PR Ramakrishnan, Bhargav Mehta, R Ravichandran, Victor Fernandez and N Bharathan.

Bhargav Mehta and Bharathan were a pair of spin bowlers who kept the AC College of Technology team competitive. Bhargav had a major role to play in Madras's maiden Rohinton Baria triumph in the 1971-72 season. He crowned a fruitful tournament with a fantastic performance in the final against Bombay, taking 14 wickets in the match. Bharathan, who also had a good tournament, a bowler I never got to watch much at his peak, as he came into the picture just after I left Madras, was acknowledged as one of the finest off-spinners Madras produced. He was also a handy batsman with a few hundreds to his credit. I saw his bowling at close quarters when he was past his best in the Madras league, and was mighty impressed by his flight and guile. At the risk of sounding immodest, I saw a bit of my own bowling in his. He was one of the spin bowlers of merit not to find a place in the Tamil Nadu team during the long period of domination of its cricket by the two world-class spinners VV Kumar and S Venkataraghavan. Venkataraghavan was still an active Test off-spinner, captain of Tamil Nadu, vice-captain of the Indian team and for a brief while its captain. Bharathan's entry into Ranji Trophy cricket was effectively blocked, just as Bhargav's was, too.

Ravichandran, who led AC Tech in local cricket and Madras University's victorious team in 1971-72, has been one of the most successful captains in this part of the world, leading teams at the school, junior, college and university levels to an astonishing number of triumphs. He was a consistent if unexciting batsman, who accumulated runs almost imperceptibly, and for some reason, never managed to earn the selectors' nod at a higher level.

Finally in the University XI

I was in II MA, my final year in college, and for once in with a sure chance to find a place in the university eleven. This time the City vs. District Colleges match took place at Madras, on the matting wicket at the University Union ground on Spurtank Road. I made short work of the District team, with ridiculous figures of 5 for 15 or something like that. When the university squad was announced, both Dayakar and I were included, but Dayakar declined. He was absolutely sure that he would not be in the playing eleven as his left arm spinner rival Bhargav Mehta was also in the team. He was probably right, but I could not see how anyone could be selected and refuse to travel. He and I had been inseparable and I would have enjoyed his company on and off the field at Dharwar in Karnataka, where the South Zone matches were played.

The tour was one of mixed fortunes for me. I bowled reasonably well without great success and totally flopped as a middle-order batsman at no. 6 or 7, but really enjoyed the experience of touring with cricketers whose company I liked besides respecting their cricket. Unfortunately, the captain TE Srinivasan, a fine batsman and the character of the team, did not make the best use of me as a bowler, and I was therefore less effective than I might have been. TE, who is no more with us, was the life and soul of the party on the tour, and a happy-go-lucky captain, and certainly did not have anything against me. It was just that the chemistry between us as captain and lead bowler was inadequate. I think we beat Mysore and Bangalore Agricultural on the way to the zonal final versus Bangalore, which we lost. I picked up a few wickets in the first two games, but was only moderately successful against Bangalore, for whom Brijesh Patel, fresh from a successful tour of Australia with the Indian Schoolboys, scored a hundred and skipper Dinkar Rai 90 odd runs (Bangalore met host Karnatak University in the zone final. TE's classic comment to an optimistic university registrar on the eve of their match was: "B...s, you'll win. You f.....s arranged a favourable draw for your team. You think you stand a chance tomorrow?")

The undoubted highlight of the tour was P Mukund's batting for UAS Bangalore. Captaining a side that was below club standard, this tall right-hander batted like a champion making 97 and 61 against us in a hopelessly losing cause. A couple of shots—including an imperiously flicked six off my bowling—he played were so breathtaking that I was convinced I was in the presence of a future Test batsman. Unfortunately, though he had a splendid run for Madras University—having joined a master's course in agriculture at Coimbatore—and South Zone Universities next season, Mukund never quite reached the great heights I expected of him. Always a contributing performer, with his off-spin and medium pace as well as brilliant close-in fielding, he nevertheless acquired the reputation of a utility player rather than a leading batsman for Tamil Nadu in the years to come. (A cruel sidelight of the match involved our reserve wicket keeper-opener KR Sundaresan who came into the eleven as Ravichandran was indisposed. Sundaresan scored a double century in his inimitable style of inordinate delay between deliveries, with several glances at the sun god and little preparatory adjustments of cap, pads and so on. When a fit Ravichandran came back into the side for the next match, Sundaresan had to make way for him. I don't think he ever played a representative match again in his entire career).

Another consistent batsman during that Dharwar sojourn was opener V Krishnaswamy, whose brilliant innings against Bangalore University hinted at a bright future, but he too did not quite live up to that early promise. This was not entirely the fault of the players, for every cricketer needs the benefit of a combination of circumstances to help him reach the ultimate goal of playing for the country. In the case of Mukund, his all round ability perhaps stood in the way of his focusing all his attention on his batting. In a strong line-up of specialist batsmen Tamil Nadu boasted in the Ranji Trophy, he tended to bat in the lower middle order, and his off-spin too was overshadowed by his own captain's undoubted ability in that department. Krishnaswamy gained initially from being a cousin of Venkataraghavan, as pedigree is often a useful asset in the early years of your career, but it probably went against him in later years.

MISSED OPPORTUNITIES

There is a tide in the affairs of men,
Which, taken at the flood, leads on to fortune;

These words of Brutus in Shakespeare's Julius Caesar are probably the wisest ever spoken in history. In my cricket career, I did not pay heed to the tide at more than one crucial juncture, though the first time around, I was more to be pitied than censured, when well-meaning but incompetent seniors saw the tide in my affairs and neatly deflected it.

The first hint that I was perhaps capable of competing with professional cricketers came on a tour of Bombay a month after my 17th birthday. I was in the midst of a successful 1963-64 season as an off-spinner for Jai Hind Cricket Club in the First division 'B' zone of the Madras league. My performances led to my inclusion in the Madras Cricket Association Colts team selected from the B and C zones of the First Division. It was then customary for the Colts team to undertake a ten-day tour of Bombay, where it played some strong teams. It was a wonderful experience for players who otherwise never had any exposure to cricket outside Madras.

The tour was off to a superb start, with our opening match against Cricket Club of India at the famous Brabourne Stadium, the venue of many a stirring international contest. The excitement of playing at the historic ground was enhanced by the personnel that did duty for CCI. The team was led by Vinoo Mankad, now retired from first cricket, and had a few Ranji Trophy players and at least one India cap in Arvind Apte. It was a proud moment for all of us when our manager asked Mankad to hand us our Colts caps. Unfortunately, to our great disappointment, the former India captain neither bowled nor batted in the match, though two of his sons, Ashok and Atul, played in the eleven. Ashok went on to captain Bombay and pile up runs at an average of over 70 in the Ranji Trophy, and though less successful as a Test batsman, had his moments in international cricket.

Winning the toss, CCI batted first. I came on to bowl when the new ball was barely ten overs old, as was often the practice those days. With the ball still shiny, I was getting quite a bit of bounce and frequent away movement while bowling my off spin at a slightly quicker pace than I would with an older ball. With my brisk run-up, high arm action and attempt to impart sharp finger spin, I was proving quite a handful to the batsmen. Arvind Apte was one of them, and he was all at sea, not knowing which of my deliveries would turn and which would go the other way. I was finding the edge and hitting him on the pads frequently, and feeling quite on top of the world. It was so exciting to know that a Test batsman was struggling against my yet unproven spin bowling. I was thrilled that I seemed to belong at that level.

It was too good to last. My captain SV Narayanan, an amiable chap who could bat a bit, did not seem to know much about spin bowling, unlike my Jai Hind captain Raman. "Toss it up, toss it up," he kept pestering me, when he should have let me continue to bowl the way I was bowling. The batsmen were sooner or later bound to make a fatal mistake, the way I was dominating them. I had frequently come across such ignorance in collegiate cricket, but also knew how to ignore gratuitous advice and do my own thing as far as bowling was concerned. This time, unfortunately, I succumbed to pressure from the skipper, who was ten years older and more experienced. I sent down a couple of lollipops, which were duly despatched to the boundary. The same captain, who had exhorted me to squander my advantage away, now took me off. I never bowled again in the match, in fact almost never again on the tour.

You don't show your disappointment on a cricket tour, and I had wonderful company in some of my teammates, but I realised that every passing day without an opportunity to bowl against the high quality batsmen the Bombay teams had lined up for us was seriously hampering my progress. I was still playing in the second division (First Division B Zone those days) of the Madras league and would never have such chances back at home. The indifference of the team management really hurt me. The manager of the team, Mr S Annadorai, was an eccentric old man, who, because he was distantly related to me—I guessed—decided he must be sternly impartial towards me. He decided to find fault with me constantly and even made fun of me more than once in public.

I must hand it to him, though. Mr Annadurai was an excellent manager of a young team, when it came to looking after our comforts on the tour. The dormitory of the South Indian Education Society's school at King's Circle, Matunga, where we stayed, was spacious, clean, and cool. We slept on our own hold-alls spread on the floor in the assembly hall, and as the school was closed for Christmas holidays, we had the whole school to ourselves. The bathrooms were spotlessly clean and that really helped our morale. Breakfast and dinner were usually at a nearby cafe or South Indian Concerns, a popular hostelry catering to people from our part of the world as the name suggests. Lunch was at the ground where we were playing and the manager also treated us to ice cream, movies, or even dinner at some relatively posh joint. In this, he was generous to a fault, often spending his own money on us.

My problems with him started, I think, with my smoking cigarettes. The habit was a few months old, and I probably smoked two or three cigarettes a day, but I hated doing it in the sly. The manager saw me light up a couple of times, and was duly shocked. He made it a point to declare in the team bus what an unworthy member of what a worthy family I was. I did not realise that a case was being built up against me, and it was exciting to be seen as a rebel in public—though one without a cause, for sure.

The second nail in my coffin was struck by a girl my family knew back in Madras, when she joined me—and the whole team, manager and marker—at the movies the one afternoon we were free on the tour. The last straw for the manager was when I returned from my teammate Lakhi's cousin's flat on Marine Drive and vomitted violently. The villain was a particularly greasy peas masala we ate that evening, but my manager refused to believe I was as yet a teetotaller. "He smokes, he drinks, and he womanises!" he announced to an irresponsible group of young rascals, who enjoyed my discomfiture instead of rising to a man in support of me.

Annadurai—bless his departed soul, for I hold no grudge against him—haunted me throughout the short tour with sarcastic remarks. "Ramnarayan's top spin is as inconsistent as his off spin", he declared at the table tennis table one evening. I had hardly any chance to prove my ability on that tour. In hindsight, I realise I was one of the few players in the squad who could have gone on to higher levels of cricket. As events turned out in the long run, I was, in fact, the only one to do so, but I had to endure a very long wait, as this was my last opportunity for the next five years. Annadurai's tour end assessment of my performance saw to it.

The highlight of the tour was the opportunity to rub shoulders with some of the greats of the game. And, when I landed at Madras and found that my father had been hospitalised, it was a rude wake-up call. He recovered soon enough, but it was my first hint of some of the hard times to come.

MADRAS MEMORIES

What a far cry today's cricket scenario is from Madras cricket of yore. Just to give you an idea of the kind of spirit that pervaded the game as it was played there in the 1950s and sixties, even the seventies, let's join the action in the first ball of a limited-overs match back in the sixties. The new ball bowler KSS Mani is known for movement and intelligent variation rather than speed. The batsman is R Vijayaraghavan, an entertaining strokemaker. To 'Viji', if a ball is there to be hit, it should be hit, even if it is the first ball of a match. Mani's first delivery is an inswinging half volley, and Viji flicks it imperiously over square leg for six. The crowd is on its feet, but look at Mani's reaction. He runs to the batsman and pats him on his back, shouting, 'Great shot *da*, Viji.'

Though such extreme acts of sportsmanship were not a daily occurrence, most of the cricket of the time was played in a spirit of friendly combat.

Madras cricket began as an elitist pursuit, learned originally from the British by the landed gentry and educated upper crust and then percolating to the middle class. It was Buchi Babu Nayudu, a dubash well versed in the ways of the ruling British at the turn of the century, who first assembled an Indian outfit capable of beating the

'European' at his own game. Soon the game spread far and wide in Madras — from Purasawalkam to Perambur, Triplicane to Mylapore and beyond, with caste Hindus and Anglo-Indians the most prominent practitioners of the game.

'Curdrice cricketers' was the epithet still reserved for Madras cricketers of my time, the 1960s, especially of the Brahmin variety (the upper castes formed a substantial percentage of the cricket playing population of the city well into the last decade). It was a sarcastic reference to the soporific effect of the staple diet of the majority back then. We were said to lack the steel for stern battle, our artistry and skills no match to the aggression of cricketers elsewhere. The demographics of the game were however gradually changing, with many of the Anglo-Indians leaving India, and more and more of the 'backward communities' taking to the game with each succeeding generation.

Brilliant strokemakers and spin bowlers in local cricket, we were considered no-hopers when it came to locking horns with the more robust if less stylish combatants from Delhi or Bombay. Fielding was at best an unavoidable nuisance and the slips the preserve of seniors, with the babies of the team banished to the distant outposts of long leg and third man. Fast bowling was too close to real work, left best in the hands of those endowed with more brawn than brain.

The local league then was relatively informal. No registration of players by the clubs was required, and you could walk in a few minutes before the toss and join the eleven. There was much banter and fielders and batsmen often traded jokes or gossip, with the umpires sometimes joining in. The action rarely approached the frenetic, and the accent was invariably on style rather than substance. The spinner who did not turn the ball and the batsman of dour defence or crude power was treated with contempt by all these different constituents of the game in my youth.

On most grounds, the shade of a large tree served as the dressing room and facilities were generally primitive. Lunch involved a hurried dash to Ratna Café, Udipi Sukha Nivas, Shanti Vihar, Udipi Home or Dasprakash and back, depending on the venue of the match. The effects of the blazing sun were countered by glasses of unboiled, unfiltered and often multihued water stored in mud pots or brought in buckets that resembled relics dug out by archaeological expeditions.

Most Madras cricketers were unable to afford high quality gear. In fact, you needed contacts abroad or access to visiting Test cricketers to buy bats and other gear from them at fancy prices. A Gunn and Moore, Gray Nicolls or Autograph bat could cost upwards of a hundred rupees and that was a lot of money for the average cricketer. The gloves, leg guards and shoes worn by most of us often performed a psychological rather than protective role. At the lower levels of cricket it was not unusual for batsmen to wear a single leg guard rather than a pair because that was all the team could afford. The bats could be handcrafted things of beauty, but they did not possess the carry of contemporary bats that can send a top edge out of the ground.

Despite these constraints, or possibly because of them—for they served to make playing cricket seem an adventure, a privilege earned by the worthy, not something handed to you on a platter as it is today—the enthusiasm for the game was plentiful and infectious among players and spectators alike, not to mention the men behind the scenes like club secretaries, scorers and markers. Of humour, there was never any shortage and the spirit of competition was always softened by a sense of camaraderie that went beyond team loyalties.

There were countless private grounds which the young cricketers simply entered one day and occupied, so to speak, until the Rip Van Winkle who owned the plot woke up suddenly to build his dream house, in the process shattering the dreams of many prospective Prasannas and Venkataraghavans, Pataudis and Bordes—only for the dreams to be resumed in technicolor as soon as the intrepid young cricket warriors conquered their next new territory.

Cricket did not stop even in the classroom, where boys played 'book cricket', by opening pages at random and affixing runs or dismissals to the two imaginary batsmen — they could be Mankad and Roy in one generation and Gavaskar and Viswanath the next. If for example you opened page 54, the second digit was the reference point for the scorekeeping, and the batsman got four runs (or two, under a different set of rules), if the page number ended in a zero, the batsman was declared out and so on.

In my extended family, we invented our own brand of home cricket, an ingenious adaptation of the bagatelle board in which we gave cricket values to the various points on the board. 150 was six runs, 125 was four, LTP was bowled, 75 was two runs, 90 three, and we had different positions for different kinds of dismissals, caught, lbw, stumped, run out, even hit wicket. A skilful player, experienced in steering the little steel ball bearings we used for marbles, could make his team score 300-400 runs if he held his nerve, and score those runs pretty rapidly. It provided perverse pleasure to make Laker and Lock or Desai and Surendranath score centuries after the top order failed.

Madras cricket of those days had its share of characters. PR Sundaram, a first rate fast medium bowler and an entertaining wielder of the long handle, was also one of the funniest men seen on a cricket field. He kept up a fairly constant chatter on the field, and was not above laughing at an umpire after he had given a dubious decision. He once informed an umpire after he had lifted his finger in response to his own loud appeal, that the poor batsman had not played the ball on its way to the wicketkeeper. On another occasion, he bowled a googly as his opening delivery of the match and laughed with his arms akimbo at the batsman who had been bowled shouldering arms.

Some others raised a laugh without intending to. There was 'Kulla Kitta' Krishnamurthy, who opened the innings for Crom-Best Recreation Club, one of numerous short statured players known by that nickname over the years, who, dismissed off the first ball of a match once, told the incoming batsman as they crossed: “Be careful. He moves the ball both ways.” ‘Dochu’ Duraiswami bowled a series of full tosses in a junior match at the Central College ground in Bangalore and later declared to his teammates: “I have never bowled on a turf wicket before.”

Opening batsman Balu sat up all night reading Don Bradman’s ‘The Art of Cricket’ with every intention of putting precept into practice, only to be run out first ball next morning, his partner’s straight drive brushing the bowler’s fingers on its way to the stumps, and catching him out of the crease! ‘Clubby’ Clubwalla was another popular character whom the crowds loved to boo, for his slow batting and fascinating contortions whether batting at the top of the order or bowling his alleged off spin with a most complicated action. He was a stonewaller par excellence who once made 37 runs in a whole day of batting.

On my first cricket tour, I came across some entertaining characters. It was a ten-day visit to Bombay with the Madras Cricket Association Colts, during December 1964. I was one of the two babies of the team, Rajkumar Manradiar being the other one. Some of our teammates were colts only by a liberal interpretation of the word whose dictionary meaning is a young male horse. Of course every member of the team was young, in that he was below 30! The uncharitable instead called us the *Kezha* Bolts, the rhyming slang for long freely used in Madras to describe seriously old cricketers. The captain SV Narayanan was a pleasant, well-mannered bank officer, but though he did have a sense of humour, he was not one of the funny men of the team. Leg spinner all rounder KC Krishnamurthi led the gang of comedians who kept up our spirits throughout the trip. Chandramouli of Salem was another rather voluble member of the team, but he chose his moments of light-hearted badinage while KCK was constantly frisky, with a fund of jokes and anecdotes. Neither is, alas, with us now. Young Srikanth of Chengalpattu was my buddy on the trip and he offered his share of mirth as well. Much of the humour was directed at the late S Annadurai, our redoubtable manager, with his quixotic ways and absolute devotion to cricket. The high point of the tour was when Perumal, our gentle, emaciated marker, got high on Christmas night, and declared to the manager: "Annadorai, I the manager, you the marker!" He was severely reprimanded, but responded with a beatific smile even as he was locked up behind a grille door for the night. He was shame-faced the next morning, but he gave us all some wonderful entertainment as he questioned the manager's parentage several times through the night in a loud, high-pitched voice.

There were other unforgettable characters in Madras cricket. Probably the best known was KS Kannan, the veteran all-rounder who became one of the best-loved coaches of the state, more famous for his original English than his undeniable cricket skills. Fluent in Tamil, his mother tongue, he could barely pass muster in English, yet he loved to express himself in the Queen's language, with invariably hilarious results. "Give me the ball to him," he would tell one of his wards, and "ask me to pad up one batsman." "Thanking you, yours faithfully, KS Kannan," were the famous last words of a speech he made at a school function.

In more recent years, the stylish right hand batsman TE Srinivasan was famous for his wit and eccentric behaviour. On an Australian tour, his only one, TE allegedly told a local press reporter, 'Tell Dennis Lillee TE has arrived.' On the same tour he persuaded a security official at a Test match to warn innocent Yashpal Sharma that he would be arrested if he continued to stare at the ladies through his binoculars. Yashpal's panic and the resultant roar of laughter from the Indian dressing room caused a stoppage in the middle as the batsman Gavaskar drew away annoyed by the disturbance.

League matches often attracted crowds in excess of a thousand and the 30-overs a side *Sport & Pastime* (later *The Hindu*) Trophy final invariably drew five or six thousand spectators. Many finals were played at the Marina ground on the Beach Road, now Kamarajar Salai, which wore a festive appearance on such occasions, with every seat in the gallery taken, every treeshade occupied and dozens of cars and scooters parked on Beach Road, providing a vantage view of the match from just beyond a low wall. If you were patrolling the boundary line, you could eavesdrop on the most knowledgeable cricket conversations among spectators who knew not only the finer points of the game but also the relative merits of all the league teams and their players backwards. You could even receive some useful advice *gratis*, but God save you if you misfielded or dropped a catch!

Devoted spectators sometimes went from ground to ground watching more than one match in a single day. 'IOB 73 for 4 at Viveka, State Bank 100 for no loss at Marina, Jolly Rovers 82 for 2 at Pachaiyappa's,' one of them, a league cricket fanatic of many years' standing, would announce even before parking his scooter. Quickly collecting the scores at this new venue, he would troop off to provide similar information to players at another ground anxious to learn how the competition was faring elsewhere. Today, coaches and managers carry cell phones and information is exchanged instantly and effortlessly by all the protagonists involved in the chase for match points. I recently ran into another old faithful, a slim, bearded man always neatly turned out in a white shirt sleeves rolled up, and a dhoti he wore tucked up at knee level, who was a silent spectator at every one of Alwarpet Cricket Club's matches. He told me he had stopped watching cricket, which was "no longer worth watching, even though the players were much better looked after now."

A Ranji Trophy match between Tamil Nadu and Karnataka or Hyderabad could draw a crowd of

20,000-30,000 paying spectators. A match at Chepauk, with all its historic association with the 'Pongal' match of yore, was a most enjoyable spectacle, watched by somnolent vacationers seated under the trees surrounding the ground. That was before the concrete cauldron of the 1970s came up, effectively reducing cricketers to dehydrated invalids in a matter of hours, to dominate the landscape.

It was an occasion to pack your *puliyodarai* and *thair sadam* and set out on a daylong excursion to catch up with old friends, and in their company, dissect the doings of the protagonists of the drama being enacted before you, to applaud or barrack bowlers, batsmen and fielders.

Madras crowds are not only knowledgeable but generally hard-to-please as well. They will never accept Anil Kumble as a better bowler than their own VV Kumar, a wrist spinner in the orthodox mould unlike the Karnataka express googly specialist. Gundappa Viswanath of the steely wrists and the nonchalant artistry ranks higher with them than Sunil Gavaskar, for all the Little Master's achievements and peerless technique.

Oldtimers even today experience goosebumps when they recall a magnificent innings of 215 played at Chepauk by the Ceylon stylist Sathasivam in 1940. According to many, no better innings has ever been played at Chepauk, though post-War cricket enthusiasts rate GR Viswanath's unbeaten 97 against West Indies in January 1975 as the greatest innings in living memory, better than the best Gavaskar and Tendulkar knocks played at the same venue—and there have been plenty of those at Chepauk. The Triplicane crowds still wax lyrical about EAS Prasanna's deadly spell in 1969, when he had Australia reeling at 24 for 6, and will be the first to admit that their own local hero Venkataraghavan could not have hoped to equal the magic of that afternoon.

That is the one feature of the Madras crowd that you will rarely find elsewhere in India—the ability to transcend regional, even national bias to appreciate true sporting endeavour and artistry. This sportsmanship was never more in evidence than when the Pakistanis under Wasim Akram did a victory lap at the end of a pulsating match India almost won in 1999. I remember the drama of that afternoon as though it happened yesterday. The crowd had been roaring its approval all morning as Tendulkar led an incredible assault on the rival bowling, supported by the gallant Nayan Mongia. Unfortunately, with victory seemingly within easy reach, Sachin succumbed to the strain of the painful back injury he had been carrying throughout the innings, and soon it was all over for India.

There was a stunned silence, as if the huge crowd was still waiting for a signal from the small but significant saffron brigade in the stands that had been shouting anti-Pakistan slogans on the last day of the match (Bal Thackeray had earlier called for a ban on the tour). Like many others in the pavilion terrace, I looked back anxiously at the leader of the group, who, after what seemed like an interminable wait, gave the thumbs up to his followers. They burst into applause and the rest of the stadium joined in thunderous ovation as the victors did their triumphant march around the ground. It was a moment to make every Indian proud.

HYDERABAD DAYS

MIGRATION

A minor miracle took me to Hyderabad, and a renewed cricket career, in July 1971. As a Probationary Officer of State Bank of India, I had been working at a small town called Anakapalle, some 20 miles from Visakhapatnam. I hadn't played cricket for more than a year, when I was transferred to Vijayawada, the second of the four branches I had to serve at in an 18-month training period.

The great leg spinner VV Kumar, a State Bank officer at Madras, had advised me to contact Habib Ahmed, former captain of the bank's team at Hyderabad if I wanted a Hyderabad posting, but I had done nothing of the sort, being the introverted chap I was then. Now a string of coincidences, in which my benefactor S Satyadev, captain of the SBI Vizag team—someone I have never met—played a key role, led to the cancellation of my Vijayawada posting.

"Report to Personnel Department on July 1," said the telegram from our Local Head Office at Hyderabad. The cryptic message left me wondering whether I was now transferred to Hyderabad or summoned there on a brief errand. With hope in my heart and disbelief that my fortunes were taking a turn for the better, I duly met the Personnel Officer at the appointed hour. "It seems the cricket team wants you," the old man—he couldn't have been older than 55, but he looked ancient to my young eyes — told me with about as much enthusiasm as if he had found a fly in his soup.

The reason for the SOS was that the strong SBI team at Hyderabad was now without five of its regulars, with the new season about to start in a week's time. Three of them, Manohar Sharma, G Mohan and Mumtaz Husain were touring East Africa as members of the Hyderabad Blues team and two others, D Govindraj the fast bowler, and P Krishnamurti the wicket keeper, were in the West Indies with the Indian team that was making history under Ajit Wadekar's leadership.

My joy knew no bounds, as I hadn't played the game for two seasons since joining the bank as a probationary officer. My benefactor Satyadev was someone I had never met; he was working at SBI, Vizag, and I had written to him from Anakapalle, asking if he, as the secretary of the local welfare committee of the bank, could help me get transferred to his branch where I could resume my cricket. The letter had been forwarded to him while he was attending a training course at the training college there. His friend and colleague MN Prabhakar Raju also attending the course was at the time on the lookout for a substitute player to replace the five players on tour abroad. Satyadev told Raju about me, and he in turn informed his boss the personnel officer! Raju, a state level left-arm spinner, was soon my teammate and I don't know if he and Satyadev knew that they had changed my life forever with that single act of kindness. Another guardian angel in the personnel department was VS Sudhir, who made sure I did not get transferred out of Hyderabad during the days I was yet to cement my place in the SBI team.

It was exciting to walk into the Local Head Office of State Bank of India and meet so many outstanding cricketers there. Perhaps the first player I met was Nagesh Hamand, an attacking batsman who had pulverized university attacks in the Rohinton Baria championship in the three preceding seasons. He was also a more than useful off spinner, capable of sharp spin and thinking batsmen out. A brilliant fielder anywhere, Nagesh had been hugely successful at that level of cricket. We had played against each other at the Marina ground the previous season, when he had led Hyderabad juniors in an Inter-Association match for the P Ramachandra Rao Trophy. There was Ali Hassan, an opening batsman, who too had played in that match which Madras had won by an innings. Soon I was sitting down in the bank canteen and enjoying a coffee with these two, when we were joined by another talented cricketer, Lyn Edwards, the tall, handsome medium pacer.

I didn't know it then, but Nagesh, Lyn and Sultan Salim were to adopt me soon as their responsibility to shape as a bowler, because they believed in my talent. Not long afterwards, Krishnamurti, the wicket keeper, would join that band of young mentors. It was quite extraordinary that these cricketers took such an active interest in a fellow player, considering that each of them was no more than 23 to 25 years old.

The SBI team of that year was pretty formidable. At full strength it read: D Govindraj (captain), P Krishnamurti, Murtuza Ali Baig, Manohar Sharma, Nagesh Hamand, Sultan Salim, Mumtaz Hussain, Ali Hassan, M N Prabhakar Raju, G Mohan, Lyn Edwards, Mazhar Ali Baig, and Abid Zainulabuddin, with me bringing up the rear. Most of the players had played for their state or zone in the Ranji and Duleep Trophies, and Govind and Murti had already represented India. Add veteran Habib Ahmed, occasionally taking a break from his official responsibilities to assist us, and we had perhaps the strongest outfit in Hyderabad, closely followed by State Bank of Hyderabad, led by the redoubtable all rounder, Syed Abid Ali.

I am sure I am forgetting a couple of names, but there were a few guest players like Inder Raj, Muthukrishnan and Ali Hussain, Hassan's twin brother, who did duty for us sometimes, as though the regular galaxy wasn't enough to keep me out of the eleven!

Once the initial excitement wore out, I realised that I was no more than a filler in the team, especially as skipper Govindraj preferred G Mohan's off spin and occasional skipper Habib Ahmed, already a veteran, did not know much about me. The many-splendoured Mumtaz Husain too did not approve of my bowling for a long time to come. My cricket career in Hyderabad would have died even before it was born but for the fantastic support I enjoyed from the likes of Krishnamurti, Nagesh and Salim and to some extent from Lyn, before he left for Australia. I will be an ungrateful wretch if I do not dedicate any success I enjoyed later in my cricket entirely to these wonderful friends, who, though of my age or thereabouts, mentored me and encouraged me, literally bullying me to keep fighting, when I was about to give up cricket altogether. This was after two years of hard work had not won me a regular place in the Bank's eleven, my earlier experience as a Madras University bowler and the zillions of overs I was sending down in the nets not seeming to count at all.

This superb trio of friends would keep my spirits up by telling me I was good enough to play for India, leave alone the State Bank team in the local league! In fact, I had sort of 'retired' from cricket for a few months, when one Sunday morning in the 1973-74 season, some four of my teammates landed up at home and literally abducted me to play a match against Gujarati XI in the first round of Behram-ud-Dowla. I won't go into the details, but that was the turning point in my cricket, because I took six wickets that day and never looked back. The team management had met a few days earlier and decided that I should be brought back into the team, by force if necessary and given a fair trial until I fulfilled my potential. By this time my seniors Manohar Sharma, Murtuza Ali Baig and Habib Ahmed had recognized the merit in my protest and decision to exit league cricket.

Other unforgettable personal memories are those of the great time I had playing for Hyderabad XI in the local zonal team under the captaincies of Abbas Ali Baig and Abid Ali, and the year I broke into the Ranji team as the 16th member of an already picked squad after taking 8 for 75 against JK XI in the final of the Moin-ud-Dowla Gold Cup, which Hyderabad won after a gap of 11 years. The captain was again Abbas.

Abbas's younger brother Murtuza Ali Baig was already a part time cricketer by the time I started playing for SBI, but I caught a few glimpses of the calm, correct batsmanship that had stood him in good stead in his Oxford Blue days. I liked his quiet humour too, and many were the occasions we enjoyed smiles if not a laugh together. He was a manager and I a field officer at the time and I remember one league match when he and I left for the bank while the rest of the team decided to enjoy a nice communal beer after a match was rained off. The opponents too joined in the festivities and their captain could not resist taking a dig at us. "State Bank will collapse if Murtuz and Ram don't go back," he sneered. It was none other than Murtuz's elder brother Abbas.

I happened to play for two brilliant sides in Hyderabad—State Bank from 1971 to 1976 and Andhra Bank from 1976 to 1980. I enjoyed both stints. It was a fantastic experience to share the spin attack with Mumtaz Husain and Nagesh for State Bank, and Bob, Meher Baba and MN Ravikumar for Andhra Bank. Mumtaz was a phenomenon in the 1960s when he wove magic in inter-university cricket with his bewildering mixture of orthodox left arm spin, chinamen and googlies, all bowled in a variety of ways. For most of his distinguished Ranji career, he stuck to orthodox bowling, but displayed his entire range in his last season for Hyderabad. Those lucky enough to witness his bowling against Kerala and Tamil Nadu in the 1978-79 season will never forget it. Nagesh was a brilliant off spinner, but luckily for me, he concentrated on his batting. He was also an effective medium pace bowler when in the mood, and a shrewd captain to boot.

PR Man Singh, then secretary of the Hyderabad Cricket Association, gave me my first break courtesy P Krishnamurti's hardsell, when I was an unknown. He picked me in the Hindustan Breweries XI in the Gold Cup, but I got switched on the day of the match to the opponents State Bank of India, my employers.

It was a great experience to bowl my first ball in that match to Rohan Kanhai and impress my captain Hanumant Singh, who taught me more about my own craft than any off spinner ever did. My cricket in Hyderabad gave me a chance to meet the great off spinner Ghulam Ahmed, and it was indeed a memorable experience. There were so many officials with whom I got on well and whose affection I enjoyed. I had the pleasure of travelling with the Hyderabad Blues when I got to know Ranga Reddy well, though I never toured with Man Singh whose hospitality was legendary. Ranga too was an excellent companion and made our life on tour pleasant and comfortable. Among the journalists, I remember Pillai of *Deccan Chronicle* and Radhakrishna of *The Indian Express*, not to mention photographer Srinivasulu, who refused to acknowledge that his photo of "Sarfraz Nawaz" that the paper carried during the Jaisimha Benefit Match in 1978 was in fact mine!

I played with many fine young cricketers after the Jaisimha era came to an end after the 1976-77 season. Saad bin Jung was perhaps the best of them all, closely followed by Shahid Akbar, both openers, one right handed and the other left handed. It's a pity neither of them made it big. Another Hyderabad cricketer who should have by right played for India was off spinner Kanwaljit Singh. He was as good as any after the greatest of us all—Ghulam Ahmed.

I have a few regrets. I only caught a glimpse or two of young Azharuddin, when he used to bowl in the SBI nets, and again in a local match, when I bowled to him. Unfortunately, I left Hyderabad in 1981, and therefore did not have any close encounters with him thereafter, nor did I ever get to play with or against Venkatapathy Raju or VVS Laxman, one of the finest batsmen India has produced. His 281 at Kolkata in 2001 will remain the high point of any cricket lover's watching career.

I would have never played first class cricket if I had not moved to Hyderabad. It was my wonderful second home and I can never forget the many kindnesses of people connected with its cricket.

NAWABI CRICKET

There was an air of aristocracy about the cricket played at Hyderabad in the 1970s. The most influential figure in the cricket of the twin cities was Modganahalli Laxminarasu Jaisimha, tall, slightly built but strong of muscle and lithe of movement, an aesthete in all he did on the cricket field, tennis court or golf course. He was the undoubted nawab of Hyderabad cricket, with his Marredpalli Cricket Club a throwback to the village cricket ambience of the England he had last visited in 1959, as a member of Dattu Gaekwad's Indian team (thrashed 5-0 by Peter May's England).

Quintessentially amateur in its membership and the cricket it played, Jai's MCC was a collection of Sunday cricketers coming together for the love of the game and not for any trophies. It would surprise you every now and then with the high quality of the cricket it played, depending on the availability on the day of players of calibre—for example Cambridge blue Santosh Reddy, or the Nawab of Pataudi on a rare visit to the city.

Jai himself added a touch of class by his impeccable batting, rarely allowing even the best bowlers in Hyderabad to get through his defences, and playing breathtaking shots of beauty, precision and power. He was also a clever bowler of medium pace swing or off spin, as the occasion demanded, and an astute strategist as captain. Though the rest of the eleven could be made up of strictly club level cricketers and his son Vivek was not yet into his teens, Jai marshalled his resources quite adroitly to beat the top teams of the city whenever he caught them napping.

Hyderabad cricket also allowed schools and colleges to field teams in the league. The year I went to Hyderabad, Nizam College had more than a couple of stars in its eleven. Kenia Jayantilal, the stocky opener, who had scored tons of runs for Osmania in the Rohinton Baria, and made tremendous progress in the Ranji Trophy, had just had a disappointing tour of the West Indies, where he was not given a fair trial. Playing in the first Test, he was caught brilliantly close-in by a certain Garfield Sobers before he had scored too many runs, the same Garfield Sobers who would drop young Sunil Gavaskar more than once as the young Bombay batsman made history scoring 774 runs in four Tests. Jayanti had been panned by the press some of whose members gunned for him without consideration for his youth and inexperience. He would never play for India again, but in domestic cricket, he continued to amass runs for years.

Abdul Jabbar was another talented Nizam College youngster. The left hand batsman made an enormous impact with his studious but fearless approach to batting, marked by powerful pulls and cuts, as well as brilliant running between the wickets. He was also an impressive medium pacer those days, and an excellent fielder anywhere. That was to be his last season at Hyderabad. He soon migrated to Madras, where he joined State Bank of India. His career mirrored mine—while I never played for Tamil Nadu, turning out instead for Hyderabad in the national championship, in Jabbar's case, the exact reverse was true.

In the very first match I played against Nizam College, I won a bet with a friend of mine by dismissing Jayanti early, but returned footsore and legweary at the end of a long day, with Abdul Jabbar making 172.

I spent almost all of the 1970s in Andhra Pradesh, most of it in the twin cities of Hyderabad-Secunderabad, a tranquil, overgrown village back then. I was shocked to learn on arrival there in July 1971 that cricket matches—the last bastion of punctuality—did not always start on time there. Sometimes the umpires came to the ground late, and could then be persuaded by the rival captains to wait for all the players to arrive. There was an air of informality about the proceedings, occasionally extending to a single scorer or kitbag being shared by the two teams. In a completely unexpected theatre of the absurd amidst the most laidback nawabi sloth on the field, there was this unlikely provision for two innings in a single day, with bonus points awarded to a team which won the match outright—invariably an innings win. Incredibly, there were teams weak enough to be so defeated in the A division of the league. When I was playing for State Bank of India, I was often witness to—and participant in—reckless attempts to win a match outright without losing points for not maintaining the requisite over rate. My friend Nagesh Hamand was an expert at running through his overs in a matter of seconds, often riling the hapless batsman no end by rushing him to take guard. These were sheer bullying tactics by the big teams against the poor, defenceless weaklings of the league. It took me a couple of years to establish myself in the State Bank team, and I rarely bowled in matches during that long wait for recognition. Yet, amidst the drought of opportunities, I once managed to take three wickets in a single over—my only over in the two innings of the match — when defiant opposing batsmen were frustrating our efforts to enforce the follow-on—all to no personal avail, as the whole thing was no more than a laughing matter for my seniors. "Ramnarayan bhi kaam me aya (Even Ramnarayan came in useful)!" my captain Habib Ahmed guffawed.

Unlike Madras, Hyderabad did not enjoy sizable crowds at the league and other local matches—at least in the 1970s, when I landed there. We had some decent grounds, like Fateh Maidan, the Secunderabad Gymkhana, Parade Ground (the Hyderabad equivalent of Azad Maidan of Bombay, where several games could go on simulataneously), the Railway Recreation Club, the Police grounds, Nizam College, Hyderabad Public School, the cantonment grounds at Trimulgherry, ECIL, Osmania University, and so on. Unlike Madras, we had school and college teams participating in the league so that youngsters enjoyed early exposure to senior cricket. Nizam College, Hyderabad Public School and Osmania University produced some excellent cricketers, some of whom have gone on to play for the state and beyond. Saad bin Jung was a young prodigy who scored a hundred against the touring West Indies team in 1977-78 while still a student at HPS.

Hyderabad cricket too had its share of characters. There was Kalim-ul-Huq the leg spinner, of the film star looks, Elvis Presley hairstyle and flamboyant ways. A leg spinner of merit, he had a bustling action and ability to turn the ball, but alas, was past his best by the time I landed at Hyderabad. Like SK Patel and V Kannan of my college days at Madras, Kalim was the most industrious nets bowler, someone who never missed a practice session. Among his State Bank of Hyderabad colleagues he enjoyed a bit of a reputation as a raconteur of stories starring Kalim-ul-Huq. "Kalim just completed his 100th wicket of the season. In the nets!" they would cackle. AR Bhupathi was a coach and umpire of Tamil origin, whom I had known briefly when he was doing a coaching stint at Madras. He was a firm believer in my bowling ability, independence and integrity, but constantly warned me that I had no future in Hyderabad cricket. His sons Mohan and Muthukrishnan were good cricketers who managed to play first class cricket, but they did perhaps suffer from the after-effects of their father's indiscreet comments in cricket circles.

There were some incredible characters like the cricket-mad PR Man Singh, whose cricketing ambitions were thwarted by poor eyesight and the resultant risk of serious injury, and who diverted all his energies to a life in cricket administration. The stories of his wheeling and dealing were as prolific as those of his chivalry and valour, depending on which of two rival camps you belonged to—Man Singh's or Jaisimha's. You had to support one or the other, not both, if you wanted to amount to much in Hyderabad cricket of the 1970s. Each was a great contributor to Hyderabad cricket but a whole generation of cricketers suffered as a result of this rivalry, real or perceived, between the two of them.

The cricket conversations of Hyderabad often revolved around past greats, especially those who did not make it to the highest level despite their undoubted gifts, and (this is more important) because of the evil machinations of some villain or other! The one and only Eddie Aibara, a fine all rounder in the early years of the Ranji Trophy, and during my time in Hyderabad, a kindly, wise coach who guided many young cricketers, was one such unhonoured hero.

Tales of skulduggery were told with great relish on the lawns of Fateh Maidan Club over several intakes of the golden liquid. "Munna, the day you stop being the honest, principled cricketer I know, I'll stop recognizing you on the street," my footballer friend Rammohan—once an India prospect—admonished me on more than one occasion after long hours at the watering hole.

I was lucky to experience the different ethos of these two cricket centres of the south. My cricket thinking was shaped by the company I kept in both cities, though ever so slightly dominated by the greats with whom I rubbed shoulders in the twin cities. And, of course, despite all these influences, you are what you essentially are, and some of my adamant shortcomings as much as my rare flashes of inspiration were of my own doing. You cannot blame Madras or Hyderabad for them.

To my great regret, many of my friends and mentors—from Hyderabad in particular—are no more today. I like to believe they would have enjoyed reading this book or at least wholeheartedly approved my initiative. Habib Ahmed, Jaisimha, Pataudi, Krishnamurti, Abid Zainulabuddin, Nagesh Hamand, Mumtaz Hussain,CR Chandran, Inder Raj... the list is long and depressing.

FATEH MAIDAN

Today, it is an anachronism as a cricket venue, as the current home of the Hyderabad Cricket Association, the Vishaka Stadium is where all the action takes place. For decades, however, Fateh Maidan, where stands the Lal Bahadur Stadium, was synonymous with Hyderabad cricket, though it belongs, not to the cricket association, but to the Andhra Pradesh Sports Council. I began to hear of this much loved cricket venue when I first read newspaper reports of the Moin-ud-Dowla Gold Cup tournament. I was at the time in college in Madras, and it was quite thrilling to read of the exploits of some of my friends and rivals—in a cricketing sense—at this prestigious competition, in which the cream of Indian cricket took part.

AG Satvinder Singh was one cricketer picked to represent the Vazir Sultan Colts that I particularly admired, and his engineering college teammate S Venkataraghavan too made a mark in the Gold Cup. I imagined then a tree-shaded ground where the aristocracy of Hyderabad gathered to watch the sleepy proceedings of cricket of an altogether more leisurely vintage than we are now accustomed to watching. I was not very wrong, as I found out years later when I actually entered the ground, except for the concrete and steel stadium. The shamianas in front of the pavilion seated the beautiful people of Hyderabad—the most stylish, the most elegant and the best looking men and women of the twin cities.

This was the ground where India was accused of wasting time to save a Test match against New Zealand, led by Graham Dowling. With India merely a couple of wickets from a defeat, the game was interrupted by a brief spell of rain — it was one of those freak showers which sometimes struck the stadium alone, leaving all other parts of the city dry. The ground staff, showing a remarkable tardiness in getting the ground ready, Dowling and a couple of his men entered the field, mop and bucket in hand, but were prevented by the umpires from doing any ground duty.

This was also the ground where I watched a number of Ranji Trophy matches before I myself started playing in them. One unforgettable memory is of Abid Ali and a couple of his teammates waving furiously at me, signalling for me to join the players in their enclosure while I sat in an adjoining stand, entry to which my complimentary ticket — courtesy the same players — entitled me. I had in the previous week played my first match at the ground, not counting an earlier one in which I did not get to bowl, and had so impressed Abid and Co., that they arranged for me to bowl in the state team's nets prior to the match I was now watching. This was a Ranji knockout match against Delhi, and though not in the original squad, I nearly played the match, I was told, with off spinner Noshir Mehta breaking a finger a day before the match.

Fateh Maidan offered a beautiful batting wicket, though it could be quite a sporting surface, whenever groundsman Venkatswami was allowed to leave some grass on it. At different times, the authorities experimented with different approaches to laying the wicket, including a brick base once, but as an off spinner, I always enjoyed playing there, though not once during my career did it present a turning track. At its benign best, it was a challenge to bowl on, an interesting one because you knew its nuances and knew how to adapt your bowling to suit them. When it offered some purchase, it was a pleasure to bowl on, with the ball hurrying off it; sometimes the batsman could be bowled off the middle of a defensive bat, the ball spinning back on to the stumps.

The stockily built Venkatswami was quite a character, very authoritative sounding, and inscrutable most of the time. Whenever players sought prior intimation about the behaviour of the pitch, his invariable reply was: *Khelke dekho* (Play and see)! At the end of the match, whichever way it went, he always told his audience: "Didn't I tell you?"

It was inside Venkatswami's little office that Abid Ali sometimes took his morning tea, either after practice, or before a match. This is where I received some sage advice from the squat, solemn looking groundsman, including the intriguing tip that it helped improve your fitness and concentration if you ran barefoot on the dewy grass of the ground on the verge of an important game. This is where I watched many a Moin-ud-Dowla match in the company of some of Indian cricket's greats like Salim Durrani, EAS Prasanna, VV Kumar and Rajinder Goel, sitting in the balcony of their rooms overlooking the ground, and listening to some delightful, if frequently apocryphal, cricket stories.

Hyderabad plays its first class matches at the new stadium at distant Uppal, but for many of us old-timers, our cricket memories are inextricably intertwined with our memories of Fateh Maidan.

THE PRINCE OF BANSWADA

'Chhotu there wants you to go and bowl in his nets,' the man I had watched lead India from afar told me, his face an impassive mask, completely oblivious to the shattering impact of his words. He was the Nawab of Indian cricket, Mansur Ali Khan, and until the previous moment, my captain for the next three days. I had been catapulted from the Hyderabad league to what was beginning to assume international dimensions, a first round match in the Moin-ud-Dowla Gold Cup, between Hindustan Breweries XI and State Bank of India. I, a lowly reserve player in the local SBI team, had been picked for the star-studded Breweries XI which also had Pataudi (captain), Rohan Kanhai, Budhi Kunderan, Gopal Bose, Anura Tennekoon, David Heyn, Duleep Mendis, P Krishnamurthi, Kailash Gattani, DR Doshi, and WA Bourne. For that singular honour I owed a huge debt of gratitude to my senior in the bank's local team, Indian wicket keeper P Krishnamurthy, who had recommended my name to selector PR Man Singh.

But now, my dreams of turning out for an international eleven came crashing down as I learnt from Chhotu, aka Hanumant Singh, former Prince of Banswada, former India batsman and the captain of the all India State Bank team, that I was to defect to his team. I, who was not even a regular in the local SBI team, was hijacked by the national bank squad, thanks to all rounder Syed Abid Ali, who had alerted Hanumant to my presence amidst enemy ranks.

The blow was softened somewhat as I bowled to class batsman after class batsman in the SBI nets. Hanumant himself had been the hero of my teen years when he launched an incredible assault against Bob Simpson's Aussies before Norm O'Neill caught him brilliantly on the boundary for 94 at the Corporation Stadium, Madras. And there were little Gundappa Viswanath, Abid Ali, Ambar Roy, Gopal Bose, Syed Kirmani, VS Vijaykumar, Abdul Jabbar and Madhu Gupte, all making for a formidable batting line-up.

Hanumant, I found out, was a shrewd captain, but his skills were not tested, as, helped by great batting by his top order, and ineffectual bowling by the opponents on a friendly pitch, State Bank made over 400 runs. (My contribution was a stylish zero). When the Breweries batted, I bowled the last over of the day, beating Rohan Kanhai outside the off stump with my first ball at that level. It was an ordinary delivery, but the great West Indian was rather rusty from a long layoff.

Then the heavens smiled on us and laughed a rather cruel laugh at our opponents. A sharp overnight shower rendered the wicket wet and soft, and when the sun shone on it in the morning, the drying surface was quite unplayable. I twiddled my thumbs going from mid-off to square leg between overs while the other off spinner Arun Ogiral grabbed five wickets. By the time I came on to bowl, the wicket had dried completely and I managed to get a couple of tailend wickets. I had done nothing spectacular, but did not disgrace myself either. We won the match comfortably.

With that win, State Bank entered the final of the Gold Cup, where it would run into UFoam XI, led by ML Jaisimha, and including a number of top performers like Brijesh Patel, Parthasarathi Sharma, Prasanna, BS Chandrasekhar, Mike Dalvi and so on. I was eagerly looking forward to the final and bowled long and hard at the nets the evening before the match. So, pleasantly tired after my exertions, I was delighted to accept an invitation from Chhotu to have a glass of beer in his room. The players stayed at the ground those days, and the rooms, belonging to the Fateh Maidan Club, had sitouts enjoying a superb view of the cricket. I joined Hanumant in his balcony after a shower in the dressing room.

Even before I started enjoying the cold beer, the captain dropped a bombshell. As our ace left arm spinner Rajinder Goel was available for the final, he was dropping me. 'You are a far better off spinner, but Arun has just taken five wickets, and poor chap, he could do with some morale boosting, after being dropped by his state." Hanumant went on to predict a bright future for me and even wagered that I would soon be picked for Hyderabad in the Ranji Trophy.

It was a crushing blow, being dropped from the team just when I was beginning to believe my cursed luck in cricket had finally begun to change. I did not know it then, but this was to become a pattern for the rest of my cricketing years. Every time I thought of hanging up my boots, there came that unbelievable break and for a while I enjoyed the rarefied atmosphere of success. But the moment I thought I had arrived, fate had a habit of cutting me down to size, as if I needed to be told repeatedly that life wasn't a bed of roses.

But this is not about my cricket. It is about that prince among cricketers of that generation, Hanumant Singh, who thought it was important to spend a whole evening talking to a younger cricketer he was about to drop from his team. Not only did he offer balm to my wounded spirits, he also took me on a conducted tour of the finer points of cricket, with special reference to off spin bowling, my field of specialisation. What I learnt that evening about my craft was more than a lifetime of learning, formal and informal. For Hanumant was an all round expert on cricket, and a storehouse of its history, especially, Indian and central Indian. His first hand accounts of the daring deeds of CK Nayudu and the thrilling batsmanship of Mushtaq Ali not only entertained but also educated.

I met Hanumant again a couple of years later at a Duleep Trophy match at Bangalore. He was leading Central Zone, and I was a reserve player in the South Zone squad, with two other off spinners,

Prasanna and Venkataraghavan in the playing eleven. He was delighted that I had received recognition as he predicted, though a season later than his prophecy.

My last meeting with Hanumant was a few years ago, once again at Bangalore, at the National Cricket Academy, which he headed. He was as always dedicated to his task, and had many great ideas for our young cricketers. Unfortunately, his old-fashioned insistence on discipline, decorum and sincere effort did not go down very well with some cricketers whom the media seemed to back. In this matter, I am not sure Hanumant received the support he might have expected from the cricket board.

In his playing days Hanumant Singh received the roughest treatment from the selectors and the board. For someone of extraordinary talent, he played only 14 Tests, and never toured anywhere after his impressive showing in England in 1967. Every time the Indian team was picked to go abroad, Hanumant was found mysteriously unfit, once with a congenital condition that had never troubled him! He never complained and he hated it if young cricketers did, about their own bad treatment at the hands of selectors. He believed in doing his job without expectation of reward, and he expected youngsters to do the same. He worried about them, especially if they did not realise their potential, or did not know how to channelise their talent. Knowing him, I am sure he worried about some of his wards to the very end.

THE RAINMAKER

There was a popular theory in the 1970s that the Moin-ud-Dowla Gold Cup was Hyderabad's answer to drought. Usually the season opener, the tournament fought for a gold cup in the name of a former local aristocrat was held in September, and invariably rain interfered with the progress of the event. Even on the few occasions it was conducted at other times of the year, the rain gods decided to visit Fateh Maidan where the cricket was in progress. When in 1972 or thereabouts, a severe drought was broken by thundershowers and a truncated final, people were convinced that it was divine retribution or mercy at play, depending on whether they belonged to the cricket association or the water-starved general public.

It was without doubt the premier cricket event in India outside of Test matches. All the Test players and the best of the rest took part in this invitation tournament. The Lal Bahadur Stadium wore a festive look for a fortnight, all the matches being played at the same venue up until the 1980s. They were three-day affairs and regarded as first class fixtures until over limitation was introduced in 1974 to make for results and exciting finishes as opposed to drawn games. These were not slam-bang affairs, at least in the first innings of 90 overs each, but sometimes the second innings of 40 overs could produce exciting run chases.

I played in the tournament for five or six years in the seventies, bowling my first ball at that level of cricket to Rohan Kanhai, and forcing my way into the Hyderabad Ranji Trophy team by taking eight for 75 against JK XI. That glamorous side was led by Pataudi, and included the likes of Surinder and Mohinder Amarnath, Salim Durrani, Abdul Hai, Karsan Ghavri and Laxman Singh. I played under a number of excellent captains like Abbas Ali Baig, Hanumant Singh and Ajit Wadekar and rubbed shoulders with several cricketing greats. On one of those occasions I was a member of the State Bank team, when, in one sensational burst of left arm medium pace bowling, young left arm swing bowler Abdul Wahab took a hat trick against us, dismissing Ajit Wadekar, Ambar Roy and Hanumant Singh.

Moin-ud-Dowla was dominated by the powerful State Bank of India. The eleven often read like the Indian Test team, boasting such names as Ajit Wadekar, Hanumant Singh, Abid Ali, GR Viswanath, Syed Kirmani, Gopal Bose, BS Bedi, Rajinder Goel, and VV Kumar, and, in later years, Roger Binny, Mohammad Azharuddin, Yashpal Sharma and Ashok Malhotra. Yet, with all those stalwarts around, less known players sometimes came up with match and tournament winning performances. The most notable of them was left arm spinner Ashok Joshi who frequently bowled State Bank to victory.

Other strong teams, especially in the early years were ACC, Nirlon and Mafatlal. Great players like Polly Umrigar, Vijay Manjrekar and Bapu Nadkarni were seen in the Gold Cup, and during the years when Sunil Gavaskar led Nirlon, Ashok Mankad captained Mafatlal. A very popular outfit was U-Foam whose captain ML Jaisimha collected a galaxy of stars around him. Salim Durrani, Tiger Pataudi, Mike Dalvi, Parthasarathi Sharma and Brijesh Patel (when their team Mafatlal was not competing), EAS Prasanna and BS Chandrasekhar were regulars in his eleven. My brother, V Sivaramakrishnan made a spectacular hundred on his Moin-ud-Dowla debut for U Foam against a Syndicate Bank attack that included Roger Binny and B S Chandrasekhar, and that's how he came into the limelight.

Vazir Sultan Tobacco, the local patrons of cricket, always fielded a youthful team with an eye on the future, and many Test players began their careers turning out for the VST Colts team in the Gold Cup. Dilip Vengsarkar, Kapil Dev and Arun Lal are names that readily come to mind.

My most pleasant memories of Moin-ud-Dowla are those of sitting on the balcony outside the rooms at the Lal Bahadur Stadium and watching cricket in the company of India's best cricketers and listening to cricket talk, eagerly absorbing some priceless cricketing wisdom from them. It was something my generation of cricketers was privileged to enjoy.

VISHY AND SALIM

"Match nahin dekha to hum ko bahut dukh hota ba," little GR Viswanath said in his pidgin Hindi to an intruder into the players' enclosure blocking his view as he sat with pads on. The place was the Lal Bahadur Stadium, Hyderabad and the occasion a Moin-ud-Dowla Gold Cup match. His teammates in the State Bank of India team knew that Vishy simply had to watch every ball while awaiting his turn to bat, getting up from his perch only during the drinks break to go into the dressing room to do some shadow practice or wrist exercises with the steel presses he constantly carried with him. This was around 1974 or so, and Vishy was already a Test veteran of some six summers, but he was still a boy at heart, polite, humble, his quiet, mischievous sense of humour part of his charm.

An apocryphal story of the time had it that he turned up for a game without a thigh pad, and was wandering around trying to borrow one from one of the other players, when one of them advised him to ask Salim Durrani. To Vishy's innocent query, Durrani's alleged retort was revealing if completely unhelpful. "Look young man, do you see that huge picture in the dressing room? (He was referring to a blow-up of Wesley Hall). I never wore thigh pads when facing him. Do you expect me to wear one now?"

The left-handed genius was the author of one of the many great stories you were privileged to listen to during that golden era of the Gold Cup, if you happened to be a player taking part. When we were not playing we watched other matches in rather distinguished company including the likes of Salim Durrani and ML Jaisimha, VV Kumar and EAS Prasanna, to name a few. The conversation on one occasion veered around to the practical jokes MAK Pataudi reportedly played on some of his cricket friends. Durrani came up with this particularly diverting version of a popular episode of that genre. (The story of a stage-managed dacoity in the vicinity of Bhopal, Pataudi's maternal ancestral home has been told elsewhere. Palace servants disguised as dacoits came rushing to where the young Karnataka players Viswanath and Chandrasekhar were in the woods after a gunshot was heard and announced that Prasanna had been killed. The youngsters burst into tears, believing the yarn).

According to Durrani, Vijay Manjrekar, retired from Test cricket, and an officer in Air India then, handed over his watch to one of the "dacoits" and told him that that was all he possessed. "Please let me go, I'm an LDC (lower division clerk) in Morarjee Mills, basic pay Rs.300, DA Rs.225, HRA Rs.150. I'm a poor man with a family to support." At this point, Raj Singh Dungarpur, unable to control his laughter, ran off towards a nearby hideout to join Pataudi's mother and sister, watching all the fun from there. Manjrekar, who Durrani said maintained to his dying day that it was a real dacoity, is said to have insisted later that Raj Singh had beaten a cowardly retreat. “Sala, Rajput bolta hai, darke bhag gaya.”

A GOLDEN OPPORTUNITY

I made my first class debut at a time most not-yet recognised cricketers would have called it a day and I myself had almost given up all hope of making the grade.

The heavy cricket calendar of Hyderabad in the 1970s meant I spent all my holidays and many weekdays at the ground, with a wife and baby daughter at home. I was almost 28 and with my cricket confined to the local league, I saw no point in spending so much time away from home. It was also time spent away from work at the State Bank of India (SBI), where I was employed.

But for my father's insistence that I try for one more season before hanging up my boots, I would not have been around in competitive cricket to be picked for the Hyderabad XI for the Moin-ud-Dowla Gold Cup in the 1975-76 season.

In Tamil Nadu, the state of my birth, I had stood no chance of getting into the state team, as the off spinner slot was occupied by S Venkataraghavan, my senior by three years, and already a Test player. In Hyderabad, I was kept out of the Ranji team by Noshir Mehta, an established off spinner. I had played for State Bank of India in the Gold

Cup a couple of seasons earlier, but this year my bank team decided to plump for Noshir, who, like Syed Abid Ali, was an employee of State Bank of Hyderabad, then a subsidiary of SBI.

That is how I came to be in the Hyderabad team led by Abbas Ali Baig. Six of the regulars were playing for other teams in the Gold Cup tournament, with ML Jaisimha captaining U-Foam XI. No one expected me to displace Noshir from the state team, as he was so firmly entrenched, but I proceeded to do exactly that before the end of the season.

A number of fortuitous circumstances made that possible, the first being my unexpected selection to play for Hyderabad in Moin-ud-Dowla. As the home team, we were given a bye into the quarterfinals, where we beat VST Colts, a young and talented side. Anshuman Gaekwad captained the side, which included Kapil Dev, Arun Lal, Dilip Vengsarkar and a couple of other Test prospects. We beat the Colts quite easily, skittling them out for 73 in the first innings. I took 4 for 22 and we entered the semifinals, where we were pitted against the redoubtable U-Foam XI.

The three-day match was almost washed out and would have normally been decided on the toss, in accordance with the prevailing tournament rules. But there was also a provision to play a limited overs match if some cricket was possible on the final day. That is how we came to play a 30-over match in extremely soggy ground conditions, as U-Foam felt they could beat us comfortably and persuaded the umpires to start the game. As it turned out, we were a younger and fitter side, more suited to limited overs cricket than our opponents. Our openers Chandran and Inder Raj gave us a flying start and we made 99 for 8 in the allotted 30 overs, and that was a big total on a heavy outfield on which boundaries were rare that afternoon. Our medium pacers Govind Raj and Jyothiprasad then bowled aggressively to bundle U-Foam out for 60, and we were home.

Hyderabad was in the final after a long gap. The other finalists were the JK XI, led by Pataudi. Their star-studded line-up read: MAK Pataudi. Lakshman Singh, Rajeshwar Vats, Abdul Hai, Surinder Amarnath, Salim Durrani, Mohinder Amarnath, Karsan Ghavri, Ranjan Baindoor, Rajinder Singh Hans, and their wicket keeper whose name escapes my memory now.

JK won the toss and batted first, after rain had delayed the start up to teatime. I was introduced into the attack fairly early in the innings, and managed to settle down into a decent rhythm, after a nervous start. The first break came when Lakshman Singh tried to loft me over mid-on and Nagesh Hamand took a well-judged catch after almost losing his balance on the slippery outfield.

That brought the left-handed Abdul Hai to the crease. This was my big break, a real morale booster, as I had frequently bowled to Abdul in Hyderabad cricket, dismissing him almost every time. He had always had trouble against my bowling and this psychological advantage brought out the best in me. I soon got Abdul's wicket, caught behind, if I remember right. The next batsman to come in was the great left-hander Salim Durrani. Here again, I had a psychological advantage, as I had once bowled to him at Madras, when he was playing for Jolly Rovers, a strong team in the league there. On that occasion, I had beaten him frequently and he had been dropped a couple of times. This gave me the confidence that I could hold my own against him. Soon I had him caught behind too, and in walked Surinder Amarnath. By now, I was convinced I could get anybody out, especially left-handers, that day, and sure enough, I got Amarnath's wicket too, going round the wicket, and clean bowling him with one that came in with the arm from outside his off stump.

I recall this story only to illustrate the role played in a cricketer's success by luck and memories of earlier performances against particular opponents. Several lucky breaks played their part in my success in the Gold Cup — which we incidentally won that year after a gap of 11 years — and subsequent Ranji Trophy debut.

MASCOT AT TRIVANDRUM

It was October 1975, months after Indira Gandhi had declared Emergency, and the small industries advances my colleagues and I were handling were often politicised to the extent of questions being asked in Parliament. A big hue and cry would be raised about loans not sanctioned, not disbursed or not enhanced to entrepreneur who cared to approach the government with their grievances. The Finance Minister duly queried the Chairman of State Bank of India. The Chairman in turn called the Chief General Manager(CGM), the CGM the General Manager(GM), the GM the Chief Manager(CM), and the CM the Manager.

The buck stopped with the lowly Field Officer, the grand title by which I was known. My late colleague Ronald Satur — a dedicated, brilliant young officer — and I were the whipping boys of our department.

In the midst of all these troubles, I was allowed by some strange dispensation to play cricket for the SBI and for Hyderabad, when the call finally came, dispelling my worst fears of being denied permission.

On the cricket field, it seemed I could do no wrong. With 4 for 22 against VST Colts and 8 for

75 against the star-studded JK XI in the final, I played a major role in Hyderabad reclaiming the Moin-ud-Dowla Gold Cup after 11 years. At the end of that performance, I got drafted into the Hyderabad squad going to Trivandrum.

I literally ran on to the railway platform the night we left for Trivandrum, as my boss had kept me back at the office for a last-minute discussion. As I nervously climbed into our first-class compartment, I was stunned to see my captain Jaisimha, former India captain Mansur Ali Khan Pataudi and Abid Ali already there. I had assumed that as Test stars they would fly to Trivandrum, not travel with the rest of us by train.

At Trivandrum, we stayed at the stately Mascot Hotel, overlooking the university cricket ground where the match was to be played.

Several mental images of that debut season have stayed with me. The first memory is of Jaisimha, Tiger and Abid joining me and my roommate Prahlad in the balcony outside our room just as we were about to turn in, the night before my debut at Trivandrum.

"Nonsense," Tiger's and Jai's voices boomed as I said good night. "Have a drink with us."

I didn't realise it then, but it was their way of ensuring that in trying to sleep early, the nervous debutant did not toss and turn all night in anticipation of the morrow.

Woken up by an insect bite at five in the morning, I was dismayed to find that it was pouring cats and dogs outside. When I went out to the balcony to take a closer look at the rain, I found almost the whole team there. Here goes my debut, I thought to myself, expecting the deluge to wash the match out.

I didn't know the Trivandrum soil, which absorbed all the rainwater by the time we reached the ground. The match started on time!

The new ball bowlers Abid Ali and Jyoti Prasad had hardly bowled 10 overs, when the captain handed over the ball to me and Noshir Mehta, my rival in the off spin department, as if to say, "May the best man win."

I was in a daze, the sudden realisation of my forgotten ambition almost paralysing me. On a bouncy new matting wicket, I was tossing the ball up gingerly, forgetting to bowl in my usual sharp style. I still managed to land the ball on the right spots and the even more nervous batsmen let me off with timid defence. In my third over or so, I got my first wicket: M Soman bowled V Ramnarayan 25.

'Tiger' Pataudi, fielding at mid-off was the first one to run up to me. "Well done, Ram, and wish you many more." He slapped me on my back and said, "And for God's sake, stop bowling rubbish." It was the wake-up call I needed. I started bowling my normal stuff and ended the innings with 6 for 33. I had arrived.

Tiger's sense of humour and his pranks were well known. During that match at Trivandrum, he quickly sized up as a cricket ignoramus a magazine journalist who sought an interview with him.

What followed was so hilarious it was difficult to keep a straight face.

Poor Mr Pillai! What horror he must have undergone when he filed the story of Pataudi's great successes and failures as Test batsman and captain—such as a double century against Belgium, an innings victory over Argentina and defeat at the hands of Netherlands!

THE DREAM CONTINUES

After the Kerala match, my friend and rival Noshir took ill and did not play in the Ranji Trophy league matches that season, coming back into the squad only in the quarterfinal round—against Bombay. My good form continued in the second match of the season against Andhra at Fateh Maidan, when I took 6 for 41 and 1 for 1 in a drawn match. Next, against Karnataka, again at home, I started on a bright note, dismissing GR Viswanath for seven, caught at forward short leg, one ball after he drove me to extra cover for four ("Stop experimenting!" was mid-off Pataudi's unfair rebuke). I had to wait a long time for my next wicket, which was Syed Kirmani (35). In between newcomer Sudhakar Rao made an unbeaten 200 to seal a batting place in the Indian squad that toured the West Indies later that season. He was out a number of times, but the umpires thought otherwise. I finished with figures of 2 for 126 in 45 overs.

I was keyed up more than usual before the next match. It was at Chepauk, against my home state. I was fiercely determined to do well proving a point so to speak, for Tamil Nadu had ignored me completely. I suppose most cricketers go through that kind of anger, and I was no exception.

Unlike my first three matches, this one kept me waiting for a whole day, as we won the toss and batted first. We scored 422, with Tiger Pataudi making 198, his highest against Tamil Nadu, while Jayantilal and Abid Ali scored 45 each. When we fielded, I was anxious to bowl, but I had to wait a long while, something I was not used to, as I had always bowled first change so far. To everyone's surprise, Jaisimha replaced Jyoti Prasad the seamer, after he had sent down five overs, and straightaway struck, clean bowling opener P Ramesh. Jai continued to bowl beautifully, claiming the wickets of Mike Dalvi and TE Srinivasan, and Mumtaz Hussain dismissed Satvinder Singh. When I came on to bowl, Krishnaswamy was playing a lone hand, now joined by the left-hander Abdul Jabbar. All the waiting and tension must have affected my bowling, for I was bowling well below par. I still managed to create a problem or two for Jabbar, who was lucky to be dropped at second slip off my bowling by Abid Ali. Abid spilled the chance after diving in front of first slip Abbas Ali Baig, for whom it would have been a simple catch.

At the end of the second day, the Tamil Nadu score stood at around 100 for the loss of five wickets. I was totally despondent that I had not had my great moment against my home state. I went to my sister Sarada's house for dinner in a miserable frame of mind. My brother-in-law Nataraj was in the reserve bench of the Tamil Nadu side, and he must have sensed my disappointment. We had a couple of drinks, and I was soon in a reckless mood, and decided to make a night of it, cricket be damned. I returned to the hotel past midnight and went to bed quite certain that the end of my cricket was nigh! I woke up next morning fresh as a daisy, with not a sign of a hangover, and feeling generally cheerful and optimistic. Jaisimha and I opened the proceedings in the morning, and when Tamil Nadu's innings closed at 207, I had 3 for 40 in 20 overs, a vast improvement over my brief spell the previous afternoon. Jai's 6 for 75 in 30 overs was his best analysis in a while; it was the only occasion in the season when he bowled so much. Being the master tactician that he was, he must have decided that he must take advantage of the psychological hold he had over a few Tamil Nadu batsmen—and proceeded to do just that. Ramesh, V Krishnaswamy, TE Srinivasan, Mike Dalvi and Abdul Jabbar were all victims of Jai's superb one-upmanship—which included elaborate rearrangement of the field for each batsman, with close-in fielders often breathing down the batsman's neck, creating the illusion that the wicket was spiteful.

We were through to the knockout. Our first opponent was Railways, a team we were expected to beat comfortably. The match, at Fateh Maidan, turned out to be an exciting affair, which we won miraculously after being hopelessly outplayed in the first innings.

Winning the toss, and electing to bat on a perfect strip, Jai—and our other batsmen—were shocked to discover wet spots on it from excessive watering the previous night. The Railways left arm medium pacer Anil Mathur was virtually unplayable. There was a steady procession of batsmen and soon we were 50 for 8, well before lunch.

That is when Jai declared. His move paid off as our medium pacers too posed problems to the Railway batsmen. Soon they were 65 for 7, but the wicket improved and a record eighth wicket stand between tailenders Hansraj and Shamji Dhobi helped Railways reach a total of 270.

Hyderabad piled up quick runs in the second innings and bowled the opponents out in about three hours of play to win the match with minutes to spare. It was among MLJ's finest moments as captain. (I only took one wicket in the match, with medium pacers Abid Ali and Jyotiprasad doing most of the damage, but I can never forget a catch I took in the second innings, which was described in a newspaper report as 'incredible', while it should actually have been the simplest of sitters. While we were racing against time trying to rout the Railways, middle order batsman Mohammad Tarif, father of Test player Mohammad Kaif, who was offering stubborn resistance, top-edged a bouncer from Jyoti. The ball was in the air for so long that it could have been held by any one of three fielders—me at silly mid-on, Mumtaz Husain at forward short leg or Abid Ali at backward short leg, but Abid repeatedly called Mumtaz's name. Unfortunately, Mumtaz stood rooted to his spot, and so did Abid, even as the ball was on its way to the ground. Realising what was happening at the very last moment, I dived desperately forward and came up with the ball miraculously lodged in my fingers!)

Fielding at mid-on, Jaisimha perhaps did not hear Abid's call, so he was naturally infuriated by my late dive, and let me have a generous piece of his mind in some colourful Hyderabadi after he had exhausted his English vocabulary. I remember Tiger Pataudi intervening to explain why I reacted so slowly.

Once the match was over, Pataudi ran towards Abid (and literally into him, as the hardy medium pacer also ran towards the nawab) in a rare show of elation on the field. Thanks to poor timing of the intended hug, Tiger suffered a dislocated finger, which affected his batting in the next match against Bombay.

Abject Surrender

When we assembled at the Wankhede Stadium in January 1976, we were still euphoric from our incredible victory over Railways in the pre-quarterfinals after yielding a first innings lead of 220 runs. The day after we arrived in Bombay by train, I went to Mulund to spend the morning with a cousin and came back just in time for practice. I didn't know it then, but I was perilously close to being dropped for the match in favour of the other off spinner Noshir Mehta, though I had had a good season so far. He had been out of action ill, and the team management discussed bringing him back for this match. To make matters worse for myself, I bowled badly in the nets, tired from the long ride by suburban train to reach Wankhede. I remember Jaisimha letting me have a fusillade of harsh words when I blithely assured him I would bowl OK in the match next day. Came the morrow, Hyderabad kept its faith in me, Bombay skipper Ashok Mankad won the toss and elected to bat, and just as I promised Jaisimha, I managed to find my rhythm straightaway when called upon to bowl after about an hour's play in the morning session. The promising Bombay University lad Vijay Mohan Raj was my first victim caught behind by Vijaya Paul deputising for P Krishnamurti, away in New Zealand with the Indian team. Left-handed Vijay Mohan Raj nicked one to the keeper and pretended he had missed the ball altogether in typically *khadoos* Bombay style, but luckily for me, the umpire was not fooled.

The Bombay team that day had a number of newcomers and soon I was dominating the batting despite impressive contributions from opener Sudhir Naik and skipper Mankad. Both their dismissals gave me great satisfaction. In the case of Naik, it was one of those rare dismissals resulting from a plan that actually succeeds. The beauty of it was that my captain Jaisimha and I were in perfect non-verbal communication, with the skipper slowly but steadily moving over after over into a position at midwicket where we both wanted him. We managed to lure Naik into mistiming an ondrive, the flighted delivery drawing him forward and dropping just short of where he expected it to be, and Jai was by now standing precisely where the miscued ondrive was landing.

Ashok Mankad was a master batsman in Indian conditions, against spin in particular. That I was able to get past his impeccable defence and force him to edge one to backward short leg was a matter of great satisfaction to me. His younger brother Rahul Mankad, making his debut, charged out to the first ball I bowled to him, but the ball dipped and spun viciously to ricochet off his bat towards short leg Jyotiprasad who threw the stumps down. Rahul was run out without attempting a run! Here was a wicket that was morally mine, at least partially, though it was Jyothi's brilliant reflex action that really dismissed him. Sandip Patil, also making his debut, was out to the same bowler-fielder combination, again off the first ball he faced, but he was out caught by Jyothi—a short-leg fielder in the same class as Eknath Solkar.

When the ninth Bombay wicket fell, with seven of them falling to me, Jaisimha walked up to me and instructed me not to get the last man out! He wanted to prolong the Bombay innings to close of play so that our openers would not have to come out to play out an awkward few overs that evening. I did not know how to bowl not to get a wicket and the aggressive tailender Abdul Ismail made merry at my expense. I was also tired from bowling more than 30 overs on the trot in hot, humid weather. Bombay were eventually all out for 222, with my bowling analysis reading 35-7-68-7. It was a proud moment for me, but the *Times of India* correspondent had a slightly different view of the proceedings from the general perception that we had bowled Bombay out on a perfect first day wicket. Among other things, he said I was helped by an unusual Wankhede wicket that took turn surprisingly on the first day, and that I stopped flighting the ball the moment Ismail launched into my bowling. Thus are reputations made and broken by our experts of the fourth estate!

We took a lead of 59 runs. Hyderabad had won the Moin-ud-Dowla Gold Cup that season, and I claimed in a boast to my friend Mumtaz Hussain that as I had brought the team luck, we would also win the Ranji Trophy, now that we had gained a first innings lead. "You don't know Hyderabad cricket, Ram, we can still lose this match," Mumtaz said, dampening my enthusiasm. I was really upset with this negative approach, but Mumtaz's words proved prophetic and we lost the match, thanks to a combination of negative tactics, timid batting and total lack of self-belief. In the second innings, Mankad hit a glorious century and declared, leaving us just over three hours of batting. We folded up without a fight against bowling that never rose beyond the accurate. Leg spinner Rakesh Tandon took six wickets, at least three of them with full tosses or long hops, and veteran Padmakar Shivalkar mopped up four more, to leave us losers by 70-odd runs. It was abject surrender of the worst kind. Mumtaz was right and my dreams came crashing down.

IRANI CUP AND THE REST!

The next season opened on a high note for me. At the end of a pre-season Moin-ud-Dowla match, I received the glad news that I had been picked for Rest of India to play Ranji Trophy champion Bombay. I remember running into EAS Prasanna at the Lal Bahadur Stadium and his telling me, "Bishan and Anshu (Gaekwad) are the only deserving players in the team." He was referring to the fact that the ROI squad was at least partially experimental inasmuch as it did not seem to be the best of the Rest, the selectors perhaps wishing to take a good look at future prospects. It would have been much more sporting of him if he had wished me luck as well. As it turned out, Prasanna was proved right by a dismal performance by the Rest, though my own bowling had been creditable if not spectacular. Bombay beat us by an innings.

The Rest of India team read: Palash Nandy, AD Gaekwad, H Gidwani, Mike Dalvi, Yajurvindra Singh, Mohinder Amarnath, Sambaran Banerjee, B Burman, BS Bedi, V Ramnarayan, A Minna. Reserves: Bharath Reddy, KA Qaiyyum, V Krishnaswami.

Bombay, led by Sunil Gavaskar, was at full strength, and Rest of India was as always a ragtag-bobtail outfit, with some of its players with very little match practice before the all-important game. In Bengal, for instance, the season had hardly begun, and its batsmen were rather rusty. Barun Burman, the pace bowler, was however in full flow and bowled very well, including the prize scalp of Sunil Gavaskar in his bag of four victims.

Batting first, we were bundled out for 173, and missed a trick or two when Bombay was in trouble after the early dismissal of Gavaskar by Barun Burman, letting them put up a total of 327. At one stage the scorecard had read 215 for 5 and 249 for 6, despite nineties by Ashok Mankad and Dilip Vengsarkar, but we allowed wicket keeper Bandiwadekar and paceman Abdul Ismail to put on 76 runs, thanks to the captain claiming the new ball with the spinners still on top. Bedi and I had two wickets apiece when the sixth wicket fell, but we did not bowl again. We collapsed again in the second innings, Paddy Shivalkar taking ten (4 + 6) wickets in the match and off-spinner Ranjan Baindoor five (4 +1). Both spinners were immaculate, but poor batting was the real culprit in ROI's massacre. The only batsmen to make runs were Yajurvindra Singh in the first innings, and Madan Lal in the second.

I have always been a great admirer of Bishan Bedi, the bowler, perhaps the greatest left arm spinner of all time, and also Bishan Bedi, the plain speaker. He was a wonderful leader, ever concerned about the welfare of his men, I found out almost as soon as I met him in that Irani

Cup match. That his actions could sometimes be incomprehensible, I found out too, the day before the match. He had seen me briefly in action in the nets at Hyderabad during the Test against Sri Lanka there, when it struck me that my bowling did not greatly impress him. That was bad news as he was India's captain! Now on the eve of the Irani Cup match he marked me out for special attention during fielding drills. I thought he was overdoing it to the point of completely exhausting me before an all-important match. Mohinder Amarnath was laughing at me all the time and saying, not without sympathy, "Bishan has obviously taken a liking to you."

Amarnath pulled out in the eleventh hour citing a fitness issue, and Madan Lal, the local lad, was fortuitously available as a replacement. Bishan seemed fond of Ashwini Minna, the young leg spinner. He was touted as a future Test bowler based on his exploits in school cricket, and I like many others was eager to catch a glimpse of this prodigy.

As it turned out, Minna appeared to be an ordinary bowler, with nothing remarkable about his unorthodox flight; it looked different only because it was of a flat trajectory. There was no sharp turn or bounce, there were no variations. Perhaps the occasion was too big for the lad, but he just faded away after that match. He was a cheerful fellow with a nice sense of humour, and a man of great courage, I was to learn later. He was from the third generation of a family that owned the newspaper group *Punjab Kesari,* and had lost his father and grandfather to assassin's bullets. Like his ancestors, Ashwini continued running the newspaper which was boldly critical of terrorist and anti-national elements. He published his newspaper fearlessly despite receiving several threats to his life. Today he is the owner of the group, and he as well as his son continue to be targetted by anti-social elements.

Unfortunately for me, everytime I was beginning to dominate the batsmen, I was removed to bring on Minna, who was less effective. I actually ended up bowling 25 overs in about five spells, thanks largely to vice-captain Anshuman Gaekwad's constant conversations with Bishan. Handicapped by a stiff neck after the evening's exertions and a disturbed night's sleep on a foam mattress in an air-conditioned room, I did not quite bowl at my best, but impressed people so much that the *Times of India's* headline read: *Ramnarayan impressive*, even though I took only two wickets. *The Hindu* was quite critical of the captain for underutilizing me.

But for dropped catches, I should have had the wickets of Ashok Mankad and Dilip Vengsarkar, both of whom were among the runs. Incredibly the brilliant fielder Madan Lal dropped a sitter off Vengsarkar and I dropped a stiff return catch myself. Bishan himself was not at his fluid best, and Barun Burman was our best bowler, with a four-wicket haul that included the prize scalp of Sunil Gavaskar. Madan Lal, brought on with the second new ball, perhaps with the hope that he would bring the Bombay innings to a swift end after I had just collected my second (and Bombay's sixth) wicket, met with no success, and it was Burman who finally cleaned up the tail. Bombay had made 327 by that time. I was fairly convinced that that was some 70 runs more than they deserved.

One of the funniest episodes of the match was when both my captain and I, with upset tummies, were in the toilet with pads on while wickets were tumbling. Bedi who wanted to bat at no. ten to my nine, had to charge ahead of me as he was quicker off the mark than I was! Later, I chose to chase a cup of tea with a glass of beer during a team meeting, because I was too polite to waste the tea that arrived late, resulting in Bishan raising an extremely puzzled eyebrow. I don't think the two incidents did anything to earn me respect from the captain!

I had bowled exceptionally well to Gaekwad in the Moin-ud-Dowla Gold Cup when he led VST Colts against us, and that was perhaps the reason why he spoke up for me during the match. Anshu, as we all know him, was to do that again a few years later, when he felt S Venkataraghavan, the captain of our team (Andhra Bank Invitation XI in the Moin-ud-Dowla Gold Cup), was underbowling me. I found him to be a genuine friend, a frank and honest one, who spoke his mind no matter who his audience might be. He cared enough about my future in cricket to offer me a job in Baroda so that I could play for Baroda and West Zone, without having to contend with world class rivals as I had to in South Zone.

Though I liked to think of Anshu as a true friend, I tended to suffer a minor trauma every time he was around. On the first occasion, as he and I were walking towards the dining room of Oberoi Maidens in Delhi, I puked on its beautifully manicured lawns, after a single shot of some exotic whisky that my friends Viji and Bharatan had plied me with during the Irani Cup match. The second instance was even more dramatic. Anshu, my brother Siva and Tamil Nadu medium pacer Bharath Kumar came home for dinner one night at Hyderabad, and we repaired to my friend Vaidy's house, as we found my wife studying for an exam on the morrow. There, I had exactly two drinks before sitting down to dinner. Next thing I knew I woke up in the guest bedroom at 4 am. I had apparently fallen asleep on the drawing room divan and with my feet sticking out across the front door, I forced my friends to carry me to the bedroom so that the guests could open the door and go home.

By now I had grown quite superstitious about the effect Anshu's company had on my sobriety. So the next time we met—during a GR Vishwanath benefit match dinner at Chennai—I made a quick exit when Anshu innocently asked me, "What's your poison?'

That Irani Cup match was probably the closest I came to a place in the Indian team. My story might have turned out different had I taken four or five wickets in that Bombay innings, but at the end of that match, I realised that I might be good enough for the Rest but was nowhere near getting into the South Zone team. I found that out soon enough even as I reached the airport, where *The Hindu's* Rajan Bala gave me the news that I was not included in the team for the Duleep Trophy that season. (In my first season, I had been unceremoniously kicked out after warming the reserve benches for three matches). It was hardly surprising considering that both the skipper S Venkataraghavan and Prasanna were off-spinners and played for India. My first appearance for the zone came a few years later when I had no realistic chance of making it to the Indian team, and that too only because Prasanna and Venkataraghavan were away in Pakistan with the Indian team.

I almost forgot. I was in the reserves of the South Zone team that played England (rather, MCC as it used to be called) at Hyderabad. There was some excitement about my chances on the eve of the match, with Venkataraghavan the skipper a doubtful starter with a finger injury. There was no sign of him till late that evening, and with Prasanna and Chandrasekhar rested in favour of Meher Baba and Narasimha Rao, my friends and well-wishers started congratulating me, in the belief Venkat too would rest, giving all three of us a chance to bowl at the tourists. I was the one sceptic in the crowd. I was absolutely right. Venkat arrived on the morning of the match and promptly tossed for the match. He played a minor role as a bowler in the match, and I sat twiddling my thumbs. Meher and Bobjee made no impact on the English batsmen, of whom Dennis Amiss and Derek Randall made hundreds. In my form then,

I was suffering from a massive case of itching fingers and no chance to do anything about it.

Those days, the local players commuted from home to the match, not moving into the team hotel as they do now. On the first day, I rode my Enfield motorcycle to the ground, with Meher Baba my pillion rider, only to be told by the traffic police to park the bike nearly a mile away from the ground, as I did not have a vehicle pass with me, though we were both already in our whites and had player passes. I asked Meher to go ahead without me, and was in a foul mood, as I entered the ground a full 20 minutes later. To make matters worse, I was greeted with a scowl and a sharp rebuke for being late, besides being told I would be warming the reserve bench. It was one of those moments you wished you had never played cricket!

The consolation was that my brother Sivaramakrishnan opened the innings and gave a very good account of himself, negotiating the swing and seam of John Lever, Mike Selvey and Bob Woolmer quite capably, before being run out for 27 some 20 minutes before lunch. He was sent back by GR Viswanath after he charged down from the non-striker's end as Vishy played to near Derek Randall prowling in the covers and called him for a quick single. Randall proved true to his reputation as a brilliant fielder. The other opener, P Ramesh, another talented left-hander, bagged a pair in the match. My brother missed a golden opportunity to become Sunil Gavaskar's opening partner in Test cricket.

(The group photograph of the two teams has two Derek Randalls. The moment he knew the camera was of the panning variety, Randall ran behind the players from one end of the group to the other).

A nice moment during a later zone game against Kallicharran's West Indies XI, was when Tiger Pataudi introduced me to Robin Marlar, an England off spinner turned journalist as an off spinner who should have been playing the match rather than watching it. As I had been the zone's most successful bowler that season and omitted for the tour match, it was indeed balm for my wounds. "The competition must be intense," Marlar said to me, but as I was apparently no longer on the selectors' radar, I thought it was non-existent.

ABBAS AND TIGER RETIRE

The season was a pretty good one for me, but not so good for Hyderabad. When I was playing the Irani Cup match at Delhi, Hyderabad was losing first innings points to less fancied Andhra at Eluru, collapsing for 120 against the pace of H Ramprasad and DGCA Varma and the spin of Meher Baba. Batting first Andhra had made 229, and though they were in a sorry state at 25 for 5 in the second, they drew the match.

There was tension in the air as I landed at Warangal for the next match—versus Kerala. There had been a recent attempt at a captaincy coup according to my teammates, one of whom, Mumtaz Hussain, warned me not to be seen in the company of my good friend P Krishnamurti. I was quite stunned by this sample of Hyderabad cricket politics, as I never played a part in any of it and was not even aware of the undercurrents. The match itself went well for me. I took 4 for 30 in 19.2 overs in the first innings, and one for 13 in seven in the second. Kerala's most successful batsman of the period, Ramesh Sampath, was a good friend—he and I had been South Zone reserves the previous season—and he playfully said to me, "Ram, you'd better not get me out!" Equally playfully, I replied, "Sure, so long as you don't sweep me," referring to his favourite shot which had fetched him so many runs against the likes of Prasanna and Venkataraghavan. As it turned out, Sampath swept the very first ball I bowled down square-leg Noshir Mehta's throat! Sampath, one of Kerala's best batsmen in the 1970s, and originally from Tamil Nadu, was a scientist working in ISRO, India's space programme. He died in tragic circumstances a few years later in Goa, drowning in the sea while out on a swim.

In the second innings of the match, Jaisimha was absent ill, and Abid Ali deputized for him as captain. Abid had a knack for confusing you so that you could rarely bowl at your best. It was difficult to pinpoint what exactly he was up to, but he managed to demoralise everyone, while trying to do the exact opposite of that. Strange as it seems, I was never the sole off-spinner in the Hyderabad XI, and good old Noshir Mehta was still among us, though since my arrival he had hardly had anything to do in the side. In the second innings, I think both of us were below par, and though I had very impressive if not productive figures, I was quite rattled when OK Ramdas pulled a half-volley from outside the off-stump slamming a powerful shot on to shortleg Jyothi Prasad's head, the only such instance in my career. Ramdas was caught off the rebound at slip, but Jyothi went down like a pack of cards. It was the worst moment of my life as a bowler to watch a scene like that. I was a nervous wreck after that, though the brave guy that he was,

Jyothi bore the injury like a true warrior, gulping down a quarter bottle of brandy neat. He gave us all many anxious hours, but recovered reasonably enough to travel to Ahmedabad to play for South Zone versus West Zone. He did well in the one-day Deodhar Trophy match but dropped an extremely tough return catch offered by Sunil Gavaskar off the very first ball of the Duleep Trophy match. Gavaskar went on to make 228.

I had only two more Ranji Trophy matches that season, as we did not qualify for the knockout as a result of our setback against Andhra. We once again yielded the first innings lead to Karnataka, thanks to centuries by Brijesh Patel and Syed Kirmani. After a promising start when I clean bowled Roger Binny and took a diving return catch to dismiss GR Viswanath (featured on the cover), I finished with figures of 3 for 98 in 40 overs. Brijesh was a scratchy starter, who gave the bowler a real chance early in the innings, but when set, arguably India's finest player of spin during his era. I had AV Jayaprakash caught behind off a thick inside edge—a brilliant legside catch—but the umpire thought otherwise. Such decisions sometimes are the difference between a match-winning performance and a steady one; I had to cause to believe that I might have restricted Karnataka to a manageable total that day had I won that legitimate appeal. By the time I took my third wicket—to an extraordinary catch by an airborne Rajan at short midwicket to get rid of the dangerous Vijayakrishna—Karnataka had already wrested the initiative from us. A five or six-wicket haul in that particular game would have surely strengthened my case for a place in the South Zone team.

I bowled my best spell of the season in the match against Tamil Nadu at Hyderabad, but suffered an injury in the second innings that put me out of action for a while. Luckily it was the last Ranji Trophy match of the season. Against Tamil Nadu I had the impressive figures of 4 for 49 in 28 overs, a spell which one newspaperman described as superior to the bowling of Test off-spinner Venkataraghavan in the match, high compliment indeed. One of my victims was my brother Sivaramakrishnan who charged out to me after making 61 brilliant runs, to be stumped by my good friend Krishnamurti. One of my other wickets was that of young PS Moses, who looked very promising in his quick 30. Having batted first and taken a lead of 59 runs, we made a sporting declaration, setting Tamil Nadu a target of 276 runs. The only way we could qualify for the knockout was by beating Tamil Nadu outright. They were 191 for 6 at one stage, despite a fine 109 by opener P Ramesh, but Mukund and Venkataraghavan put on an unbeaten 52 to save the match. TN were never in with a real chance to win the match. Unfortunately, I dislocated my little finger after my initial spell of nine overs, diving forward foolishly to attempt an impossible catch at leg slip off a thick inner edge by Ramesh off fastish leg spinner Narasimha Rao that was going down rapidly. Three newspapers the next morning added insult to injury by describing it as a dropped catch. When I confronted Radhakrishna of *The Indian Express* a few days later at a local match, he said, “All of us had stepped out for tea, and photographer Chari told us you dropped a catch.”

HYDERABAD WITHOUT JAI

The next season dawned with a major change in the Hyderabad cricket team: ML Jaisimha had retired from first class cricket after captaining Hyderabad for 23 seasons. It was a situation that we all knew was inevitable but had difficulty adjusting to. We would certainly miss his strong presence, his sharp cricketing brain, his charisma and the tremendous confidence all that gave us as we stepped on to the field.

My first reaction to the news that Syed Abid Ali was to be his successor was one of happiness—for Abid, and all of us—though I had vague apprehensions about Abid's temperament that could on occasion be fragile.

Abid was a well-meaning captain who sometimes got confused about what was the best course open to him as the leader of the team, such that he made some strange decisions, most of which demoralized most of us. Personally, I had a new off spin bowling rival in the team in Shivlal Yadav who had replaced Noshir Mehta, which made things rather awkward as Abid often decided to bring on Shivlal for no rational reason and denied me the opportunity to finish off the job I had begun.

Typically I might have taken two or three of the first six wickets, but would not bowl another over in the innings, finishing with far fewer wickets than I normally would have. These eccentric bowling changes must have put a great deal of pressure on young Shivlal as well, because throughout the time I was in the eleven along with him, he was rarely among the wickets. (It was quite another matter that he was still selected to play for India against the touring Australians on the strength of 13 Ranji Trophy wickets; and went on to claim 100 Test wickets in a successful career). The eventual sufferer was of course the Hyderabad team, which performed below its own potential. The worst part of the experience for me was that Abid, my erstwhile mentor, was a good friend and often my roommate on tour.

Abid was not available for the knockout phase of the Ranji Trophy in his first season as captain, and I enjoyed considerable success under the captaincy of Narasimha Rao who led us in his absence, with seven (5 + 2) wickets against Bengal and 4 against less fancied Uttar Pradesh, who beat us, only to lose by a big margin to Karnataka in the final.

I was particularly proud of my bowling against Bengal as I took five wickets with what I thought was intelligent use of the conditions of slow, low bounce on an uncharacteristic first day wicket. Bengal had a strong batting line-up that included Gopal Bose, Raju Mukherjee, Ambar Roy and Michael Dalvi, and I relied on subtle variations of pace and trajectory rather than any sharp spin in trapping well set batsmen into mistakes. At the other end, interim captain Narasimha Rao was at his brilliant best with his pacy leg breaks and googlies and bounce, but he finished with only three wickets to my 5 for 51. Next morning, KN Prabhu, writing in the *Times of India*, was quick to point out that the better bowler on the day picked up fewer wickets, and I made it a point to agree with him when I met him in the evening. I also asked him why it never occurred to his tribe to comment on the occasions when I bowled better than the more successful bowler of the day!

This was the match I first met the Bengal left-arm spinner Dilip Doshi, whom I had admired from afar for years. I first watched him in action in the Duleep Trophy match I had watched in 1968-69 at Eden Gardens, when he had looked unplayable on a helpful wicket. (Though he bowled with great skill as a late entrant to Test cricket to earn worldwide respect, I believed that he had been at his sharp-spinning best before he entered the Test arena). He came up to me after the Bengal innings, and asked me how I bowled the ball that took the outer edge of his teammate Raju Mukherjee's forward defensive bat to result in a slip catch. He was surprised and pleased when I confessed that I had attempted a normal off-break, only to find the ball go the other way. "Some other bowlers would have claimed they bowled the floater!" he said. A couple of years later, Dilip was to offer to find me employment in Calcutta to enhance my chances of playing Duleep Trophy cricket, hampered as my prospects were in the South Zone, with two Test off-spinners in the team. I foolishly declined the offer, unwilling to give up my 'proper' job as a senior bank officer in favour of a 'cricketing' one.

For someone who played so little of his cricket against Bengal or at Calcutta, I had quite a few friends in the Bengal team. In a ridiculous show of mindless aggression during that match, after being hit high on my shoulder by a Barun Burman bouncer, I took a golf swing at the stationary ball and sent it flying past the bowler, who was so shocked that he was in a rage throughout the time I was at the crease. True, it was an instinctive reaction on my part, but I would have been fined heavily or suspended under today's rules. It's a wonder that no one appealed. Had they done so, the umpire would have had no option but to rule me out. I remember that former India captain Shanta Rangaswami—a star woman cricketer—who was doing the radio commentary had a thing or two to say about my behaviour.

Barun was a very good friend of mine and so was his captain, the late Ambar Roy, who invited us both to his room that evening, when we had a few beers and shook hands. On the few occasions we met, Ambar was kindness personified, as gentle as his stroke play on the field. His became one of the prize scalps of my career when I bowled him in the second innings of a State Bank of India inter-circle match between Hyderabad and Calcutta. "What kind of off spinner are you, bowling bloody outswingers?" was his friendly complaint after the match. Coming from such an outstanding batsman, I thought it was high praise. That was my last match for State Bank as I had put in my papers, and it was a memorable one. I took ten wickets in the game (medium pacer VS Patel was the other successful bowler) while we put up a decent, but losing, fight after veteran Subroto Guha had demolished us in the first innings with a magnificent spell of swing bowling, claiming eight wickets for next to nothing. He was moving the ball so prodigiously that some 50 byes contributed to our first innings total of 105. As we were coming off the ground at the end of the match, the Calcutta skipper Chuni Goswami walked towards me and enveloped me in a warm embrace. "Great bowling. Hope you play for India soon," were his words. TJ Banerjee, a fine medium pacer who played that day, was another close friend from Bengal.

Our victory over Bengal took us to the semifinal round, where we were to meet Uttar Pradesh. Though UP had quite a few good players in its ranks, we were the favourites as we took them on at the picturesque Mohan Nagar, Ghaziabad, ground owned and maintained by the Mohun Meakin Breweries. An indifferent, timid batting display by us on a sluggish surface led to our being dismissed for 247, with the slow bowlers—left armers Haseen Ahmed and Rajinder Singh Hans and veteran leg spinner Anand Shukla—taking three wickets each. Skipper Narasimha Rao played a lone hand with an unbeaten 80.

UP started their reply fairly strongly, and, while Bobjee continued his good bowling form, I was ever so slightly below par. I was unsettled by the umpire repeatedly suggesting—without actually warning me--that I was running on to the danger area of the wicket. I was less penetrative than usual and occasionally lapsed in direction. My good friend Abdul Hai, the brilliant lefthander from Hyderabad, was now playing for UP, and he played some excellent positive cricket. He and one-drop Shashikant were involved in a fruitful partnership, and UP were well placed overnight for the loss of only two wickets, with Abdul unbeaten with a half-century. A few chances went abegging, but I knew that had I bowled better than I did, we might have finished on a stronger note.

That night, Bobjee, manager Murtuza Ali Baig, senior player (and my roommate) Mumtaz Hussain and I met in my room to discuss the strategy for the morrow. The thinktank approved Mumtaz's plan that he and Bobjee open the proceedings, with Mumtaz shutting up one end with some accurate defensive bowling, with me coming on after we made a breakthrough. Though I was slightly disappointed to be so 'sidelined,' I realized that the idea made sense. I was up until quite late trying to figure out a way of regaining some of my sharpness off the wicket, and went to sleep only when I thought I had the answer to my bowling problems.

Wonder of wonders! Things went exactly according to plan, and UP were struggling to accelerate against some very precise bowling by Bobjee and Mumtaz (17-5-29-0). True to the agreed plan, I came on to bowl as soon as Abdul was caught at shortleg by Jyotiprasad off Bobjee for 91. The scoreboard read 172 for 3 at the end of a 130-run partnership. I had surmised that my run-up had slowed down as a consequence of over-long spells in local cricket, and tried to run in faster this morning. The move paid off and I was back to my best bowling. I clean bowled Shashikant for 50 and UP were now 176 for 4. With Bobjee and I attacking from both ends, UP were soon 193 for 6, but several missed chances facilitated a seventh wicket partnership of 48. 241 for 7. More spilled chances ensured a 20-run first innings lead for UP, though Bobjee (4 for 81) and I (4 for 90) toiled manfully.

We batted badly a second time and UP won the match outright chasing a target of 156, to enter the final, which they lost to Karnataka at Delhi.

It was an unpopular Hyderabad team that returned home after yet another lost opportunity to be a finalist. Our former skipper Jaisimha, now the chairman of selectors, invited the senior players and Murtuza Baig to dinner. He was in no mood to listen to our explanations for our defeat, and Bobjee and I were at the receiving end of a fierce tongue-lashing. Not having won the Ranji Trophy in his career as a player, he had had great expectations from us after our good showing during the season. He was deeply disappointed.

The confusion and demoralization in the Hyderabad team continued through the next season. We did not qualify for the knockout, and our losses (by virtue of first innings leads) at the hands of Tamil Nadu and Karnataka were extremely depressing experiences. The one bright spot was the opportunity to watch EAS Prasanna's fantastic bowling against us at Bangalore in his final Ranji Trophy outing. I vividly remember the new delivery he unfurled in the nets during that game—one that turned like a leg break—which he refused to try out in a match because he had not mastered it. That would probably have been the first *doosra* in cricket—bowled with a clean action to boot!

That was Abid's last season for Hyderabad, and despite all the unhappiness he caused himself and his teammates in the last two seasons, we would all miss him. He was a truly great champion at his best: attacking batsman, brilliant fielder, shrewd medium pacer, and affectionate friend. As a bowler he always performed above his capacity, but as a batsman I think he was an underperformer. With his superb eye, immense power and twinkling footwork, he should have been a much more successful batsman than he proved at the international level. He would have revelled in today's shorter format cricket. He was a loyal soldier of Hyderabad cricket for the best part of his career, despite all his idiosyncrasies and insecurities.

If some of the matches during his years at the helm had been forgettable—like the time he unsuccessfully tried to bounce out TE Srinivasan who loved the short stuff—the next season with Narasimha Rao wholly in charge was not much better. I was dropped for the first match of the season at Nizamabad against Andhra—with off-spinner-all rounder Arshad Ayub joining Shivlal in the eleven—and came back into the eleven when Shivlal was unavailable doing Test duty. Though I bowled well in every match that season, it seemed the captain was making sure I did not meet with success in the last league game of the season—against Kerala—perhaps so that the selectors would not face any embarrassment when Shivlal came back for the knockout phase of the Ranji Trophy. I had played my last match for Hyderabad.

SWEEPING DEFEAT

Sometimes you do something innocent on a cricket field and it results in disastrous consequences for your team. In my case, back in 1979-80, it was a full-blooded sweepshot I played off Shivlal Yadav's bowling that led to my team Andhra Bank's defeat by a Hyderabad Cricket Association XI.

Ours was a star-studded eleven led by S Venkataraghavan and including guest players Anshuman Gaekwad, Surinder Amarnath, Duleep Mendis, and Ved Raj. Andhra Bank's chairman O Swaminatha Reddy, who desperately wanted to enter a team in that year's Moin-ud-Dowla Gold Cup, fulfilled the HCA's stipulation of at least four Test players to qualify for entry into the tournament by inviting these high-profile cricketers. I had been totally against this move, as this would mean dropping some of our leading players, all of them state or South Zone cricketers. I even offered to stand down to enable our vice-captain CR Chandran to take his rightful place in the team.

There was much unhappiness all round as the guest players kept five of my teammates out, and none of them was released to play for other teams in the tournament. This made ML Jaisimha, captain of the F D Stewart XI, very angry as he badly needed players for his side and we refused to part with any. Adding to the confusion was the replacement of our captain Vijay Paul by S Venkataraghavan, with my manager asking me to request Venkat to play under Paul's captaincy. As it turned out, Venkat did lead the side, all five guest players took the field and Chandran refused to let me yield my place to him.

Batting first, we were caught on a drying wicket taking appreciable turn. Shivlal, who was in the Hyderabad XI only because I was turning out for Andhra Bank, struck gold against some extremely poor batting by our star imports and we were soon 70 odd for 9, when I walked in to bat. I was determined to stick around with left-handed Meher Baba, a homegrown Andhra Bank cricketer, and we managed to add nearly 50 runs for the last wicket. My contribution was some 15 to 20 runs and I remained unbeaten, if I remember right.

The crucial act of mine that had such a telling impact on the match was my powerful sweep off Shivlal Yadav which hit forward short leg L Rajan on his knee and rendered him hors' d' combat for the rest of the match. Rajan was Hyderabad's opening batsman, whose place at the top of the order was now taken by skipper P Krishnamurti, well past his best playing days, and originally slated to bat at No. 10. Now, Krishnamurti had a few points to prove against the Hyderabad Cricket Association and also enjoyed playing against

Venkataraghavan, whom he was determined to collar to demonstrate his batting prowess in the evening of his career. He launched a sizzling assault on the bowling, reserving his worst for Venkat, and made a swashbuckling 126 at more than a run a ball.

Krishnamurti's onslaught meant that HCA took the first innings lead despite effective bowling by Meher and me that troubled all the other batsmen. Catches were spilled frequently, leading to no more than respectable figures for me and Meher, while off spinner Shivlal Yadav, my replacement in the Hyderabad side, hit the headlines and went on to play for India not long afterwards. When the list of Indian probables prior to the tour of Pakistan was announced, my name was a prominent omission.

IT'S A TIE

It had been a difficult couple of years for me in cricket. Competition, some of it unfair, was breathing down my neck, and I was suffering from the first major injury of my cricket career, without realising how serious it was. Constantly wearing inferior cricket shoes as I did, I had developed an Achilles tendon problem, medically known as bursitis, which gradually grew unbearably painful. Off-season, I had trained harder and harder, somehow gritting my teeth and ignoring my pain, thinking this was the usual temporary soreness of muscles. I even ran with my awful cricket spikes on the gallery steps round and round the stadium when it rained. My condition naturally grew worse. The new season was about to start and at 32, I had serious cause to worry about my future in the game, if this injury was going to lay me low. And all this after I had been dropped - from the Hyderabad team in the previous Ranji season and I had sworn to get back into the team, come what may.

That is when my friend Dr Harsha, an orthopaedic surgeon, arrived on the scene like some angel of mercy. He correctly diagnosed my condition and offered to give me a cortisone injection in the affected part. "The injection pain will kill you but after a couple of days of that hell, you will have a new heel. If you are lucky, the relief could be permanent."

I took the chance and decided to brave the injection pain. Just as Harsha had promised, the pain was real hell, and I wondered if I had made a mistake. Two days later, I woke up in the morning, completely free from pain! It was as if I had a new heel, a new foot, a new left leg!

I was then playing for Andhra Bank, led by Vijay Paul in the absence of Narasimha Rao who was away playing league cricket in Ireland. We had stars like Jyotiprasad, Ravi Kumar, H Ramprasad, Meher Baba, Chandran and many more and we were about to play the first round of the Ghulam Ali memorial knockout tournament. I don't remember the early rounds, but I clearly recall our encounter with the Jaisimha-led Marredpally Cricket Club in the quarterfinals. I was delighted to claim Jai's wicket for the first time and finish up with five wickets. We won despite a fighting, elegant 85 by Vivek Jaisimha. In the semifinals, I took seven wickets against State Bank of Hyderabad, another star-studded team, and we entered the final in style.

Syndicate Bank were our opponents in the final, which was a 2-innings match limited to 75 (8-ball) overs a side in the first innings and 35 in the second. Our opponents were a strong outfit, even though their Test player Shivlal Yadav was away playing for the country. Led by Vinod Reddy, they had in their ranks Jugal Kishore Ghia, Chamundeshwarnath, Sainath, Shivkumar, Moses Nityanand and several other talented cricketers.

Winning the toss, we batted badly and were soon in a bad way. As our manager, the late CS

Shyam Lal, and I took a walk around the boundary line, I told him, "Don't worry, if we make 150 we will win," so confident was I with my bowling form after the recent treatment. We managed to reach 169 with a small contribution from me in partnership with Jyoti and we were soon on the field. We claimed a couple of early wickets but the obdurate Shivkumar tested our patience with his complete mastery of whatever we sent down. In the last over before stumps, I managed to get one past him (by sheer mind power, I think) and we went home in a reasonably happy frame of mind. Next morning, our bowling really clicked and we bowled Syndicate Bank out for 125, with 7 wickets my share of the booty.

When we batted a second time, we fared much better, and I was again involved in a rearguard partnership with my good friend Jyoti. Syndicate Bank had to make 224 in 35 (8 ball) overs to win the match. Moses Nityanand and his partner (whose name I don't recall now) blazed away, but our left arm spinner Meher Baba and I were able to put the brakes on the rampaging batsmen, and though Moses made a hundred or thereabouts, we managed to peg Syndicate Bank in their run chase. I bowled the 34th over, yielding only three runs and helping effect a run out (my second in the innings). I had taken six wickets, totalling 13 for the match. Meher bowled the last over with Syndicate Bank needing six runs to win the match. The batsmen ran like crazy between the wickets, there were run out attempts that missed the stumps by a whisker, until the last ball target was a mere two runs. The batsman swung and missed and they ran a bye. It was a tie!

Once the significance of the result sank in, disbelief and joy replaced the disappointment of not winning and both teams were able to enjoy the rare occasion. I invited all the players of both teams home for beer and dinner, and my wife had the shock of her life when some 30 bedraggled, dirty, tired cricketers landed at her doorstep. The celebrations went on till well after midnight and many of the guests stayed overnight. Rarely in my personal experience have two rival teams enjoyed each other's company as we did that night.

SACKED!

"F... cricket." It was probably the only time I had used those two words together, and a rare occasion when I swore. Ranga Reddy had the most shocked expression on his face. He was deeply offended too, because he heard "you" instead of "cricket". Once I repeated the expletive, he was quite relieved and happy. I, in sharp contrast, was deeply unhappy, beyond rage, my entire cricket career in a shambles, for no fault of mine, but as a result of the machinations of the cricket bosses, their pawns the selectors, and the captain who had sacrificed some of us at the altar of his own progress.

Ranga Reddy and a couple of senior cricketers of the Hyderabad team were my drinking buddies that unhappy night, when it became crystal clear to me that it was indubitably the end of the road for me. I was one of about 25 cricketers training at the unlikely outpost of Nizamabad in a two-week conditioning camp leading to the selection of the team to represent Hyderabad in the Ranji Trophy in the forthcoming season. I was all of 33, the oldest member of the team—though some of my teammates were not very much younger, if you ignored their concocted dates of birth and did a bit of investigation. The whole team had been sacked on the morning of a Moin-ud-Dowla cricket match at the start of the season and all of us banned for an indefinite period of time.

The ban was lifted in record time—about two weeks after it was announced—once the administration realised that the whole cricket community and the corporate supporters of the game were up in arms against what they saw as a draconian measure by an uncaring administration indifferent to genuine player grievances and demands. Once the ban was removed, all the affected players were included in a squad of 25 or so named to attend a pre-season conditioning camp at Nizamabad, the same venue I had experienced the humiliation of being dropped from the Hyderabad team to meet Andhra in the previous season's opener, after a similar 3-week-long camp.

I participated wholeheartedly in the camp. A couple of days into it, some of us came to learn during after dinner conversations with the manager of the camp and Ranga Reddy, the vice-president deputed by HCA to spend a few days at the camp, that three of us had been identified as the villains of the whole drama and targeted for eventual removal from the team. Jyotiprasad and Vijay Paul were the other two.

Heated words were exchanged as the players and the officials blamed each other for the sad state of affairs in Hyderabad cricket. Ranga Reddy even suggested that I should be grateful to Hyderabad that it afforded me a chance at all in first class cricket while I had been rejected by my home state. That is when I swore at cricket, and Ranga thought I was cursing him. "What did you say?" he demanded in a most agitated voice, and was quite relieved when I repeated "F... cricket." So long as I was not swearing at him, it was all right with him.

It was one of the lowest points of my cricket life. I knew in my head that my dream of a comeback to first class cricket was effectively over, though my foolish heart did not agree. I had had a splendid local season after cortisone injections had given me a new left foot as it were, relieving severe pain caused by tendonitis. Dropped from the Ranji team in the knockout phase of the previous season, I had been picked in the Hyderabad squad to play against Mafatlal in the Moin-ud-Dowla Gold Cup, after a succession of top performances in the Ghulam Ali and Behram-ud-Dowla knockout tournaments. And I had really been looking forward to returning to the arena I knew so well—especially as I had a psychological advantage against the Mafatlal players. I had dominated most of them earlier in the Ranji Trophy and the Deodhar Trophy.

The camp had come a couple of weeks after one of the most dramatic developments in Indian domestic cricket, when the entire Hyderabad team was sacked on the morning of its match against Mafatlal Sports Club in the first round of the Moin-ud-Dowla Gold Cup. There went the chances of my comeback!

Trouble had started the day before the match, though it had been brewing from the time the Hyderabad boys under M Narasimha Rao went to Srinagar to take part in the Wills Trophy. Rumblings of some form of player rebellion had begun to be heard, catalysed by the brave noises made by the captain, disgruntled at being left out of the South Zone squad, and blaming the Hyderabad Cricket Association (HCA) for it.

I had been out of the Hyderabad team since the previous season's knockout round, when Shivlal Yadav came back from Test match duty, and I had not been selected for the Wills Trophy. I had, however, worked hard to reclaim what I regarded as my rightful place in the state team, and had a bagful of wickets in the tournaments leading to the first class season. My performances had been quite spectacular, with 5, 7, 7 and 6 wickets in the last four innings before Moin-ud-Dowla, and the selectors were virtually forced to include me.

Arriving ten minutes late for morning net practice the day before the Moin-ud-Dowla opener, I was surprised to see the whole team trooping back into the dressing room. For a moment, I wondered if I had been so hopelessly late that my colleagues were already taking a drinks break.

I soon found out that the players, led by their captain and the hugely talented batsman Saad bin Jung, were actually staging a walkout in protest against coach K Premji's instructions to those two players to leave the nets and change from their tracksuits to cricket 'flannels', to fall in line with the HCA's dress code.

'The coach insulted our captain and senior player,' was their vociferous claim, and there was bedlam in the dressing room. "Ram, are you going to talk some sense to your teammates or are you too going on strike?" Premji had asked as soon as I entered, and now it all began to make sense to me.

Once I had a chance to talk to my colleagues, I tried to do exactly what Premji had asked me to do. But my advice fell on the deaf ears of a very worked-up group of young firebrands, or so it seemed. "That's the trouble with you old guys, you have no guts," one of the youngsters told me, and a couple of his friends nodded in agreement.

I still persisted that confrontation would do us no good. "We can't walk out of practice a day before an important match. We should instead try to sort out our differences with the association across the table," I tried to reason, but again, I met with stiff resistance. Finally, I warned my friends that we could all be dropped en masse on the morrow, and asked them, were we prepared to face such a consequence? A loud 'Yes' in chorus was the reply.

"Now that all of us are prepared to accept the worst punishment, I am fully with the team," I assured them and we all dispersed, amidst much nervous giggling and palpable excitement.

Mafatlal Favourites screamed the sports page headline next morning, even as I was getting dressed to go to the ground, and I was wondering how *The Hindu* could so blatantly disregard the all round strength of the local team. Just then I noticed the box item next to it, which said: *Hyderabad team sacked.*

Once I recovered from the shock, I decided to act perfectly normal. I started packing my kit bag—a small affair unlike the 'coffin' favoured by present-day cricketers—and getting ready to leave for the Lal Bahadur Stadium. The doorbell rang. My visitor was the Hyderabad captain Narasimha Rao, laughing and hyper, outwardly excited by our unusual status on the morning of an important match. Soon we were joined by a few more players, including my good friend Jyotiprasad, who had for long been Narasimha Rao's bosom pal, until differences had gradually crept in between the inseparables. As we chatted nervously, now giggling, now laughing out loud, I was getting increasingly anxious. I was furious that the HCA administration had acted unilaterally in dismissing an entire team without giving the players a chance to defend themselves. I was keen that we report at the ground and be sacked in full view of the crowd.

I was annoyed with my teammates, the captain in particular, for delaying our arrival at the ground until the match was well under way. We lost a great chance to win the sympathy of the crowd—small as it was—by trying to enter the dressing room and getting ejected by the officials. Little did I realise then that the association had asked the captain the previous evening to bring all the players to the ground to explain our stand to the officials, and that he had told them none of us was interested in talking to them. He had allegedly put his feet up on the table in front of him while

Mr. V. Ramnarayan (aged 17 years), son of Mr. P. N. Venkatraman, Madras Branch, was selected to play for Madras Cricket Association 'Colts' XI. He is a student of B.Sc. class at the Presidency College, Madras, and was awarded the Government of India Scholarship for proficiency in Hindi. **Our congratulations to Mr. Ramnarayan and good wishes to him for further successes.**

Beginnings

The author's first steps in cricket lauded in the in-house magazine of his father's employer, Bank of India

Presidency College team (1965-66)

Seated (L to R): R Sridhar, VM Raghupathi (Physical Director), Dr BGL Swamy (Principal), **N Ram (captain), V Ramnarayan (vice-captain),** John Alexander

Middle row (L to R): Ramadurai, Kamalakar Tapkire, PS Ramesh, SP Balachandran,NP Balasubramaniam, Chinnikrishnan, Prakash

Last row (L to R): CV Tyagarajan, CS Dayakar, Mohan Krishniah, Jayaraj

Andhra Bank XI with guest players

Seated (L to R): D Meher Baba, P Jyotiprasad, AD Gaekwad, **S Venkataraghavan** (captain), Surinder Amarnath, T Vijaya Paul, Duleep Mendis

Standing (L to R): MN Ravikumar, CR Chandran, KN Charan, V Ramnarayan, CS Sham Lal (manager), Ved Raj, Bhaskar Ramamurti, H Ramprasad, D Inder Raj

Andhra Bank with all the trophies it won in the 1978-79 season

Standing (L to R): Mallick Dev, Bhaskar Rammurti, V Ramnarayan, Dilip Reddy, Mujtaba Ali Baig

Seated (L to R): CR Chandran, T Vijaya Paul (captain), CS Sham Lal (manager), ML Jaisimha & PR Man Singh (honoured guests), P Jyotiprasad

Hyderabad vs. Kerala at Warangal 1976-77

Seated (L to R): Ramesh Sampath (4th), **ML Jaisimha** (7th), **JK Mahendra** (9th), S Abid Ali (11th), P Krishnamurti (12)
Squatting (L to R): P Jyotiprasad (1st), Khalid Qaiyyum (4th), Abdul Bari Wahab (5th), T Vijaya Paul (6th), Mumtaz Hussain, Noshir Mehta, Shahid Akbar, V Ramnarayan (7th to 10th)
Standing (L to R): A Satyendran (1st), MV Narasimha Rao (3rd), OK Ramdas (11th), L Rajan, CR Chandran

The Press and Two Cricketing Greats

Berry Sarbadhikari (radio commentator), Dicky Rutnagur (Correspondent, Daily Telegraph, UK), Tiger Pataudi, KN Prabhu (Times of India), KN Chari (Photographer, The Hindu), Garfield Sobers, Pearson Surita (Radio commentator), PN Sundaresan (Spl Correspondent, The Hindu, and my paternal uncle).

Hyderabad vs. Karnataka, 1975-76

Seated (L to R): BP Patel, BS Chandrasekhar, GR Viswanath, Official (O), **ML Jaisimha**, O, O, **EAS Prasanna**, O, S Abid Ali, AA Baig, MAK Pataudi

Standing (L to R): Umpire I Ramana Rao, ?, ?, ? V Ramnarayan, , Prahlad, P Krishnamurti, T Vijaya Paul, MV Narasimha Rao, P Jyotiprasad, SMH Kirman, Nagesh Hamand, ?, K Jayantilal, Abdul Hai, Sultan Salim, Mumtaz Hussain, CR Chandran, ?, Umpire KB Ramaswamy

Hyderabad vs. Andhra 1975-76

Seated(L to R) : Sultan Salim, Syed Abid Ali, MAK Pataudi,P Krishnamurti, official, RVVK Prasad (Andhra captain), official, ML Jaisimha (Hyderabad captain), official, official, AA Baig, K Chandrasekhar Rao, B ramprasad, K Jayantilal

Standing (L to R) : Umpire, CR Chandran, Abdul Hai, P Jyotiprasad, T Vijaya Paul, V Ramnarayan, H Ramprasad, MV Narasimha Rao, Prahlad, Others in the picture include from right DGCA Varma (11th), D Meher Baba (10th), T Sridhar (8th), Mumtaz Hussain (4th), MN Ravikumar (2nd) and umpire Kasturi

In action

V Ramnarayan in his pomp – all fire and concentration

From the author's first Moin-ud-Dowla match. A picture of opponents Hindustan Breweries XI

Standing (L to R): PR Man Singh (manager), Kailash R Gattani, P Krishnamurti, AV Jayaprakash, DR Doshi, ?, Venkat Sunderam, Gopal Bose

Seated (L to R) : Budhi Kunderan, WA Bourne, Duleep Mendis, MAK Pataudi, Rohan Kanhai, Anura Tennekoon, David Heyn

Conditioning camp before the 1977-78 tour of Australia

Dhiraj Parsana, Chetan Chauhan, GR Viswanath, S Venkataraghavan, Kapil Dev, BP Patel (half hidden), Yajurvindra Singh, BS Chandrasekhar, Barun Burman, P Sharma (hidden) Raju Jadeja (hidden), AD Gaekwad, EAS Prasanna, V Ramnarayan, SMH Kirmani, AV Mankad, RS Hans, Sambaran Banerjee, DK Tandon (trainer), SM Gavaskar.

Siva

My brother V Sivaramakrishnan, Tamil Nadu and South Zone opener

Last Hurrah

The TVS team that won the Hindu Trophy, 1984-85.

Seated (L to R): MO Parthasarathi, V Ramnarayan, VA Parthasarathi (manager), K Bharath Kumar (captain), PK Dharmalingam (coach), AG Harjinder Singh, R Madhavan

Standing (L to R) WV Raman, S Hemant, M Venkataramana, R Pattabhiraman, L Rajkumar, K Srinath, Lalith Kumar, Rajaram (scorer), KS Dharmesh, PR Venkatasubramaniam, Bhasker (WV Raman and M Venkataramana later played for India.)

addressing Surendar Reddy, the President of HCA, who sat on the other side of the desk. In fact it was to be months before I learnt that Narasimha Rao had told the association we were uninterested in talking to them, while at the same time, informing us that HCA had given us no chance to talk it over.

Events overtook us from then on. There was an unexpected groundswell of support for the sacked players, with the public, our employers, and several cricketers past and present lending their voices to what grew into a minor protest movement of sorts in no time at all. We had former players on our side, ML Jaisimha, my former captain who was then a South Zone selector, but was not part of the Hyderabad selection committee, the left arm spinner Mumtaz Hussain, VM Sham Raj, and Munim Siddiqui among them. We all had a series of meetings of 'the rebel players', the first of which took place at Saad bin Jung's residence at Begumpet. Many of our supporters were with us not because they believed in our cause but because they saw in the moment an opportunity to settle scores with PR Man Singh, the presiding deity at the Hyderabad Cricket Association.

(The night before the meeting, the captain's brother and senior HCA official Ranganadha Rao and his friend Gopal had come to my house and asked me to advise my teammates to tender apologies to the HCA and seek an official pardon. I had willingly agreed, and when I told Saad I was going to bring that up in the meeting, he thought it was a good idea. His initial ardour had obviously cooled now to a pragmatic attitude. At the meeting, however, my fellow rebels shouted me down angrily when I suggested we all apologise en masse to Man Singh).

Soon we started meeting at ML Jaisimha's residence at Marredpally—the venue of many wonderful evenings of hospitality—where a cricketer was always welcome. The Nirlon cricket team was in town playing in the Gold Cup. Their captain, Little Master Sunil Gavaskar, came up with a brilliant idea, which we unfortunately could not translate into action. As Mafatlal CC had won their first round match against the second-string Hyderabad team that replaced us, they had three free days before their next game. Sunil suggested that the sacked Hyderabad XI play a one-day match versus Mafatlal at the South Central Railway ground at Secunderabad, which was outside the control of the HCA. We were all excited about this dramatic gesture cocking a snook at authority, and the match nearly took place. The preparations of course had to be carried out in secrecy, and this is where we ran into trouble. The Mafatlal opening batsman K Jayantilal was the younger brother of Premji, the Hyderabad manager, and that is how we guessed the news of our plan was leaked out to HCA. The upshot of it was that the Railway authorities denied us permission to stage the match at their ground, apparently nudged by HCA to withdraw their earlier concurrence.

I had the unusual experience of being summoned by the Chairman of Andhra Bank, O Swaminatha

Reddy, along with our cricket manager CS Sham Lal, to draft a strongly worded letter to the cricket association slamming its decision to suspend an entire team of cricketers. I realised that I was gradually being seen as the hero (or villain, depending on your loyalties) of the movement, notwithstanding my conscientious objection to the protest in the first place. I wrote a suitably pompous sounding letter to the Hyderabad Cricket Association, which the Chairman signed in his capacity as a member of its executive committee. The gist of it was that the bank would withdraw its support to the present cricket administration unless the action against the players was withdrawn.

Soon, some other key members of the committee including the State Bank of India and State Bank of Hyderabad expressed their displeasure to the cricket association, leading to some rethinking on the part of the administration. The sage counsel of former BCCI secretary and India captain Ghulam Ahmed, still an official of the Andhra Pradesh government, was sought, and he summoned all the players to his office for a meeting. The interesting part of the meeting, personally for me, was that Ghulam, and therefore, most in Hyderabad, had identified me as the arch villain of the whole protest movement.

To cut a long story short, the Hyderabad Cricket Association realised it had gone too far in suspending so many players, and soon announced the withdrawal of the action against all of us, including us in a list of 25 players selected to attend an 18-day conditioning camp at Nizamabad, the scene of my famous conversation with Ranga Reddy of the opening paragraph. Later, the majority of the suspended players made their peace with the HCA during or immediately after the camp.

There was a dramatic development before the first Ranji Trophy game. All three villains were included in the South Zone team in the interim between the camp and the start of the Ranji season. I was completely unprepared when my friend Vaidy called one day to give me the news I was to go to Kanpur as a member of the South Zone squad for the Duleep Trophy match versus Central Zone there, as the original off spinner and skipper S Venkataraghavan was unavailable. Vaidy was with Jaisimha, South Zone selection panel chairman, when he broke the news to him. He had had a phone conversation with Kripal Singh, the Tamil Nadu representative on the committee, and had prevailed on him to include me, rather than Arshad Ayub, who had replaced me in the Hyderabad team. It was obviously a swipe at Man Singh and HCA as much as it was a vote of confidence in three genuine cricketers.

Soon I was on a flight to Delhi en route to Kanpur. I met the boys from TN there: my brother Sivaramakrishnan, K Bharath Kumar, TA Sekar and S Vasudevan, if I remember right. We spent the morning having breakfast and a lovely cup of south Indian coffee at the residence of Mr Sundaresan, soon to become the father-in-law of

K Srikkanth, who did not make the trip to Kanpur because of his engineering exams.

The evening before the match, I badly bruised a finger during fielding practice, and was a doubtful starter—which would have been a disappointing end to my comeback dreams. As it turned out, I recovered enough to play, but in hindsight, always wondered if I might have bowled better than I did. When we lost the toss and fielded first, I did bowl quite well on a flat track so typical of that part of the country, though my 50 overs fetched me only 4 wickets for 144. When Central Zone were at 250 plus for 6, we stood a decent chance of bowling them out under 400, but Narasimha Rao, at slip, still apparently angry with the world, was literally caught napping, and he dropped the no. 8 batsman, left-hander Anil Mathur before he had scored a run off my bowling. It was a sitter of a catch, and the fielder had no business to stand with his hands literally in his pockets as Bobjee did.

With opener Sanjeeva Rao (188) and Mathur (50) putting on 99 for the seventh wicket and Central Zone finishing on 445 all out, the match was literally taken away from us. We yielded a large first innings lead, though Narasimha Rao (67), Vijay Paul (51) and tailender TA Sekar (58) batted delightfully for half centuries. In the second innings, Sanjeeva Rao made 95 and the second century-maker of the first innings, Parthasarathi Sharma, 87. My brother Sivaramakrishnan scored a hundred in the second innings and MN Ravikumar was unbeaten with 69, but it was all too little, too late. The two redeeming features of the South Zone performance were the brilliant wicket keeping of 16-year-old Sadanand Viswanath and the hostile fast bowling of TA Sekar, who took four second innings wickets. The other medium-pacer K Bharath Kumar was also impressive.

The hotel we stayed in was probably built by the British soon after they landed in Calcutta and neglected forever after that. It was a disgrace of a lodging for a zone team, low on comfort, hygiene and safety. One afternoon, I found a stranger using the toilet attached to my bedroom! He had got in through a huge hole in a door that opened on to the street.

Some of us decided to have our bit of fun in the surrounding gloom and the camaraderie in the team was quite uplifting. Bharath Kumar and I even attended a wedding reception on the lawns of the hotel clad in our rather garish lungis. The food was a distinct improvement on what the hotel served the team.

As I said before, I bowled reasonably well, and TA Sekar and I were clearly the most successful bowlers of the team. Unfortunately, my dream run had to end there. When the selectors met to pick the South Zone team to participate in the Cricket Association of Bengal Jubilee tournament, they omitted me, and if I remember right, Jyothiprasad as well.

The new Ranji Trophy season opened with a match against Tamil Nadu at the Lal Bahadur

Stadium, and as expected, Hyderabad excluded the three villains identified by the administration—Vijay Paul, Jyothiprasad and me. In my case, it could really have been a comeback, now virtually ruled out by my missing the Moin-ud-Dowlah tournament, a spectacular show in which alone could have helped my cause. Paul and Jyothi eventually came back into the team and enjoyed a successful second lease of life. They too must have extended the olive branch to HCA and Man Singh at some point, though I was no longer around in the twin cities to witness that.

The most disappointing aspect of the team selection after the camp was that at yet another meeting involving the players and Man Singh and Co., the venerable Ghulam Ahmed changed his tune to say that the three of us had not been 'victimised' as he had himself claimed at our last meeting. Addressing me directly, he said, "Ram, you must admit you are too old to be in the selectors' reckoning. In my playing days, I retired the day I felt I was over the hill." This was a resounding slap in the face. I made up my mind to leave Hyderabad then and there, though not to pursue a cricket career elsewhere. I wanted to quit the scene of my bitter defeat.

LEADERS

THE SKIPPER

"Do you remember that evening in Bangkok in January 1978 when we had some 12 bahts between us and needed to buy a bottle of soda?" my former captain would ask, recalling the experience of temporary poverty that had had a couple of thirsty souls seeking desperate measures on alien soil. He would then proceed to describe the clothes you wore, the décor of the hotel room and the brand of nectar you shared, even the name of the angel in uniform who rescued you from dehydration.

This eye for detail and unusual memory marked every shrewd move Motganahalli Laxminarsu Jaisimha made as captain of Hyderabad for over two decades. Each nuance of the leading batsmen of the day was filed away in his mental database for future action. Often, when one of them took guard against Hyderabad, the field was elaborately rearranged; and with Jai's reputation for cunning on a cricket field, the ploy invariably sowed doubt in the mind of the batsman.

A man of strong likes and dislikes, Jaisimha abhorred cricket that was aesthetically objectionable. He was impatient with players whose methods were crude even if effective and who were better appreciated by other captains.

Jai was the most feared captain of his time in Indian cricket, someone the Indian captain `Tiger' Pataudi was happy to play under in the Ranji Trophy. Any Hyderabad player of the time can vouch for Pataudi's admiration for him and total acceptance of his leadership. The 1975-76 season arguably featured Jai's finest hour as well as his worst match as captain. That season, we saw how a masterstroke by him gave Hyderabad victory after we had conceded a lead of 220 runs in the first innings of a three-day match.

If in the match against Railways, we prayed desperately for the fourth day that was not there, towards the end of the next match, we wished there had been only three instead of four days of play. We took a first innings lead of 59 runs against Bombay in the quarterfinal round, but eventually lost the match. I took seven wickets in the first innings, and their captain Ashok Mankad decided to go after my bowling in the second, in the hope that my captain would remove me from the attack. It was a tactical move that paid off as Jai walked into the trap, bringing on his medium pacers from both ends and setting ultra-defensive fields. Mankad made a brilliant unbeaten hundred and declared the innings, leaving us with less than four hours of batting on the last day.

We collapsed like a deck of cards against the spin bowling of Rakesh Tandon and Padmakar Shivalkar, and Bombay won a thrilling, unexpected victory. Ashok Mankad's captaincy in the match came in for praise all round, while Jaisimha acknowledged that he had blundered. By his own admission, it was by far his worst piece of captaincy.

ML Jaisimha was a stylist par excellence, with his immaculate grooming, graceful walk and copybook technique. Nothing ugly marred anything he did on the cricket ground, tennis court or golf course. Even to friendly arm-wrestling, in which I recall no youngster ever defeating him, he brought an elegance and nonchalance that could compare with the seeming effortlessness of his cricket.

Jaisimha left behind him a way of life steeped in sport, and a host of friends and acquaintances replete with memories of the fantastic hospitality of the Jaisimha household.

PATAUDI

Hyderabad's cricketers and cricket lovers had the redoubtable Ram Prakash Mehra and his fiefdom, the Delhi and Districts Cricket Association, to thank for MAK Pataudi's transfer from Delhi to Hyderabad in the Ranji Trophy.

He was already India captain when he fell out with the DDCA administration and his close friendship with ML Jaisimha, the Hyderabad skipper, brought him south, with his sister's address in Begumpet giving him the necessary residential qualification.

Thus began Tiger's over-a-decade long love-hate affair with Hyderabad cricket, with most of his new teammates and the local crowds welcoming him with open arms and a lunatic fringe of sons-of-the soil partisans opposing the transplant.

What Tiger's arrival in the twin cities did to Hyderabad cricket was to double the glamour quotient of the team, which already had Jaisimha—with his matinee idol looks and inimitable swagger—and Abbas Ali Baig with his boyish charm.

At times there were as many as six Test cricketers and almost the entire South Zone eleven in the squad — Tiger, Jai, Abbas, Abid Ali, Jayantilal, Krishnamurti, Govindraj, Mumtaz Hussain, Abdul Hai, Narasimha Rao, Noshir Mehta and so on—who formed as exciting a line-up as anywhere.

The seniors were naturally older and altogether more experienced and polished than the rest of the team, but for all the awe that their stature demanded, we were a remarkably relaxed lot in the dressing room if generally on our best behaviour.

Tiger, who never led Hyderabad, was ever mindful of who the boss was, not once hinting by action or word at his own exalted position in the cricket world.

In fact, some of us were once witness to what came close to a ticking off by the captain, when he pulled up Tiger for going off the field without sufficient cause, suggesting that he had taken a cigarette rather than a toilet break during a painfully long session.

On a personal level, I was his teammate for exactly one season during 1975-76, though we remained in touch afterwards.

My first season for Hyderabad was his last. He had just retired from Test cricket after a thrilling series as captain against Clive Lloyd's West Indies, though a poor one as batsman.

The rapport between us was instant, and his approval of my cricket did wonders for my morale.

Imagine coming into a team with at least four stars you had watched and admired from a distance—in my case at the ripe old age of 28, when I had given up all hope of playing first class cricket!

It was nothing short of a dream, to drink in the special atmosphere of the Hyderabad dressing room, to enjoy the long train journeys to Ranji

Trophy matches, the interesting, sometimes electrifying conversations about cricket and cricketers that taught you more about the game than any coaching manual, the card games from bridge and rummy to the most absurd games of pure chance that Tiger invented, the conviviality inspired by Mr. McDowell, in short, the sheer camaraderie of it all, with every member of the team included in all the fun.

"When I saw the English bowling," was Mansur Ali Khan's pat reply to a British journalist at a press conference immediately after his maiden Test hundred at Madras against Ted Dexter's visiting England side in 1961. The question had been about when after the loss of one eye he had started believing he could play Test cricket again.

In his autobiographical *Tiger's Tale*, Pataudi recounted how he decided to have some fun in the middle in that game. "The crowds here have rarely seen Indian batsmen take the aerial route," he told his batting partner and skipper Nari Contractor, and proceeded to play some delightful lofted shots, including a couple of sixes, in an innings that broke away from the defensive mould of the time.

Pataudi was the first superstar of Indian cricket, arguably more charismatic than anyone before or after him to don India colours. The reasons were not far to seek: his brilliant wit and repartee as much as his striking good looks, superb athleticism and positive cricket.

He was the first Indian captain to demand consistent hard work in the fielding department, though there had been the occasional flash in the pan before his time. He set a marvellous personal example, patrolling the covers with lissome authority—those fortunate enough to watch the early Pataudi believed that he was not only a genius of a batsman but also a world class slip fielder, before he became blind in one eye. One of the first things he is said to have told his team after taking over as Sussex captain was: "Gentlemen, let's see some scuffed trousers and bruised knees and elbows."

Acknowledged as one of the world's best fielders of his time, he was once invited by a television channel to compete in a fielding contest with Colin Bland, South Africa's original Jonty Rhodes, to be telecast live, but Tiger declined because it involved getting up early on a non-match morning!

Pataudi's heroic exploits in a losing cause once earned him the newspaper headlines His Magnificence The Nawab of Headingley. This was during the 1967 tour of England and he made 64 and 148 as India scored 510 after following on, forcing England to bat a second time. Next year, he was leading India in Australia, where after being forced to miss the first Test by a hamstring injury, he earned the sobriquet of Captain Courageous with his brave batting in the remaining three Tests— "with one good eye and on one good leg."

It has been suggested that his 2793 runs at an average of 34.91 are ordinary figures, but these statistics have to be seen in the right perspective. For the major part of his career he averaged around

40, which was not far behind the performance of the leading Indian batsmen of his period. His failure against the West Indies at both the start and end of his career it was that brought down his average considerably. At the peak of his career, he modestly dismissed any excessive praise of his batting by claiming that most of his runs were scored against medium pace bowling! In rare moments, he however admitted that with two eyes, he might have equalled the great batsmen of the game.

Two memories linger from my first season for Hyderabad: one a totally unexpected cameo by Pataudi in a match against Andhra, when following an off-drive off my bowling, the batsman MN Ravikumar dived back to his crease after starting a second run as he saw Tiger pick up the ball in a feline swoop and fling it—feign a throw, in fact—only to see him walk up to where the ball had actually stopped on a damp outfield and retrieve it casually; another a masterly 198 against Tamil Nadu after demanding a promotion in the batting order and promising the captain a double hundred.

I remember suggesting to Pataudi that his decision to retire from Test cricket at the end of the 1974-75 series India lost 2-3 to Clive Lloyd's West Indies. His reply was heartbreaking. "I don't want to be killed on a cricket field, Ram," he said, referring to his inability to see the express deliveries of Andy Roberts and Co.

My thoughts keep going back to a moment at the end of my first Ranji Trophy season. We were sitting on the terrace at the Wankhede Stadium after losing to Bombay a match we should have won. I had had a good match personally, and Pataudi was quietly happy about it in the manner of a kindly senior. "Seven wickets against Bombay!" he repeatedly muttered, but adding a disclaimer. "Next year, wickets will be harder to come by, because every batsman will take you more seriously." Prophetic, those words turned out to be, though I did not take them seriously then.

What he said next devastated me. "All the best, Ram. I won't be playing next year. I am announcing my retirement from first class cricket."

PLAYING FOR SOUTH ZONE

Fast bowler CR Rangachari was one of the more outspoken Tamil Nadu cricketers I knew. I had the pleasure of getting to know him when he officiated as the manager of the South Zone cricket team for its Duleep Trophy and Deodhar Trophy matches during the 1978-79 season. The venue, Nagpur, was notorious for being somewhat player-unfriendly. The Indian captain Bishan Bedi for instance had to face the firing squad after he had demanded orange juice for his team at breakfast and hot water for their bath at the MLA hostel where they were staying during a Test match.

The manager spared nobody with his sharp comments made in a loud voice, be it star batsman Brijesh Patel or the brilliant TE Srinivasan. The all rounder Roger Binny came in for special mention (remember he was some distance from playing for India). Rangachari told me, "This Binny, do you call him an opening bowler? He has no pace and no skill. Later he told Narasimha Rao, "What kind of opening batsman is Roger Binny? He has no technique." That night, Roger, suitably lubricated during the team meeting in my room, knocked continuously on Rangachari's door with the long pole kindly provided by the management for us to hang and unhang washed clothes in the tall clotheslines that decorated every room (Yes, the noises made by Bishan Bedi a few years ago had had no effect on the Vidarbha Cricket Association, our hosts, who believed that spartan conditions brought out the best in cricketers; hot water continued to be a distant dream, and orange juice was still not part of the menu).

Rangachari was particularly harsh on the newly married TE Srinivasan who had brought his wife with him. “Has he come to play cricket or enjoy marital bliss? He should have self-control,” he thundered. “When I had a Ranji Trophy match to play soon after marriage, my wife told me, “No mischief (I have censored the word Rangachari actually uttered) before the match!” He was indignation personified when Brijesh Patel was late for a team meeting. “Mr Patel may be a Test player, but I do not tolerate indiscipline from anyone,” he told the assembled team. However, we discovered that Mr Rangachari was something of a paper tiger, because he stopped all the ranting and raving the moment the player in question entered the room.

The team meetings were the best part of that trip, and they invariably took place in my spacious room, which the leg-n-leg players used as their watering hole every evening after a long day in the sun, with the two umpires Piloo Reporter and Rajen Mehra joining us and trading several rollicking stories with us. Reporter’s humour and flair for anecdotes are well known.One of his favourite stories of Bombay cricket was about a stout umpire who fell down in a heap everytime he signalled a leg bye. He also loved to recall a batsman who would shout 'Mind your end' to his partner, only to be run out himself.Reporter grew fond of a totally inappropriate story I liked to tell about a big game hunter, the most desired woman in the state of Texas and a wild bear, and made it a point to ask me. "How's the Texan woman?" as an opener for years afterwards.

For all the leg-pulling we indulged in at the manager's expense, we had healthy respect for his cricketing prowess. His exploits for Madras were good enough for him to lay claim to being the best fast bowler his home state has produced.

With MJ Gopalan, he formed a deadly pair of opening bowlers, with Gopalan growing with the years into a seam and swing specialist and Rangachari himself remaining wedded to sheer pace for most of his career.

As a selector, coach and manager, Rangachari was known to be a good sport who spent considerable time mentoring his young wards, lightening the mood in the dressing room with entertaining if apocryphal stories from his own youth.

During the match at the beginning of this story, I asked him if he was quicker than Kapil Dev. "Have you seen Wes Hall? Same speed!" was Rangachari's instant response. Only it sounded like shame shpeed, thanks to the tobacco he was chewing.The resultant giggles and tittering were understandable as the young listeners had never seen him in action or even read about his sterling deeds in first class cricket. Those who actually did, remembered him as a speed merchant, tireless and persistent, even on dead wickets. He was a brave soldier of Madras cricket.

Personally, I had mixed fortunes in the game, with only one wicket for over a hundred in the first innings and 3 for 34 in the second. That was to be my last chance in the Duleep Trophy for a couple of years more as we lost the match to Central Zone. I fared better in the Deodhar Trophy match that followed, with figures of 3 for 42 in 12 overs (those were 60-over matches).Later that month, I fared even better against West Zone at Bombay, claiming 4 wickets for 35 in my allotted 12 overs, only to be dropped for the final versus North Zone. My career figures of 7 for 77 in 24 overs in the Deodhar Trophy must be some kind of record, if it was any consolation to me.

Central Zone had two fine left arm spinners in Suresh Shastri and Rajinder Singh Hans. Both were quality bowlers, and Hans was distinctly unlucky to miss out on India selection, as he was in the middle of some great bowling form when the selectors plumped for the more experienced Dilip Doshi while picking the team to face Kim Hughes's Australian team that toured India in 1979-80.With Doshi succeeding straightaway and going on to take more than 100 Test wickets, Hans, later a national selector, never made it. He and I got on very well as spinners sailing in the same boat, and I remember his little acts of kindnesses from time to time. During that Nagpur game, for instance, he ran on to the field when his side was batting with a supply of spare studs for my cricket shoes, when I desperately needed them.

SYED ABID ALI

In addition to my own State Bank of India teammates Krishnamurti, Nagesh Hamand and others, I was fortunate in acquiring another mentor in Hyderabad soon after my arrival there. My teammates spread the word about me in cricket circles, and that is how Syed Abid Ali, the Hyderabad and India all rounder came to watch me in action in the practice nets behind the State Bank of India's local head office at Kothi, Hyderabad.

Abid straightaway decided to take me under his wing. For the next few years, I was to enjoy that protective umbrella and benefit from Abid's willingness to share his experience and knowledge with me. His way of helping me become a better off spinner was to hit my best deliveries repeatedly out of the ground during net practice, so that I learnt to adjust my flight when confronted with batsmen who could do that to me in matches. Even in matches in which we were pitted against each other, the lessons continued, ruining my bowling analysis in the process. Of course, when I got him out, he always had a perfect explanation for the accident that had nothing to do with good bowling!

Abid Ali was a genuine character among cricketers, an original in many ways. For instance, he set high standards of physical fitness for a generation of cricketers known for its lackadaisical attitude to such matters. The punishing regimen of training he followed was often the subject of anecdotes, perfect entertainment in the evening after a long day at the ground.

He practised his fielding with devotion and became an acrobatic close-in fielder and an athletic one in the outfield, with a flat, unerring throw. He developed enough variations in his military medium pace bowling to keep the batsmen guessing. He also had the knack of making the ball skid on most wickets. He was demonstrative in an age when most bowlers tended to hide their emotions. His appeals to God when he beat the edge, and his sardonic grins at batsmen blessed by the Lord—unfairly in Abid's opinion—were sights to see and remember.

When Abid took over the Hyderabad captaincy from the cerebral and celebrated ML Jaisimha, he was determined to make a strong impression. He was solemnity personified as he addressed the team just before taking the field in his first Ranji Trophy match as captain. "Boys, I want you to play tight, mean cricket. I want us to give not LESS than 40 runs in the first hour." He had of course meant to say "not MORE than 40 runs," and the giggles and suppressed guffaws that interrupted him, spoiled his speech somewhat, but it was a happy Hyderabad team that took the field that morning.

When the mood captured him, Abid could be the life and soul of the party. He was great company while travelling with the Hyderabad team, taking part in crazy card games devised by MAK Pataudi, or singing calypso songs he learnt in the Caribbean. His favourite line was "Great India bowler Abid Ali" which he sang with gusto.

Few cricketers exploited their talent better. Abid Ali was an honest-to-goodness medium pacer, who could also bat aggressively. He made a sensational Test debut in 1967 when he took 6 for 55 against Australia at Brisbane, following it up with two brilliant innings of 78 and 81 opening the innings in the Sydney Test.

"Kya bole?" (What did you say)? Abid is credited with asking this classic question of GR Viswanath, when they met three quarters of the way down the pitch, with GRV rooted to the spot and repeatedly shouting "No!" at the top of his voice, and Abid still charging down regardless for a run. This no doubt apocryphal story of an incident in a Test match was told with much relish by the Karnataka batsman, at the expense of the Hyderabad all rounder, who had a reputation for getting mixed up in run outs. The reason was simple: Abid Ali was about twice as swift between wickets as most other batsmen and was always on the lookout for quick singles. He was at least once stumped off the first ball he faced, because he had taken off for a single even before playing the ball.

Abid took his cricket with him when he migrated to the USA by the end of the seventies. There, he became an active participant in the local cricket scene in Los Angeles and coached many Indian, Pakistani and other immigrant groups still passionate about cricket. He always wanted to come back to India on a coaching assignment and has had a couple of stints as the coach of state teams. With his keen observation and emphasis on physical fitness, he will always be a good role model for young cricketers to follow.

ABBAS ALI BAIG

No one could have had a more sensational start to his Test career. 20-year old Abbas Ali Baig was a dashing young batsman at Oxford University, with a few exceptional performances under his belt in English county cricket, when the 1959 touring Indian team summoned him to play in the Manchester Test. It had been a severe drubbing for the tourists from Peter May's Englishmen, but the handsome, fleetfooted Hyderabadi made a brilliant 112 on debut and in the company of Polly Umrigar (118) salvaged some pride for the Indians. Though England beat India in that and the next and final Test to make a clean sweep of the five-match series, Baig's name was permanently inscribed in the pages of Indian cricket history.

Unfortunately, Abbas never repeated that level of performance in his Test career thereafter, though a defiant 50 by him against Australia in the Bombay Test next season brought him an unexpected reward in the form of a kiss planted on his cheek by a young female fan in full view of the capacity crowd at the Brabourne Stadium. That is the time the expert Vijay Merchant told the Australian commentator Michael Charlton, "I wonder, Michael, where all these enterprising young ladies were when I was scoring my hundreds?" in his inimitable lilting tones.

Back in his native Hyderabad, Baig played a major role in the team's consistent performances at the league stage of the Ranji Trophy for well over a decade, though neither he nor his star colleagues Jaisimha, the captain, Pataudi and Abid Ali were able to achieve a title triumph in all those years. He was stylish in all he did, be it his thoughtful yet positive batting, his sophisticated contributions to team strategy or his urbane social skills. "*Abbas angrez hai*," Pataudi once quipped, when Baig asked for a fork and knife at lunch.

His three younger brothers also played competitive cricket. Murtuza, slightly younger in age, but older-looking and more sober and conservative in behaviour, was also an Oxford Blue, who played for Hyderabad with less success than Abbas. So did Mazhar, next to Murtuza, with a reputation of being a murderer of most attacks below first class level. If Murtuza was polished and rather understated in a British sort of way, Mazhar was relatively earthy, given to less patrician ways than his elder brothers. The youngest, Mujtaba, was the tiniest of them, with a batting style reminiscent of Abbas, a very nice, simple man, lacking the self belief of Abbas to put his talent to comparable use. I had the pleasure of playing a good deal of cricket with all four brothers at different times, and it was a pleasure and privilege to be their teammate.

Abbas—nicknamed Buggy by peers like Jaisimha and Pataudi—was often my captain in local cricket, when we both played for Hyderabad XI in the Zonal Tournament, the Hyderabad equivalent of Chennai's Buchi Babu before 1968, when it changed from being a local zonal event into an invitation tournament for teams from all over India. He had great confidence in my ability, but it took me a while to realize that, as he nagged me constantly on the field of play, only to praise me generously at the end of the day's play. He also made it a point to spread the word whenever he felt a player had done exceptionally well. It was he who persuaded me to play in the 1975 Moin-ud-Dowla tournament, when I had doubts about my fitness. I did exceedingly well, finishing with eight for 75 against star-studded JK XI in the final, at last managing to convince the selectors with that performance, that I was good enough to play for Hyderabad in the Ranji Trophy. To my amazement, Abbas stopped tutoring me during that match; he must have thought I had come of age. His delight at my success in that match and throughout the season that followed was heartwarming.

As I said earlier, Abbas and Murtuza were of somewhat different temperaments, and sometimes did not see eye to eye on some matters. Once, as Murtuza and I, my senior in the State Bank, were preparing to go to the office after a match had been washed out, even as the other players decided to have a beer together, Abbas said in his most acerbic manner: "The State Bank will collapse if Murtuz and Ram don't turn up for work!"

In yet another instance of sibling rivalry, I bowled a faster ball, following a signal from Murtuza from slip, to incur Abbas's instant wrath. Marching up to me, he admonished me: "Didn't I tell you to flight every ball? Don't you dare listen to that Murtuz!"

Of the brothers, Murtuza was my closest friend, though a bit of a mentor as well. We share a birthday, but he is six years older. But the day Abbas announced he would no longer be available to play for Hyderabad was indeed a sad day. It had been a double whammy as Tiger Pataudi too had come to the same decision at the same time. It was at the end of the 1975-76 season, after we had lost a quarter final match we ought to have won to Bombay. It was the end of an era.

EDDIE AIBARA

The first time Hyderabad won the Ranji Trophy was in the 1937-38 season, when a fortuitous conspiracy of circumstances brought the state into the final without playing a single match. Those days, the whole competition was played on a knockout basis, with teams within the zones, eliminating one another for one of them to qualify for the inter-zone matches — in other words, for the semifinals, as it happened that season.

Madras beat Mysore but gave a walkover to Hyderabad, who were then drawn to meet Southern Punjab in the semifinal round. Wonder of wonders! They were given another walkover and entered the final without playing a single game en route. The other finalists, Nawanagar, were a powerful outfit with three members of the Jamsaheb's princely family Yadvendrasinhji, Indravijayasinhji and Ranvirsinhji — descendants of the great Ranji and Duleep — in the eleven, and strengthened by the presence of L Amar Singh, SN Banerjee, Vinoo Mankad and the Sussex pro AF Wensley, who later coached and played in Madras. Also in the eleven was wicket keeper Abdul Aziz whose gifted son Salim Durrani was to electrify Indian cricket stands decades later.

The final will forever be remembered as Eddie Aibara's match, for his heroism it was that won the match for Hyderabad when it had all but slipped away. After yielding a first innings lead of 39 runs, Hyderabad had conceded their opponents 270 in the second venture, and therefore, needed 310 to win. Openers Asadullah (5) and S R Mehta (24) were both run out and soon the innings was tottering at 67 for 3. Aibara (137 not out) then steadied the innings with two partnerships of 60 and 74 with Hussain (32) and Hyder Ali (46), taking Hyderabad to 244 for 5. Three wickets fell for no run after lunch, but Aibara stood firm in the company of Ten and Jack, grabbing a thrilling one-wicket win. It was a magnificent performance by a great batsman who never played for India.

There were other unsung heroes in that unlikely Hyderabad win. Pacemen Ibrahim Khan — a humble soul if ever there was one and the father of Habib Khan and Sardar Khan, two fine fast bowlers — and Hyder Ali, who bowled superbly in both innings, had match figures of 6 for 109 and 9 for 147. S R Mehta bowled his off spin with purpose in the first innings and batted defiantly in the second.

For Nawanagar, Wensley and Mubarak Ali batted and bowled beautifully even as their more illustrious teammates failed. Amar Singh had a poor match with the ball but made invaluable runs. His new ball partner Banerjee was among the wickets.

Two of the combatants of that match — A F Wensley and Eddie Aibara — went on to become much loved and respected coaches in pre-independence as well as independent India. For Aibara, it was the beginning of a successful run for Hyderabad before he joined Rajkumari Amrit Kaur coaching scheme at Patiala.

(On a personal note, I missed being coached by both Aibara and Wensley. I was already a Ranji Trophy cricketer when I first met Aibara, who was then coaching schoolboys at Hyderabad. Wensley had left Madras by the time I attended my first coaching camp. I was fortunate to come under the benign gaze of TS Worthington, AG Ram Singh, KS Kannan and NJ Venkatesan in Madras. Most of them left my bowling well alone! Two coaches helped me when I badly needed help during my first class years at Hyderabad. Rehmat Baig, an off spinner who represented Hyderabad and the Services, once helped me overcome a shoulder injury with expert advice and made me stretch as a slip fielder enough to improve my catching substantially. The late Vasant Amladi, a coach from Bombay, miraculously transformed my action which had gone all awry one season well into my first class career.He was coaching the under-12 boys of Hyderabad one summer, when I, struggling in the nets, approached him diffidently. "I was hesitating to talk to you, though I've been watching you for the last few days," he said. He then proceeded to correct me in a matter of minutes. Another coach who also encouraged me greatly was the late Bhupathi, father of two excellent cricketers, Mohan and Muthukrishnan, though he never coached me).

MATES

FELLOW TRAVELLERS

In this chapter, I try to recall my memories of some cricketers I played and interacted with, both in Hyderabad and Chennai, and whose lives and mine intersected in significant measure. Except for my seniors in the Hyderabad team, they were not Test or international cricketers. No Test player from Tamil Nadu will find mention here. I have attempted to profile Venkataraghavan and Kumar along with the other famous Test spinners elsewhere.

Bobjee And Joe

They were inseparables in the seventies, two Marredpalli lads, who wore identical clothes, went together everywhere, giggled at everything, and played brilliant, uninhibited cricket. Both were all rounders, the tall, wiry, gangling half of the pair, M Narasimha Rao, Bobjee to everyone, bowled leg breaks at a fast pace a la Chandrasekhar, and batted in a tall, erect, impressive style, driving with authority and using his feet to the spinners, while the shorter, muscular P Jyotiprasad, bowled a sharp, accurate medium pace, giving the batsman no width and cramping him with his nagging, low-slung in cutters—and, difficult to dislodge lower in the batting order, equally capable of stout defence and murderous attack, especially in a crisis.

Both were excellent fielders, could run fast, swoop down on the ball and throw hard, flat and accurate from anywhere, but were better known for their agility and dependability close to the wicket. Jyoti, or Joe, was in the Eknath Solkar class at forward short leg, capable of diving full-length forward and scooping the catch millimetres from the ground in his cupped two-handed style, unique among bat-pad specialists. Bobjee was even more spectacularly agile and flexible and could bring off unbelievable catches, but he was slightly less reliable, tending to be casual when not in the mood.

Bobjee and Joe were popular with the cricket establishment and their peers and seniors alike. They were seen as two innocent teenagers of simple tastes, totally focused on cricket and madly in love with the game. Every captain loved to have them in his team, and soon they progressed from their school teams and Marredpalli club to age group and university cricket before they both graduated to Ranji Trophy cricket and a place in the newly formed Andhra Bank team that before long launched a giant killing spree, ousting State Bank of India and State Bank of Hyderabad from their lofty pedestals.

The pair straightaway began to make an impact on Hyderabad's fortunes in the national championship, Jyoti with the ball and Bob with the bat. It was not long before one grabbed his first five-wicket haul and the other scored his first hundred. Captain Jaisimha and his senior colleagues Abbas Ali Baig, Mansur Ali Khan, Abid

Ali & Co. grew fond of the young rascals, as they were often referred to, thanks to their mischievous, leg-pulling ways off the field.

Idylls do not last forever, and the friendship entered troubled waters, as the careers of the two started following slightly different paths. The tall, lanky Narasimha Rao was the more successful cricketer of the two, recognition coming his way more regularly than in the case of Jyotiprasad. He was made Hyderabad vice captain and when the skipper Abid Ali missed the knockout, travelling overseas, he led the side for the first time in the 1977-78 season. He batted and bowled well, and captained quite capably, though Hyderabad lost in the semifinal to less fancied UP on first innings lead.

Soon Bobjee was selected to play for India and he made his debut against Alvin Kallicharran's West Indies team touring India. Unfortunately, he did not receive too many opportunities and gradually faded away from the Test scene. Bobjee's leadership was on trial from then on, but he held on successfully, negotiating challenges on and off the field with consummate skill, and eventually led Hyderabad to a title triumph, beating Delhi in the 1981-82 final. That was easily the high point of his career.

Joe's career was not quite as successful. Dropped prematurely from the state side, he fought gallantly to make a spectacular comeback and enjoy a happy second innings for the state. He never rose much higher, his few appearances in the zonal competition, though quite impressive, failing to produce statistically significant performances. Opening the bowling on his Duleep Trophy debut, he dropped an extremely difficult catch Sunil Gavaskar offered off the very first ball of the match. The Little Master went on to make 228!

Bobjee and Joe were an unforgettable pair. Though their careers panned out differently, Bob marrying an Irish girl and settling down in Ireland, and Joe continuing to work for Andhra Bank at Hyderabad, they were an integral part of the Hyderabad team at its glamorous best, often playing match winning and match saving roles, and for that, they will always be remembered.

Nagesh Hamand

Nagesh Hamand was one of those cricketers you come across often wherever the game is played, someone who is very successful at the junior and university level but does not quite make the grade in first class cricket. He was one of the first cricketers I met at Hyderabad, and one of my dearest cricket friends, who for years advised and guided me, constantly appreciating my efforts and pointing out my mistakes. He was my State Bank colleague as well as neighbour, living in a quiet residential area originally called Walker Town and renamed Padmarao Nagar.

Nagesh had captained Hyderabad Juniors at Madras in 1969 when we beat his team by an innings. He had put up a lone fight with a brilliant

80 or so, the first time I saw the raw power and aggression of his batting. What I did not know then was what a good off spinner he was, as well. He bowled with a brisk, economical action, and, while he was perhaps not so classically side-on as the purist might wish, he made up with his whippy action and the sharp tweak he gave the cricket ball. He was a confident, aggressive bowler who always believed he could get the batsman out. Also capable of bowling medium pace quite effectively when the mood caught him, Nagesh was convinced he was a better off spinner than Noshir Mehta, who formed a successful pair with left armer Mumtaz Husain for years in Ranji Trophy cricket. Happily for me, he believed I was a better bowler than both of them and never hesitated to pass me useful tips.

It was as a batsman that Nagesh made his mark in university cricket. He was an explosive middle order batsman, who would often take the bowling by the scruff of its neck and give it a mauling. He was particularly severe on off spinners, and loved to go after poor Noshir in local cricket. I too received the brunt of his fury on occasion, though I probably tamed him more often than other purveyors of my trade. The one chink in Nagesh's armour was his weakness against left arm spin, which he managed to conquer on matting, but surfaced, sometimes embarrassingly, on turf.

A shrewd student of the game and an excellent tactician, Nagesh was an astute captain, though he did not receive too many leadership opportunities in his career. He was however an invaluable part of the State Bank think tank for well over a decade. An all round sportsman who could play a very decent game of tennis or table tennis, he had the irritating habit of smiling mischievously at you after defeating you, often coming back from difficult situations.

In the cricket conversations that are part and parcel of the game at all levels, Nagesh was a frank participant who did not bother to pull his punches. Of the firm view that he was a better cricketer than a number of middle order batsmen the Hyderabad selectors preferred to him over the years, he made no secret of his feelings, regardless of who was present. Based on performance, it was difficult not to agree with him.

Inder and Chander

D Inder Raj and C R Chandran—Inder and Chander to their friends—formed one of the most devastating opening pairs I had seen in Hyderabad cricket. The two of them opened the innings for Andhra Bank in domestic competition in the seventies. Both were talented and aggressive and both loved to show off their shot making ability, often competing with each other in tempting fate with some outrageously risky strokes. The faster the bowler bowled the more powerfully they hit the ball. They usually gave Andhra Bank flying starts, even if they sometimes let down the side by getting out in quick succession, when a more cautious approach might have served the team's cause better. Both could cut, pull, hook and drive on the up like the West Indies batsmen of the day, and fours and sixes galore flowed from their flashing blades. One memorable start they provided for Andhra Bank was against the touring Ceylon Tobacco Board XI, which had the pacy Ranjan Gunatilleke in its ranks. As the young tearaway charged in and hurled his express deliveries, the ball kept disappearing into the distant shrubbery beyond the boundary at the Osmania University ground.

Chandran was tall and well built, very athletic in early youth and tending to put on weight as he grew older and learnt to enjoy the good things in life. Like me, he was a vegetarian, a rarity in cricket circles, but loved the pleasures of high quality spirits. He was also a smoker and lit a cigarette invariably with a flourish. A great fan of Amitabh Bachchan, he had the height and good looks to make a good imitation of the great film star, though he resembled another hero of the times, Vinod Khanna, more, especially after he started wearing glasses. During the long evenings on cricket tours, he frequently entertained his teammates with his mimicry of cricket commentators, John Arlott in particular.

Chandran was also a very useful medium pace bowler, with an ability to move the ball both ways. Quite fast when he was young, he later slowed down and concentrated on the fine art of swing and seam. In one unforgettable spell of bowling on the then matting surface at the Railway Recreation ground at Secunderabad, he had the stylish Sultan

Salim weaving and ducking to his short-pitched deliveries. One of his bouncers flew straight and high over Salim's head off the handle and descended on the stumps even as the batsman was trying to obstruct short leg from reaching the catch.

Inder was short and slight in stature and had the whippy reflexes of the small made. He could bowl useful medium pace but his real forte in bowling was leg spin. He toured England with the Indian Schoolboys in 1967 and performed reasonably well. He was one of the more attractive batsmen of his period and a very attacking leg spinner, capable of deceit through flight and variation. One trait he shared with his mate Chandran was a sharp cricketing brain and superb analytical ability. Both could dissect an opponent's strengths and weaknesses and think out excellent strategies to get out of tight corners in matches. Both were relatively lazy, and could easily have achieved greater success than they did had they applied themselves the way some of their les talented peers did. (Chandran once completed a cross-country run by rickshaw)!

Unfortunately, both led adventurous lives and both paid for it, getting a greater share of the rough end of the stick than they perhaps deserved. Chandran died young many years ago, and Inder suffered some setbacks in his career, and he, too, is no more. They have left a trail of wonderful memories with the entertaining brand of cricket they played and the warmth of their friendship.

Abdul Jabbar

Abdul Jabbar came to Madras some time in 1972, to join State Bank of India as a cricket recruit, leaving his native Hyderabad where job opportunities for sportsmen were limited. State Bank was a good employer and entry into the Hyderabad Ranji Trophy team did not seem easy. When the talent scouts of State Bank of India, Madras landed in the twin cities, and the captain, VV Kumar walked into the Nizam College ground where Jabbar and his mate Rashid Mirza were playing a match and made them both an offer of a job in Madras, neither had any hesitation in accepting. Jabbar had a brilliant record at the university and junior level.

The young left-hander was athletically built and quickfooted. His batting was marked by commonsense rather than any exaggerated notions of style. Compact in defence and fluent in strokeplay, Jabbar played very straight, concentrated hard, but could hit the ball explosively hard, when he chose to. He was a good judge of a single, his sense of timing and placement was sound, and his demeanour on and off the field was sober, alert, conservative. A pious Muslim, Jabbar came from a middle class family with a keen interest in sport. Elder brother Wahed was a more than useful medium pacer and younger brother Abdul Azeem, a successful batsman for Hyderabad, once scored a triple century against a Jabbar-led Tamil Nadu attack.

Once in Madras, Jabbar began to make a positive impact on State Bank's and Tamil Nadu's cricket, lending the middle order unprecedented stability. By temperament, he was a long innings player, and time and again he gave evidence of that in the league, Ranji Trophy and Buchi Babu matches. Tamil Nadu was those days in the process of developing into a good batting side, but not yet so consistent as to provide a No.6 batsman ample opportunity to build innings. Jabbar often ran out of partners, and had to be satisfied with forties and fifties. Only in 1976, did he cross three figures for the first time in the Ranji Trophy, making 201 not out against Karnataka.

In due course, Jabbar accumulated more than 3600 runs at a healthy average of 44.57, and became known for his ability to rise to the occasion whenever the chips were down for his state. Given belated recognition in Duleep Trophy, Jabbar had a reasonable run in the tournament, but it came too late in his career to take him further upwards in his career.

Jabbar developed into a very useful off spinner, in which role he was a huge asset to the State Bank team, in the local league, in the intra-State Bank competition and for the all India team in national level tournaments, especially in limited overs cricket. His state captain Venkataraghavan too saw merit in Jabbar as an off spinner in his mature years, and he was a quite a good foil to Venkat and left arm spinner Vasudevan.

Jabbar was a brilliant close-in fielder, a brave short leg in the early years, and a fine catcher in the slips later. He was a team man all through his career, someone the youngest player felt free to go up to for advice and comfort when in trouble.

After serving State Bank for 18 years, Jabbar joined the Sanmar group and turned out for its team Jolly Rovers in the league for a few years, achieving tremendous success with the bat. In the second innings of his career, he began to play some daringly attacking cricket.

After his playing days, Jabbar has turned to coaching youngsters. He is especially good with very young players, grounding them well in the basics, and motivating them with a gentle touch. His coaching clinic is one of the most popular in the city, with pupils and parents alike. He has also been the coach of the Jolly Rovers team, as well as the Tamil Nadu, Kerala and Assam state teams at different times.

Saad bin Jung

Two innings by a young batsman stand out in memory whenever I think of Hyderabad cricket. The first was a fearless century against a West Indies pace attack consisting of Malcolm Marshall, Vanburn Holder and Sylvester Clarke. The second one was another hundred, this time against Tamil Nadu on a square turner at Chepauk a couple of years later. The batsman was Saad bin Jung, Mansur Ali Khan Pataudi's nephew, barely 16 when he took on the might of the pace bowlers from the Caribbean at Lal Bahadur Stadium, opening the South Zone innings, no matter that Marshall was a raw colt and the other bowlers were not exerting themselves unduly in a tour match.

I had been silently critical of his inclusion in the zone team, following a fifty against the tourists playing for the Indian Under-19 or Schoolboys XI. He was an unknown quantity at the first class level, not having made his Ranji Trophy debut yet. The only glimpses we had had of his batting had been at the local league level, where he represented Hyderabad Public School. There were whispers that he was in the team because of his pedigree and proximity to the chairman of the selection committee, ML Jaisimha.

We, the critics, were proved wrong and Jaisimha was proved right by what happened when South Zone won the toss and batted first. The young Hyderabad batsman played the fast bowlers as though he had played them all his life. He had this uncanny ability of seeing the ball early and playing it late. Pace and bounce did not trouble him, nor movement in the air or off it. He played a calm, collected innings worthy of his seniors in the side like GR Viswanath.

Secure in defence, he was unequivocal when it came to playing attacking shots. He cut, drove and pulled with insouciance, and when he came back to the pavilion with a century under his belt, chubby cheeks and all, the crowd gave him a standing ovation.

If after this display against genuine pace, we entertained any doubts about Saad's ability against quality spin, these were dispelled a couple of years later, when he made 113 and 37 not out against Tamil Nadu in conditions inimical to batting. The wicket was spiteful minefield with the ball rearing and turning. Venkataraghavan, Vasudevan and Santosh Kumar were the spinners in operation, and especially in the second innings no batsman was secure.

The exception was Saad bin Jung, who used his feet in a masterly fashion to the spinners, dancing down the wicket and smothering the spin with his body. The second innings cameo was really worth its weight in gold, as it saved the match for Hyderabad. At the end of the match, Venkataraghavan paid Saad a generous compliment when he appreciated his batting as some of the best he had seen against spin on a turning wicket.

Saad faded away soon after that magnificent performance. Part of the blame surely lay with him, because he perhaps got carried away by all his early success and began to focus less on cricket than the trappings going with it.

The administration too was perhaps unhelpful; and uncaring, and instead of nurturing an unusual talent, came down heavily on him when he did not toe the line. An extremely promising career got cut even before establishing itself. I know I can be accused of blasphemy, but I believe that in Saad bin Jung, we had a potential Sachin Tendulkar.

The Khan Family

Every now and then in cricket, you come across truly humble folk from a working class background, who are also outstanding cricketers, quite unaware of the awe they command from fellow players and cricket lovers. The Khan family of fast bowlers of Hyderabad are an example of such quiet achievers.

The elder Khan, the tall and rangy Ibrahim Khan, was Khan Saheb to all of us, a man we respected as an elder and veteran cricketer of the past. As a member of the Hyderabad team that won the Ranji Trophy in the 1937-38 season, he had played an important role in that historic victory achieved by winning a single match, thanks to a string of walkovers. He had taken wickets in both Nawanagar innings in the final.

The other Khan Saheb was his eldest son Habib Khan, who opened the bowling for Hyderabad and Railways in the Ranji Trophy. Back in the 1970s, he was still quite a force to reckon with in the Hyderabad league, turning his arm over for South Central Railway. He bowled off a smooth run-up, a simple, economical action and nice flowing follow through. He was a tall man and extracted plenty of bounce from most pitches. On matting wickets, he was quite deadly. He was a simple soul, extremely modest and always smiling and friendly. There was something slightly deferential in his manner, and old-fashioned Hyderabadi courtesy marked his every utterance and action.

I remember one of the last matches Habib Khan played in local cricket. It was at Fateh Maidan and though I remember we were pitted against each other, I cannot recall the occasion. I was not known for my batting prowess and in that match I contrived to hook a short-pitched delivery from Khan Saheb to the boundary. In the evening, after the game, Habib sauntered over to where I was sitting and said, "*Bus, ab bahut ho gaya*! It's time for me to hang up my boots, if batsmen like you can hook me," with just the hint of a smile lighting up his sad eyes.

Another sad occasion involving Habib Khan was when Hyderabad beat Railways in a three-day pre-quarter final match in the Ranji Trophy at that same venue. He was the manager of the Railways team, and when his team took a 220-run first innings lead, he beamingly told us he had made arrangements for them to travel to wherever they were scheduled to play the next match. Unfortunately for Railways, we made an incredible recovery in the second innings and won the match. Khan Saheb was really crestfallen and my heart went out to him.

Habib's two younger brothers were also impressive quick bowlers. Majid Khan was quite pacy and a dangerous customer on matting. I was once out caught first ball in a junior match, the daredevil wicket keeper AA Asif standing up to Majid (only a madman would do that) but the umpire said not out. I am ashamed to say that I stood my ground. The next ball was another express delivery and the result was identical, the umpire once again saying not out. This time around, I walked.

Majid enjoyed considerable success at the junior level but did not progress much as he had a doubtful action, but the youngest brother Sardar Khan was probably the most successful of the siblings, as he played for Railways in the Ranji Trophy and Central Zone in the Duleep and Deodhar Trophies in the seventies. He had an action similar to that of the Sri Lankan bowler Malinga, very round arm. He was quite pacy too, and managed to extract considerable bounce. He picked up quite a handful of wickets in the Ranji Trophy as well as the zone matches for a couple of seasons before fading out of the scene, once he lost some of his pace and batsmen learnt to cope with his unusual release.

The Khans were a talented family of cricketers, two generations of honest, hard working fast bowlers, who toiled away on unresponsive wickets, enjoying precious little by way of recognition or reward. They were a fine bunch of sportsmen, well behaved, modest and always willing to give a hundred per cent. It was a pleasure to play cricket with them and interact with them.

P Krishnamurti

P Krishnamurti of Hyderabad was for a while India's top wicket-keeper, good enough to play all five Tests in the 1971 tour of the West Indies, as a member of Ajit Wadekar's triumphant team. Unfortunately, Murti never played in an official Test match again, at least partly because his keeping began to deteriorate soon afterwards.

Murti was one of my early friends in Hyderabad cricket; only he was my mentor and admirer as well, though I was never in any doubt that the admiration was rarely deserved. But for timely interventions by Murti, I would never have enjoyed the success I did as a cricketer.

When I joined the State Bank of India Hyderabad cricket team in July 1971, Krishnamurti was in the Caribbean on that historic tour. When he came back, he and his teammate on that tour, medium pacer Govindraj, who was also the new State Bank captain, were given a heroes' welcome at Hyderabad, but unlike today, all the celebrations did not translate to monetary rewards. Once the celebrations died down and the two India players joined the rest of the bank team at nets, my own bowling was met with a mixed reception. Govind did not think too highly of it, at least he thought the other off spinner G Mohan was a better bowler, while Krishnamurti was convinced I was good enough to play for India one day! He told me so constantly and egged me on to work harder and harder. Wherever he went, he spoke to people about my bowling talent, and soon a number of important cricketers started taking notice of me. One of these was Syed Abid Ali, who came to our nets, watched me bowl and straightaway adopted me as his protégé.

Yet for all the active canvassing Murti, Nagesh, Abid, Sultan Salim and other well-wishers did on my behalf, my career was getting nowhere, especially, with the captain unimpressed. It took a couple of years for Govind to be convinced of my value to the team, and by the time I began taking wickets regularly for the bank and being noticed by the state selectors I was already 27, not exactly the age to start your first-class career.

It was around this time, that my determination to make it in cricket began to flag a little. One morning, I reported for a local league fixture wearing, a thin pair of Bata keds, hardly the kind of footwear for serious cricket. One look at my shoes, and Murti was livid with anger. "What do you mean by turning up for a match looking like a G division player, when next week you are going to play in Moin-ud-Dowla?" he ticked me off in style. Though dumbfounded by the ferocity of his attack, I still retained enough alertness to ask, what did he mean I was going to play Moin-ud- Dowla?

That such an unlikely scenario actually unfolded just the way Murti told it, is part of my own cricket story, and I tell it here merely to show how, hardly a year older than I was, the wicket-keeper took an almost paternal interest in my career. For years afterwards, Murti remained my friend and guide, unswerving in his loyalty. To my eternal regret, Murti, and another dear friend Chandran, were on the other side of an unpleasant divide in Hyderabad cricket around 1979-80, and I said a few things to them that must have hurt and disappointed them. Though I did apologise to them, and we remained friends afterwards, I could never get over my feeling of guilt over that unhappy interlude. Unfortunately, both Murti and Chandran are no more today.

As I said before, Murti became a bit careless about his wicket keeping after his return from the West Indies, and this was reflected in his performances in first-class cricket. His batting however flourished and he played some delightful innings for Hyderabad, especially when the chips were down. A hundred against Karnataka was memorable, but truly scintillating was his 127 for Hyderabad XI against Andhra Bank in the Gold Cup, during which he mauled the off-spin of Test bowler Venkataraghavan.

Even during this period of relative decline, Krishnamurti had patches of brilliance. His work behind the stumps on a tour of Sri Lanka was outstanding. In one of the Tests, he kept with a broken finger and kept superbly to pace and spin alike, even standing up to the sharp pace of Pandurang Salgaonkar, and bringing off breathtaking legside stumpings.

As it happens so often in Indian cricket, Murti was caught in behind-the-scenes politics of which he became the victim. As this coincided with a fall in his wicket-keeping standards and the emergence of the brilliant young wicket keeper from Karnataka, Syed Mujtaba Hussain Kirmani, the Hyderabadi's career came to a premature end. Drinking, personal tragedy and the resultant depression took a heavy toll on this fine representative of Hyderabad cricket. His friends will however always remember his good nature and the glow of his undoubted talent.

Noshir Mehta

Noshir was a very good off spinner and a natural athlete, wiry and strong, someone who could bat and field well too. His name was invariably misspelt as Naushir by the press and the cricket administration, and he never seemed to take the trouble to correct them. The first time I saw him was at Chepauk, when he was playing for Hyderabad against Madras in a Ranji Trophy match or it could have been a Buchi Babu or state junior match at the Marina. He was, as I said, athletic and tall, smartly dressed in perfectly creased flannels and a sleeveless cricket sweater with dark blue stripes around the neck. It was as if he had stepped out of a photograph in Wisden.

There was a reason why I watched Noshir so closely. He was my rival. To put it more precisely, I was presumptuous enough to believe I could one day rival him, even prove a better off spinner. My misfortune as an off spinner was that I had been born a couple of years after a certain S Venkataraghavan, who kept me out of every level of competitive cricket, having made his Test debut at the ridiculous age of 19.

So it was, that when I came to be a college cricketer, the door was slammed in my face when it came to selection to the Madras University team. Even when Venkat moved on and graduated, I still had to contend with formidable competition in the form of the Districts off spinner P Vijayaraghavan. I was convinced that I was as good as any of these rivals, but had precious little opportunity to prove so, as I was confined to playing strictly local cricket, unable to break into university or even state junior cricket. When I eventually did, I played under the captaincy of another off spinner, JS Ghanshyam, who at that point, did not quite seem to believe I belonged at that level of cricket, though he changed his opinion over the years.

When I watched Noshir, I was impressed. For a tall man, he did not have as high an action as you might expect, as he delivered off a slightly round-arm action, but spun the ball sharply, and was extremely accurate. He could go on for long spells landing the ball with precision at an awkward length, and obtaining considerable turn and bounce. He had an effective wrong 'un too, the ball that went straight through or left the right hander's bat, with no perceptible change in action.

He was a very good lower order batsman too, with a sound defence and the ability to hit the ball cleanly. Yes, I was impressed by this young off spinner, but I was also quietly confident I was a better spinner! The frustrating thing was that I would never perhaps get a chance to show the world how good I was.

Noshir was firmly entrenched in the Hyderabad team, not least because of his brilliant displays against Madras, later Tamil Nadu, in the Ranji Trophy in a couple of matches I had watched. Years later, when I moved to Hyderabad, it took me a while to establish myself in the State Bank team in the local league, and when I did, he was my next obstacle, as I knocked at the doors of Ranji cricket. The fact that his father SR Mehta, a veteran all rounder, was Chairman of Selectors was often held against Noshir, but I knew nothing but warmth and affection from the Mehta family, even after I replaced Noshir as first choice off spinner for Hyderabad.

Noshir played for State Bank of Hyderabad for many years, and he served the team with great distinction, but that did not prevent his teammates from pulling his leg, quite mercilessly at times. Particularly mischievous were a pair of inseparables, John Tarachand and Khaja. It was their theory that though he had several hundreds to his credit for the bank, Noshir was not particularly fond of facing quick bowling. There was this apocryphal story of Noshir joining a voluntary residents' night patrol party in the suburb of Marredpally during a time when daring burglaries were being carried out with regularity in different parts of the city. "The dacoits need not carry any weapons to frighten Noshir. All they'll need is a new ball!" was their quite unfair barb.

Mumtaz Hussain

This is your last chance, Taz. You'd better give it all you've got. I don't know what you'll do, but you must get wickets. If you don't, I'll have no choice but to drop you for the next game at Madras.

Abid Ali, the Hyderabad captain, spoke these words in a matter of fact voice, but his heart must have been heavy as he uttered them, because the man he was addressing was the seniormost player in the eleven after the captain himself. The selectors had told Abid in unequivocal terms that his senior left arm spinner was on trial.

Mumtaz Hussain, the recipient of the bad news, was close to the end of a distinguished career in which he took 173 Ranji Trophy wickets at less than twenty runs apiece. He had been a vital part of the Hyderabad spin attack, forging a successful partnership with off spinner Noshir Mehta, no longer a member of the team, replaced a couple of years earlier by me. The occasion was a Ranji Trophy match against Kerala at Kollam.

Initially depressed and dejected, Mumtaz decided on calm reflection, that it was time to unveil the rare bag of tricks he had kept hidden from public view for over a decade. In his Ranji Trophy career, he had stuck to bowling left arm orthodox spin, never attempting the seemingly infinite variety he had unleashed on unsuspecting batsmen in the inter university matches for the Rohinton Baria Cup in the late sixties. He then had the standard left arm spinner's stock delivery which left the right hand batsman, he bowled a chinaman using his wrist, a googly from the back of the hand, and both these deliveries with a finger spin action for variety. Batsmen were completely foxed by his changes of grip and action, or the lack of either, as they misread ball after ball, until they were bowled, caught, lbw or stumped, simultaneously looking very, very foolish indeed.

One famous victim was Sunil Gavaskar of Bombay University in 1970. He describes in his autobiographical *Sunny Days* how he shouted to his partner Ramesh Nagdev, "I can read his googly now!' only to be stranded outside his crease, completely fooled by one that looked like a perfect Chinaman but went the other way. Wicket keepers were not immune to the Mumtaz magic either. They had to resort to secret signals to anticipate what would come their way from a Mumtaz Hussain in midseason form.

The first innings was over at Kollam and Kerala was heading for defeat. Not bringing Mumtaz on even for a solitary over in the first innings, Abid Ali was now tossing the ball, barely seven or eight overs old, to the left arm spinner. He clearly wanted his old teammate to perform well today and save him the embarrassment of being dropped.

In his very first over, Mumtaz's attempted a chinaman, despite the newness of the ball. The ball pitched short but the batsman did not take advantage of the long hop. Very soon, Mumtaz's length improved reasonably but more important, he bowled a few unplayable deliveries and ended up with a bag of six wickets, though his loose deliveries were hit to the boundary.

The next stop for the Hyderabad team was Chepauk, Madras. The Tamil Nadu batting line-up was formidable, with V Sivaramakrishnan, V Krishnaswami, TE Srinivasan and Abdul Jabbar prominent in it. Once again Mumtaz displayed his wares, for the second time after his university days. He was now up against a foe of great talent. There would be no meek surrender this time. He could not find the edge or a defensive blade as often as he encountered in the previous match.

Once again Mumtaz claimed five utterly bamboozled batsmen, including Sivaramakrishnan and Krishnaswami, who either went chasing a delivery outside the off stump like one hypnotised, or was bowled trying to withdraw the bat.

There was a brief moment in cricket history when fame and fortune flirted with Mumtaz Hussain, teasing him and cheating him in the end. He had just completed taking 48 wickets for the season in Rohinton Baria, a record until then, and had been included in the Board President's team to play against the touring West Indies led by Garry Sobers. The other left arm spinner in the squad answered to the name of Bishan Singh Bedi, a young bowler of immense promise. The chairman of selectors was former Test off spinner Ghulam Ahmed, intent on being seen to be scrupulously fair as a selector. When it came to a choice between Bedi and Mumtaz, the local boy naturally lost out, or so the story goes.

Ghulam Ahmed's decision was justified by subsequent events, as Bedi took six wickets in the match and went on to become arguably the world's greatest left arm spinner of all time. But had fate been kind to the Hyderabadi in selection terms, what might have been Mumtaz's future in the game? When Indian batsmen found him practically unreadable, what chance did batsmen overseas enjoy of surviving his wiles and tricks? Had he played against West Indies the day Bedi made such an impressive showing, would Mumtaz have made a sensational impact on the world stage?

These questions are merely hypothetical and not for a moment is it being suggested that Mumtaz was a greater bowler than Bedi, but it remains an unsolved mystery of domestic cricket why Mumtaz gave up his delightfully mysterious wares, and toed the line as an orthodox spinner in Ranji Trophy cricket, untouched by the greatness that might have been his, had he chosen the other path. Was he told to do so by his captain and seniors in the interest of economy and accuracy, as claimed by his teammates or did he do so of his own volition as some others have suggested? What heights might he have reached had he continued, when he could resume his old magic from where he left off after a gap of ten years, without any substantial loss of effect? Mumtaz Hussain is no more today, a victim of cancer.

Essentially happy go lucky, he had more than his share of woes in his short life of 52 years. The loss of a young daughter was a grievous blow. Yet the enduring image of my old teammate and colleague is that of a man of a cheerful disposition, given to grinning wickedly at batsmen he had fooled.

Manohar Sharma

Manohar Sharma was one of the senior cricketers in the State Bank of India Hyderabad team when I joined it in 1972. He was already a greying elder statesman of the side, probably in his thirties then, but alleged by leg pullers to be at least ten years more ancient. He was a shrewd, cheerful man of stocky build and healthy appetite, a Hindi-speaking vegetarian brahmin from Indore, whom wartime short service in the armed forces had brought to Hyderabad in the late 1960s. He liked the place and settled down there once he got selected as a probationary officer in the bank as part of a quota for army officers. A natural PR man, he gravitated to the public relations function in the bank after serving his mandatory stint as branch manager, one of the branches he headed being the Trimulgherry office in the cantonment area of Secunderabad.

Sharma was a sticky customer with his determined, if often unentertaining approach to batting, but great value to a team overabundant in stroke makers, as ours was. Unknown to me, at least in the early days of my career, he kept an avuncular eye on me and wished me well, seeing in me a spark of talent meant for higher honours. As at the time no honours had come my way, it meant that he believed I should at least be allowed to play some cricket.

There came a time when I had to decide to give up cricket, as I was no more than a spare tyre in the SBI team, needed only when one of our regulars (including guest players preferred to me) was not available for some reason. Having been recruited as an officer for reasons other than cricket, I could not complain if my manager did not allow me time to practise with the cricket team or play matches for the bank. My boss HV Rangaswami was a kindly man, but also a professional, so it was but natural that he asked me not to make a trip to Madras to take part in an inter-circle match unless I was sure of being in the playing eleven. It was a busy time in the office for us field officers in the small industries business division and his was a fair proposal, so I went to my captain D Govindraj and explained the situation. He promised I would play at Madras, but once we were there, promptly dropped me from the XI.

That settled it for me and when we came back, I withdrew from cricket and concentrated on my job and spent more time in the company of my young wife. It was at this time that 'Sharmaji' or 'Punditji', as we called Manohar Sharma, summoned me one morning to his cabin and tried to persuade me to change my mind, as he believed I had a bright future in cricket. I was moved by his concern but stood firm in my resolve. In a couple of months' time, however, Sharmaji and my other teammates succeeded in literally abducting me from home to play a match, which turned out to be the beginning of a new, happy chapter of my cricket career, as it turned out. So, whenever, I look back on my wonderful days of cricket under the sun, I cannot help remembering Punditji.

Punditji did yeoman service as the sheet anchor of the SBI team and he continued to play Ranji Trophy cricket for Madhya Pradesh, if I remember right. He was also a very useful off spinner, especially when we wanted the batsmen to be kept quiet. Surprisingly for a dour, defensive batsman, he could belt the ball quite effectively in limited overs cricket. Many opponents did not know this, until they found out to their own disadvantage in a match. One amusing incident involved the Andhra Bank skipper Abdul Hai and spinner Meher Baba who had strict instructions not to dismiss Sharmaji in the wrong belief he could not score quickly. Meher dutifully tried to keep Sharmaji quiet with some innocuous stuff aimed at his pads, but the batsman managed to hit it hard and straight to Abdul Hai, who took the catch, yet chided Meher for getting Sharmaji out!

Once we got to know Punditji well, we youngsters felt free to tease him and he took it all sportingly. I even forgot myself enough once to lose my temper with him, something you never did with seniors you respected, and he not only accepted my outburst without a murmur, he did not refer to it later after tempers had cooled down. It was a hard fought match we lost narrowly after four days of struggle, and I had long spells in torrid conditions in both innings. Sharmaji had left the field early in the final moments of the match because he had a train to catch, and as he came up to me in the dressing room to commiserate with me for the defeat despite my 'great' efforts, I snapped at him, as I believed we could have won if he had been on the field. I was being wholly unfair to him, but he took it on his chin like a true soldier.

Sharmaji was a great tourist, superb company on the long evenings of cricket tours. He laughed loudest and longest at the pranks his teammates played on him, as when MAK Pataudi left a dead alligator in his bed on a tour of the West Indies. (I personally do not care for that kind of practical joke, but if Punditji minded, he never showed it). His lovely wife cooked delicious meals and all of us enjoyed the lavish hospitality of the Sharma household at Begumpet, whenever we were invited there for a meal.

V Sivaramakrishnan

V Sivaramakrishnan, the tall, left handed opening batsman, who played first class cricket between 1973 and 1988, had the highest Ranji Trophy aggregate for a Tamil Nadu batsman for a long time, before another lefthander, S Sharath, went past him. My youngest brother, he had a great appetite for runs even as a boy. Five years older, I did not watch him in competitive cricket until we were pitted against each other in the Ranji Trophy. At that level, he was my senior, making his debut for Tamil Nadu three seasons before I made mine for Hyderabad. As he was playing for Bihar during my first season, I had to wait one more season before I bowled to him for the first time outside our home compound back in Madras all those years ago

(Had we not surrendered to Bombay after gaining the lead in the quarterfinal, we might have faced Bihar in the final). Fittingly as his elder brother, I got him out in that game at Lal Bahadur Stadium, Hyderabad, but only after he had made a bright 61. Thereafter, we sort of shared the honours more or less equally, with him scoring consistently and I dismissing him more than once in Hyderabad-Tamil Nadu matches.

Sivaramakrishnan represented the beginning of a batting revival in Tamil Nadu cricket which gradually turned the state's fortunes around in the seventies to a position of dominance in the South Zone, until its batting reached its pinnacle towards the end of the eighties—when it won the Ranji Trophy—and the nineties.He was a product of university cricket, an important member of the Madras University team that won the Rohinton Baria trophy for the first time in its history.The year was 1971 and under the captaincy of R Ravichandran, Madras discovered a galaxy of young stars in Sivaramakrishnan, Krishnaswamy, Mukund, Sushil Haridas, Bhargav Mehta, PR Ramakrishnan, and a whole host of others.The left-hander's best contribution in the tournament was a fine hundred in the final against Bombay. I watched most of the games Madras University played that season at Waltair, Visakhapatnam, as I was working at nearby Anakapalle. A hundred and other good scores in the Vizzy Trophy followed, South Zone winning the title.Sivaramakrishnan's good form continued the next season in which he scored a double century, besides playing several innings of character.

Making his Ranji Trophy debut against Karnataka in 1972-1973, Sivaramakrishnan wasted no time in establishing his credentials.Run out for zero in the first innings, he gave evidence of his class in the second, when he punished Prasanna and Chandrasekhar in a display of quick footwork and daring strokeplay to make 53.

With stiff competition building up for batting places in the Tamil Nadu eleven with the arrival of P Ramesh, another left hander of great promise, and a line-up that had in it Krishnaswami, TE Srinivasan, Jabbar, Satvinder Singh and Mukund, Sivaramakrishnan moved to greener pastures in the steel town of Jamshedpur in Bihar, where he played for the TISCO team and Bihar in the company of Ramesh Saxena and Daljit Singh. His consistent performances, with a highest of 99 versus Assam, straightaway won him a place in the East Zone team, and he scored runs in the Duleep and Deodhar Trophy matches against North Zone, dancing down the wicket to Bishan Bedi and Co.

Sivaramakrishnan returned to Madras in the very next season, with his reputation enhanced by his Bihar sojourn and an earlier stint in Calcutta where he had proved his competence against the moving ball, playing quality swing bowlers with consummate ease.

Back in Madras for the Ranji Trophy, the left-hander batted in the middle order against an attack that included Prasanna, Chandrasekhar and Vijayakrishna.

Sivaramakrishnan went from strength to strength from that point onwards to become Tamil Nadu's most reliable batsman and consistent rungetter.He was a strong driver of the ball and revelled in the cut. He was particularly good when the chips were down and when there was something in the wicket for the bowlers. His 5039 runs in 126 innings included 11 hundreds and an equal number of dismissals in the nineties. One of the most brilliant close-in fielders Tamil Nadu has produced, he held more than a hundred catches in the national championship, besides occasionally turning his arm over usefully with gentle in-swingers.

Sivaramakrishnan came close to being picked to tour Australia in 1977-1978, when he made 74 for South Zone against North at Bangalore. His rival to the second opener's slot Chetan Chauhan failed in that game, but North piled up a large total after debutant Yashpal Sharma made an impressive 173. The only way South could have gained the first innings lead and by virtue of it, the match, after being down at 50 plus for 3 was for Siva and TE Srinivasan (who scored a hundred) to put on a massive partnership, but Siva virtually threw his wicket away just when the attack was tiring and South Zone yielded a lead of over 100. North went on to win that match and Chetan Chauhan made a hundred in the final at Bombay, to clinch a place in the squad.The rest is history as Gavaskar and

Chauhan struck a durable partnership thereafter.

Opening the innings back in 1976-77 for South Zone against Tony Greig's Englishmen at Hyderabad (I was warming the reserve benches), Siva had negotiated the seam and swing of John Lever and Co., and been on the verge of launching an all-out attack on the spinners, when he was run out while attempting an impossible single to Derek Randall. He had made 27. In those pre-helmet days, he was out fending off bouncers from Imran Khan and Malcolm Marshall in the tour matches against Pakistan and West Indies, and failed to convert a good start against Rodney Hogg and Co. of Australia. These failures kept him out of the Test berth he otherwise richly deserved. His last chance was against England again in 1983, following a hugely successful Ranji season, but again he was dismissed for 38 and 30, though he made batting look relatively easy facing Bob Willis at his quickest.

Some of Siva's best batting against fast bowling came in Colombo in 1982, and Perth, six years later. In Sri Lanka, he batted so well in the first innings of the Gopalan Trophy match, against genuinely quick bowling on a fiery wicket, that the coach Peter Philpott advised the captain not to enforce the follow on so that the Lankan bowlers gained more practice bowling to a quality left hander, ahead of the forthcoming tour of Australia, which had a few southpaws.In Australia, playing for the Ranji Trophy champion Tamil Nadu, he blunted a pace attack which had three Test fast bowlers on the Perth wicket notorious for its pace and bounce. It was a brave counterattack amidst a general batting collapse.

Winning the Ranji Trophy that season was a personal triumph for Sivaramakrishnan.He had come back successfully into the side for the knockout stage of the championship after announcing his retirement at the start of the season, scoring heavily in all three matches he played, including a hundred in the semifinal and 94 in the final. That had been the crowning moment of this extraordinary team man's first class career— unrewarded at the highest level, but deeply satisfying at the State level. He continued to play league cricket in Chennai for many more seasons, playing selflessly for his team and amassing runs.

S Vasudevan

A more laidback cricketer may belong only to the world of fiction, but for over a decade, S Vasudevan was an outstanding performer for Tamil Nadu, partnering S Venkataraghavan, his captain and senior by several years. From the moment he came into the side in 1976-1977 to the time he retired from first class cricket a year after leading Tamil Nadu to its second Ranji Trophy title, he was a thorn in the flesh of Karnataka and Hyderabad, the two strong opponents in the zone. Batsmen like Brijesh Patel, Sudhakar Rao and GR Viswanath repeatedly faltered against Vasu's accurate, sharp spin. On the best of wickets, he made the ball hurry on after pitching, possessing a satisfactory arm ball and on a bad one, he was well nigh unplayable.

Vasu was a delightful batsman too, though he often gave the impression he was not interested. Perhaps, batting came too easily for him to take too much trouble over it, or he possessed a bowler's mind like so many others before and after him, but whatever the reason, the upshot of it all was that he never fulfilled his batting potential.Two first class hundreds, one in the Ranji Trophy and another in the Gopalan Trophy, do not reflect his true batting ability.The century against UP was made when the frontline batsmen had failed in a heap, and he rescued the team from disaster.

Vasu gave notice of his exceptional ability in university cricket. He was slightly overshadowed by fellow left arm spinner and teammate SK Patel who broke the record for most wickets in a single Rohinton Baria season (1975-1976), but soon he left his own imprint on university cricket.(He and his teammates came to watch Hyderabad's Ranji quarterfinal match vs. Bombay that season while they were waiting for their own final. That is when I met the whole team introduced to me by coach PK Dharmalingam). Succeeding Patel into the state team, just after VV Kumar quit the scene, Vasu went on to take more than 200 first class wickets. He was unfortunate to belong to the South Zone when the zone had an embarrassment of spin bowling riches, and therefore did not get to play Duleep Trophy cricket.When he was at his best, India was well served in his department, the younger Maninder Singh replacing his senior Dilip Doshi. With Ravi Shastri too contributing with the ball, Vasu was never a serious contender for a place in the Indian team, though quality-wise, he was inferior to none.

Vasudevan's greatest moment was when he led Tamil Nadu to a Ranji Trophy title triumph in 1987-1988, himself picking up seven Railways wickets in the second innings of the final at Chepauk.

A software professional, Vasudevan belonged to a generation of cricketers who often had an alternative career to fall back upon after their playing days.He made a successful transition from cricket to a rewarding professional career.

SPIN DOCTORS: THE CRAFT AND THE PRACTITIONERS

THE CRAFT

Rarely do we read sensible writing on spin bowling. A very popular—and completely nonsensical—cliché is the description of a slow bowler that he varied line and length intelligently. Nothing could be more absurd. Unless you are express fast and can bowl a good bouncer, you never vary your length except to modify it to suit the reach and footwork of the batsman. A tall batsman demands a slightly shorter length than a short one or a predominantly backfoot player; otherwise a 'good' length is sacrosanct, though a half volley is always a better delivery than a rank short ball.

As an off-spinner who began his career in the 1960s, I had part intuitively been following precisely these bowling fundamentals. Both length and direction were unvaried in my arsenal of sharp off spin, faster deliveries, floaters and leg-cutters, not to mention the occasional outswinger, and this is something I had learnt very early. My first mentor (excluding my cousin Venkatachalam who had often shared his cricket wisdom during conversations indoors when I was still in my *arai nijar*) had been medium pacer VV Rajamani, my senior in the Presidency College cricket team.

The one aspect Rajamani stressed was arm-speed from the top of my delivery stride to my finish ("that doesn't mean you push the ball through; you whip the ball as if you were spinning a top; the arm comes down fast, but the ball travels in a parabolic loop"), with my left leg ramrod straight and right arm falling to the left of my left thigh. A pivoting action was essential on your delivery stride, and for this your left foot needed to grip the ground firmly. In all these years of cricket reading, I have not come across a reference to arm speed, the Rajamani gem that helped me so much in my development as a spinner. (Among world class spinners, Shane Warne provides an exceptional example of this factor, his strong back and shoulders compensating in this regard for his short run-up; a longer, quicker run-up would normally provide the necessary momentum).

In my adult life, I learnt some of my best bowling lessons from Hanumant Singh, the Rajasthan and India batsman under whose captaincy I played for State Bank of India for a couple of seasons in the 1970s. I made my debut for the bank's all India team when he was captain; he softened the blow of my being dropped for the next game and final to make way for Rajinder Goel, by complimenting my efforts and giving me some great insights into the game, spin bowling in particular. This is when he confirmed the correctness of my instinctive understanding of the game. "Whatever you are doing, bowling at your normal pace and trajectory, flighting the ball a little extra, pushing the ball through quicker, or bowling the wrong 'un, make sure that the ball invariably lands on the same spot—same length, same line. This way the batsman is always in doubt, while you are giving nothing away by way of width or poor length."

"Length is mandatory, while line is optional," the great EAS Prasanna has been quoted as saying. This could easily be misunderstood to mean that you can change your direction from ball to ball, over to over—unless you grasped the proper import of Prasanna's words. No captain can set a field for you if you bowled on both sides of the wicket all the time. Prasanna has obviously other ideas: that you decide your line on the basis of the nature of the wicket, the amount of turn it is yielding, on whether you are attacking or defending, and on whether a right hander or left hander is batting. Once you decide your line of attack for the day (or the session in case conditions have suddenly changed) and pretty much to stick to it.

I played under a great captain for Hyderabad. Though there was not a great deal of spoken communication on the field between ML Jaisimha and the bowlers, all of us knew his cricket thinking and quickly learnt to bowl to his plans. For one thing, the field—sometimes extremely attacking—that he set for you clearly demanded a certain line of attack. Even on a typical first day wicket, he always gave me two short legs—forward and backward. We would start with a slip, point, cover, mid-off, deep square leg, mid wicket and mid-on, besides the two short-legs, with square leg the only deep fielder, some three quarters of the way to the boundary. All the other fielders except those in the close-in cordon were at single-saving distance from the bat. After a few overs, when he was confident I had settled down, he'd say, "All right, Ram?" and then proceed to bring in point to silly point, leaving that region totally unprotected. The field would then be slip, silly point, cover, mid-off, mid-on, mid-wicket, forward and backward short-legs and deep square leg. (You had to be absolutely accurate around off-stump; you simply could not afford to stray outside it the way you could with a less attacking offside field).

Once the batsman settled down, either slip or silly point was removed and only much later would a deep midwicket be added to the onside field, with the offside field reduced to point, cover and mid-off. Unless the batsmen really flourished and some 400 runs were on the board, the two short-legs were a constant. Even when one of them withdrew into the outfield, it was rarely the forward short-leg or bat-pad fielder that left his post.

This was a typical field deployed for a good off-spinner by the leading captains of the day, say Tiger Pataudi for India, Jaisimha for Hyderabad, V Subramanyam (succeeded by Prasanna) for Karnataka, or Venkataraghavan for Tamil Nadu. I have a serious suspicion that this kind of attacking field placement originated in the south, perhaps when Subramanyam was leading Karnataka, and evolved through brainstorming among all these greats of the period. And if I am not mistaken, this broadly speaking, is what Prasanna means when he says length is mandatory, line is optional).

On a turning wicket, you not only tried to turn the ball from well outside the off-stump, but often went round the wicket to make the batsman play, once he started using the pads with no fear of lbw, thanks to the abundant deviation. The trick was to still bowl around the same spot from round the wicket, the straighter angle forcing the batsman to play and increasing chances of leg before at least slightly. And a well-directed straight or away-going delivery from round the wicket could get you one of three kinds of dismissals: lbw, bowled, or a slip catch.

Playing in that era, you also learnt some superb lessons on how to bowl to left-hand batsmen from the aforesaid nawabs of cricket. Contrary to what most of today's experts advocate, our seniors encouraged off-spinners to bowl over-the wicket, and maintain a strict leg-and-middle line, thus cramping the left-hander. You often had a forward short-leg to grab the bat-pad snicks, while you could still force an outer edge to slip, especially if the pitch offered some purchase.

My career ran parallel to the golden era of Indian spin. In addition to the Quartet, there were a number of high quality spinners who would have walked into any Test side, and one of them Dilip Doshi, did play for India with distinction. Two other left-arm spinners Rajinder Goel and Padmakar Shivalkar were not so fortunate, because their tenure ran parallel to Bishan Bedi's. I watched both in their prime and enjoyed competing against them. They were great bowlers and fine men. Salim Durrani was every romantic's dream cricketer—a hugely talented, lazily elegant match-winner. Again it was my good fortune to play against him a few times. Rajinder Singh Hans, who lost out to Dilip Doshi after Bedi left the international scene, was another brilliant left arm spinner and a good friend. Add all the superb slow men I played with in South Zone and you will realise what a rarefied atmosphere pervaded our cricket, at least in the spin department.

Here is a list of some of the excellent spinners—some of them truly great bowlers—I played with and watched, other than those I cover in detail in this book: Goel, Shivalkar, Dilip Doshi, Rajinder Singh Hans, Vijayakrishna, Raghuram Bhat, Suresh Shastri, Ashok Joshi, Murali Kartik, Venkatapathy Raju, Mahendra Kumar, Anand Shukla, Rakesh Tandon, Kanwaljit Singh, Noshir Mehta.

(Here, I cannot resist the temptation to tell a couple of stories involving Rajinder Goel, one of the nicest, most innocent cricketers I have known. Two days into a physical conditioning camp for the Indian Probables in 1977, he was rendered *hors d combat* with rock-hard, extremely painful calf muscles. He was my brother's roommate in Hotel Connemara and every evening when we returned from the camp, he made anxious enquiries about some of our fellow probables. "Is Prasanna all right? Parthasarathi Sharma? Ashok Mankad?" And when we assured him that every one of them was fit, Goel's face really fell. "How can all these chaps be fit, when I am so badly off?" he kept muttering. A few years later, when he told me he was retiring from first class cricket at the end of the season, I gently reminded him that if he did that, Venkataraghavan would surely break his record of the highest number of wickets in the national championship. "In that case, I won't retire," Goel *Paaji* said determinedly. His record is still intact).

THE PRACTITIONERS

Jim Laker

His autobiographical *Over to Me* was not a book meant to inspire a young cricketer, as it contained a continuous rant against his skipper Peter May, manager Fred Brown and other cricket personalities of the time, but I read it from cover to cover because at age ten I was already an ardent fan of his bowling.

Jim Laker was my role model as an off-spinner. I never saw him in flesh and blood because he did not play Test cricket in India, never watched him in action elsewhere in the world, because we had no TV then, leave alone satellite telecasts. My only acquaintance with him was via radio broadcasts in the voices of Norman Yardley, John Arlott *et al* and photographs. His immaculate bowling action captured by still cameras was forever etched in my mind. I had a perfect image of his easy run-up, high-arm action, viciously spinning fingers, and perfect follow-through imprinted permanently in my mind's eye. Growing up in a complex of three independent houses with no compound walls separating them, I never walked between them, always bowling imaginary but unplayable deliveries in my hero's action, getting imaginary batsmen bowled, caught or leg before innumerable times every day. Years later, I was to admire Laker's dry, laconic wit as a no-nonsense broadcaster, but reading about his incredible cricket exploits (193 wickets in 46 Tests at an average of 21.24, an economy rate of 2.04, a strike rate of 62.3, best innings figures of 10/53, best match analysis of 19/90) in real time gave me a high never equalled afterwards.

A Yorkshireman by birth, James Charles Laker started his career in his home county as a batsman, but by the end of it, he had been acknowledged as arguably the best off-spinner of all time. It was Surrey that recognised his bowling potential, and invited him to join the county staff, after a sore 'spinning finger' had prevented his playing a 'trial' match for Essex.

What made Laker such a great spinner? According to John Arlott, English cricket's golden voice, "There have been off-spinners though few who spun the ball as much as Jim Laker; some of them had comparable control. But no one has ever matched him in those two departments and had also, such a quality of intelligence.

"Physically economical of energy, he walked back six paces to his mark and came in up a short-stepping run which he deliberately varied from ball to ball, changing its pace or number of steps, a subtlety which made it difficult for the batsman to time his approach.

"Without any apparent change of action he bowled a topspinner and a ball which ran away a little off the pitch but, equally dangerously and far more unusually, he could and did, control the width of his break."

Often a batsman would find Laker's first ball pitched on a length and turning relatively mildly. The next ball would look innocuous enough, quite easily defended. Nothing much would happen off the next ball either, and the batsman would, if he did not already know Laker, conclude that here was just another off spinner. The next delivery would look no different from the earlier ones but bite, turn, hurry through and hit his stumps even before his bat came down.

Laker was a good bowler on all types of wickets. He spun the ball really viciously and ran through sides on turning pitches at the lowest possible cost. On good wickets, whether in cool England or in tropical conditions, he could bowl over after over of perfect length and line. On those, he set problems of length and flight.

Like all great spinners, he achieved flight by spinning the ball hard.

The ball left his hand and travelled towards the batsman in a perfectly controlled parabola, thanks to the spin imparted by strong and determined fingers that gave the ball—and themselves—a fair rip. The flight of the ball was tantalising. Like a mirage that fools a thirsty traveller until he gets there, the Laker delivery was almost always not there for the batsman when he reached for it in defence or attack. Listen to John Arlott again: "He paid a painful price for his bowling. Like most men who spin the ball really hard, he often wore away the skin from the inside of his index finger. If he bowled on, it would harden, a corn would form and then, as it grew too hard, it would tear away, leaving the flesh exposed once more. (He) lacked the unusually long fingers of the savage off-spinners and to gain a similar degree of purchase, he had to take a grip which stretched his first two fingers to an exceptional and painful extent."

As a result, Laker's fingers became distorted and he developed an arthritic condition that ended his career sooner than expected. Yet, in only 46 Tests, he took 193 wickets at the meagre average of 21.24.

This is what a young cricketer can learn from a great spin bowler like James Charles Laker or our own great slow bowlers. When you are told to flight the ball, it doesn't mean you toss the ball up in a gentle arc. Buying wickets doesn't mean giving away free runs. The idea is to fool the batsman into believing that free runs are to be had. And that, you can do, only if you genuinely spin the ball, only if you tear the skin of your finger by rubbing it hard against the ball to make it spin like a top, only if you practise so long and so purposefully, that in a match, good line and length are automatic, and you have the confidence to try variations at will. If you have never had spinning finger problems, you have never had blood oozing from that finger, you have never spun the ball. Forget spin bowling then, and switch to something easy like batting!

S Venkataraghavan

The qualities that made Venkataraghavan a very good umpire were evident in him as early as during his schooldays, when I first met him. These were a thorough knowledge of the game and its laws, fearlessness, superb physical fitness, the ability to concentrate hard for hours, a brisk decisiveness and a commanding presence.

I played with or against (mostly against) Venkat from the time I was about 10 and he 12, but though we had occasion to meet intermittently on the cricket ground as well as socially for decades, I cannot count myself as one of his friends, for he is a very private man, with few intimate friends. On the field, however, we had some enjoyable exchanges, highly competitive and intensely fought. That is the only way the off spinner knew to play his cricket. The needle was a bit extra, at least on my part, when we competed against each other, because I was an off spinner myself, trying to dislodge him from the Indian side, though without success. Every time I faced him I was determined not to lose my wicket to him, and every time I bowled to him I desperately wanted his wicket. I do not know if he reserved any special effort for me, but the going was never easy when I was at the receiving end from him.

We both played for the same school, PS High School of Mylapore, Madras, but in college cricket, we were regularly pitted against each other. He led the formidable Guindy Engineering College against Presidency, my college, which had a number of talented players. In addition to bowling his accurate and nippy off spinners, he batted high in the order and scored consistently. He was a brilliant fielder, especially close to the wicket, a facet of his cricket for which he was admired at the highest level. (One remarkable catch I saw him take in local cricket, however, involved his running to midwicket off his own bowling and holding on to a skier, a truly fantastic effort, on the Marina ground). He was already a Test cricketer, and some of the senior batsmen in my side got out to him even before they left the safety of the pavilion, so complete was his psychological domination of them. Our first victory over Engineering was achieved only after Venkat's graduation.

My enduring memory of Venkat is one of the seriousness with which he approached net practice, bowling non-stop for three hours everyday, following that with an extended session of fielding practice. Taking a hundred slip catches a day was about par for the course for him.

Throughout his career, Venkat never left the ground citing injury. Two occasions stand out in my memory. The first was during a Duleep Trophy match against Central Zone at Bangalore in 1975. One evening during the match, Venkat met with a minor road accident, falling off a scooter. (Can you imagine a current Test cricketer on two wheels?) On the morrow, he carried on as if nothing had happened, bowling a long, match-winning spell with little or no indication that he was in any discomfort. But back in the pavilion he had great difficulty taking off his trousers to change, because he had been badly bruised from waist to foot on one side.

On another occasion, Venkat bowled a marathon 72-over spell against East Zone in the Duleep Trophy at Eden Gardens, nursing a very painful injury. Left-hander V Sivaramakrishnan, my younger brother, who played that match, rates that spell as the bravest, most disciplined effort he has seen on a cricket ground.

Around the time he made his Test debut against New Zealand, after a splendid match for Indian Universities against the tourists, Venkat's bowling was perhaps the most accurate anywhere. His sharp off spin was persistent and his occasional well-disguised leg cutter a deadly variation, invariably resulting in a catch behind or at slip when it was not clipping the off bail. Batsmen mostly played him from the safety of the crease, stretching well forward to avoid being lbw. Rarely did one of them use his feet to dance down the track. To prolong his career at the first class level, Venkat slowed down, but his trajectory was still flatter than that of the classical off spinner who flighted the ball. He was much taller than Prasanna, for instance, and therefore could not achieve the arc that Prasanna did. Still, his own adaptation of flight and spin to suit his natural endowments—which by the way included strong, long fingers, and a supple, wiry frame—was a beautiful sight on a cricket field. All his life, he remained a difficult proposition to score off, and earned the respect of many leading batsmen, including the incomparable Garfield Sobers. In fact, some of Venkat's important successes came against the formidable West Indies.

BS Chandrasekhar

Anil Kumble has earned his place in the pantheon of the greats of the game by sheer perseverance and longevity—not to mention his superb qualities of head and heart which have enabled him to triumph over the trials and tribulations that beset him through his long and distinguished career. There is no doubt that in a different time and place, his exceptional intelligence and man-management capabilities would have won him the captaincy of his country for a far longer spell. He is a man to be admired and respected, and not one for whom tears are easily shed, because he meets every adversity with courage and determination—and usually succeeds.

This preamble is necessary to explain the greater partiality many of the 1970s generation have for the unorthodox Indian leg-spinner to have attained cricketing immortality: BS Chandrasekhar. If Kumble is the perfect professional, Chandra was in many ways the antithesis, a genius with nothing workmanlike about him. If Kumble is all intellect and mental toughness, Chandra was frail and vulnerable, in both a literal and a metaphorical sense. A polio-afflicted limb gave him the unusual arm-speed that enabled him to whip googlies, flippers and the occasional leg-break at ferocious velocities. There was the air of a tragic hero about him as time and time again misfortune struck him when least expected.

His physical attributes too contributed to this less-than-aggressive image that stayed with him through his career. He remained slim, almost thin, throughout his 15 years in top-flight cricket, his intermittent beard serving to heighten that impression of forlornness.

Of the celebrated quartet (or trio, to be truthful, as only once did all four play together in a Test) of Indian spinners, none was more spectacular than Chandrasekhar. Bishan Singh Bedi's bowling action was deservedly described as poetry in motion, Erapalli Prasanna was a spinner's spinner with his classical flight, sharp spin and delightful variations, and Srinivas Venkataraghavan was a probing wielder of a surgeon's scalpel, but none of them could accelerate the pulse rate of excited spectators in the manner of a fast bowler as Chandra did.

As he measured his paces, marked the start of his bowling run, walked the first couple of steps cupping the ball in both hands, ran in with a purposeful stride, and then delivered in a perfectly side-on finish, left arm raised high, right arm coming down in a rapid whir, thudding on to his left thigh, the crowd exploded in a burst of feverish anticipation.

Slip fielders and short legs, not to mention wicket keepers belonging to any other generation would have dreaded the prospect of the fierce edges that Chandra's fizz and bounce induced. But that high noon of Indian cricket was lit by some extraordinary close-in catching fireworks, ignited by such champions as Ajit Wadekar, Venkat, Abid Ali, and the incomparable Eknath Solkar. Despite that magic ring of fielders, streaky boundaries abounded when Chandra was on song, as the edges flew through the gaps at supersonic speeds towards the boundary.

Some pundits may mock Kumble for his lack of turn. Back in the 1960s, they called Chandra the fastest bowler in the Indian XI. It was like saying that Indira Gandhi was the only man in her cabinet—sometimes it was actually true. Some of Chandra's hand grenades, which sent stumps cartwheeling, were no more than a blur to the spectator. Worse, from a batsman's point of view, he did not see them much better either. What caught batsmen unprepared was that the lead-up to a sensational Chandra spell could consist entirely of full tosses and long hops. One moment, he would be muttering to himself and working himself into a nice temper to bowl better, and in the very next, he would be firing down an unplayable Yorker or flipper. Like a man in a frenzy, he would wait impatiently for his next victim, chafing at the leash.

Unlike Kumble, Chandra was not a cerebral bowler, but it would be a fallacy to state, as many self-styled experts did, that he did not know what he was doing. If his general bowling style was fast and faster, he introduced subtle changes as he grew in age and stature as a bowler. When he held one back, it presented a much more difficult proposition to the unsuspecting batsman than the well-flighted delivery of an orthodox wrist spinner. There was only an imperceptible change of trajectory in this change of pace, which more often than not fooled batsmen into spooning return catches.

Yet another major difference between the two great leg-spinners of Karnataka is that the senior could not bat to save his life, while the younger man has on occasion shamed his frontline colleagues with his determination amidst the ruins of a collapse. Chandra is perhaps the only Test bowler in history with more wickets than runs to his credit. I believe he once made 22 in a Test innings and played two memorable supporting roles at No. 11—the first while V Subramanyam, his Karnataka captain, went from a hundred or thereabouts to 200 against Madras at Chepauk in 1967, and the second as an admiring spectator at the non-striker's end while GR Viswanath raced to an electrifying unbeaten 97 against the fire of Andy Roberts & Co. at the same venue seven years later.

Everyone knows that Chandra's greatest moment was the Oval Test of 1971, when he bowled India to an improbable first Test victory in England. Yet it would be folly to single that magical performance out in a glittering career, which included many acts of derring-do in India and abroad—against England, Australia, New Zealand and West Indies. In one memorable spell at Bombay, he took eight wickets in the first innings and four in the second. *The Hindu's* PN Sundaresan, not known for flowery prose or sentimentality, wrote perhaps his most inspired prose describing the lump in his throat as he watched the frail young man soldiering on against a West Indian batting juggernaut led by Garfield Sobers.

Personally, though never a close friend, I, like other cricketers of my generation, was witness to Chandra's tragedies and courage in adversity. We all knew of his weakness for Mukesh's hauntingly nasal voice and his guru Saigal's favourite beverage. I also had occasion to learn of his fondness for another brew—*rasam*, without which no south Indian meal is complete. In Chandra's case, it could be the meal to the exclusion of the rest of the menu, I once found out.

I wonder if Kumble would have been possible without Chandrasekhar. Were it not for Chandra's match-winning exploits in the 1960s and 70s, would any selector have dared to blood an unorthodox wrist spinner in the mould of Anil Kumble in the 90s? Would he have been dismissed as a freak bowler, unlikely to succeed on the world stage?

BS Bedi

It is one of the lovely ironies of modern cricket that great cricket writers can wax lyrical about both fast and slow bowling. Whoever described Michael Holding's bowling action as whispering death was perhaps a greater wordsmith than the man who described Bishan Bedi's as poetry in motion, but both the speed merchant and the spin wizard tended to evoke superlatives in those watching them in their prime.

Bedi at his best not only fitted that description perfectly, but was the most consummate exponent of the art of spin bowling—so much so that the question is often asked if he has been the greatest left-arm spinner in the history of the game. Certainly Sir Donald Bradman, who saw Bedi only at his best or close to his best, believed so.

He was certainly the best left-arm spinner I saw, better than Vinoo Mankad, whom I did not have the good fortune to watch in his youth, more classical than the mercurial genius Salim Durrani, more complete, especially on good wickets, than Derek Underwood of England—who could be destructive on certain types of pitches—the two brilliant bowlers he kept out of Test cricket, Rajinder Goel and Padmakar Shivalkar, his outstanding successor Dilip Doshi, and New Zealand's Daniel Vettori.

Expanding this assessment to name the best Indian spin bowler I have watched, Chandrasekhar would have been the obvious choice for being the most spectacular, and Anil Kumble for being the most consistent, longest lasting match-winner of them all, but I might have placed Bedi higher than my eventual choice Prasanna among them, but for Bedi's profligacy in the last few Tests of his illustrious career.

Though Bedi had been impressive when I first saw him—in his second Test and the third and last of that series at Chepauk—it wasn't until six years later that he was to overwhelm me with his total domination of the English openers when brought on within moments of the start of the innings. By now, he was a confident purveyor of his exquisite art of classical spin bowling. Twinkle-toed in his run-up, he was virtually airborne in his final stride to the wicket, looking over his right shoulder in side-on elegance. His incredible arm-speed in delivery completed the illusion of effortlessness that enabled him to slow the flight of the ball in the air but hasten it off the pitch with just the amount of finger spin he wanted. His arm ball, especially with the shine still on, was a veritable in-swinger that could castle the bemused right-hander or find the edge of the unsuspecting lefthander. Bedi seemed to be naturally fit, with just the right strength and flexibility of muscle for a spin bowler. If Prasanna was cerebral and Chandrasekhar intuitive, Bedi was more the artful dodger, though he too could lay an elaborate trap for a batsman when he set his mind to it. He was also the most stubborn of the Indian quartet of spinners, someone who sometimes appeared to refuse to see what was good for him or his side, as events in the evening of his career suggested.

In his rivetting *Bishan, Portrait of a Cricketer*, Suresh Menon—perhaps completely rightly—attributes this chapter of his bowling life to Bedi's adamant refusal to deviate from his philosophy of flight, but I have always wondered if the poet had simply lost his talent for verse by the time he arrived at that juncture of his cricketing journey. Was it a question of loss of spinning ability and resultant absence of loop that made the previously deceptive suddenly innocuous? (Menon does hint in his empathetic yet delightfully honest book that Bishan was physically and mentally tired by the time he toured Pakistan as India captain).

EAS Prasanna

The first time I saw EAS Prasanna in action was in the final Test of the 3-Test series between India and West Indies at Madras in January 1967. Test cricket was coming back to Chepauk after its banishment to the Corporation Stadium 15 years earlier. The Garfield Sobers-led visitors had won the first two Tests at Bombay and Calcutta, where Prasanna's rival Venkataraghavan had bowled well—without great success, if you did not count Garry Sobers's scalp, which he captured in Bombay.

The Chepauk Test, made memorable by Farrokh Engineer's near—hundred before lunch on the first day and some second innings aggression by Ajit Wadekar and V Subramanyam which served to book their berths to England in the following summer, was the first time the trio of Chandrasekhar—Bedi—Prasanna came together.

Prasanna was impressive in that game, though not incisive enough to cause a collapse in either innings. In the first innings, he accounted for the wickets of Butcher and Hall, while in the second he fared better getting Hunte, Butcher and Hendricks out. The bouncing run-up and tempting were very much in evidence, and so was a happy optimism as if he expected a wicket every ball in his approach to bowling. For someone who was making his comeback to Test cricket after a hiatus of five years, he looked comfortable in his shoes, as though he never doubted he belonged in the company of his seniors in the side. A lot of it must have been the result of the confidence he enjoyed from his captain and South Zone teammate Pataudi as well as South Zone captain and Test teammate ML Jaisimha, on the reserve bench for the match.

That Test match which ended in a draw thanks to dogged post-tea resistance on the last day by Garry Sobers and Charlie Griffith had raised hopes of a resurgent Indian team, with some exciting batsmen in Ajit Wadekar, Pataudi, and Borde and a brand new spin combination promising much. The tour of England that followed soon afterwards proved a great disappointment, with India receiving a massive drubbing despite some isolated instances of defiance. The spinners did nothing of great note, and we had to wait till the third and final Test for Prasanna to run into some form. He took 3 for 51 and 4 for 60 in the best of his outings in the series. In fact, Prasanna never did spectacularly well in England, the weather in the first half of the summer perhaps preventing him from bowling at his best, with the ball retaining its shine for long periods and the grassy wickets inimical to turn.

Prasanna was at his best on the 1968 Australia—New Zealand tours when he took as many as 49 wickets in eight Test matches. Like thousands of other Indians, I was glued to the radio every morning during that wonderful tour when India were gallant losers in Australia and deserving winners in New Zealand. Prasanna was hailed as a world—class spinner by the Australian critics and even some of the Australian batsmen.

The real moment of magic was to come soon. It was in the Chepauk Test in January 1970 that Prasanna almost single-handedly landed India at victory's doorstep—only for a missed stumping chance and fighting batting by Ian Redpath and the tail took Australia to a total which proved way beyond India's fourth innings capability. In their second innings, Australia were tottering at 24 for 6 before their miraculous recovery. Prasanna's share of victims up to that point had been four, to Mohinder Amarnath's two—incredibly, Keith Stackpole and Ian Chappell, both for duck. Prasanna finished with six wickets in the innings, and I was permanently hooked on his bowling, though I was away in Dharwar playing university cricket and only heard the match!

I remained his fan throughout the rest of his career, and had the pleasure of playing against him in the Ranji Trophy. He had a lean patch after that wonderful spell against Australia, when Ajit Wadekar took over the captaincy and led India to historic victories in the West Indies and England in 1971. India's maiden triumphs in the two continents meant that Prasanna's relegation to the background was hardly noticed. His bowling against England in the 1972—73 season and again in the 1976—77 season was outstanding, though against Tony Greig's men his spin seemed to have lost some of its sting. Jaisimha and Pataudi, my seniors, however believed he was still as good as ever, when I suggested to them that he was past his best. In between, in the 1975—76 season, he had a successful tour of New Zealand and a less successful tour of the West Indies, where he lost his Test place to Venkataraghavan after the first match.

I realised that Jaisimha and Pataudi were probably right about the continued high quality of Prasanna's off-spin when I played against him in the Ranji Trophy, which featured some outstanding spells by him. In what was perhaps his last Ranji game, he took seven wickets against Hyderabad, in a match at Bangalore. I was one of his victims, caught at short-leg while trying to drive on the offside. The ball was a perfect beauty, flight, dip, turn, bounce and all. I had hit him the previous ball for a four to square-leg, a shot he actually applauded. How he had me fooled! Around the same time, I remember the way pressmen waxed lyrical over the way he dismissed Sunil Gavaskar with a perfect straight delivery in an Irani Cup match. I had to wait for some 15 years to witness a repeat of that scene, when he bowled Gavaskar after he hit a flurry of boundaries with a similar delivery that clipped the off bail during my brother Sivaramakrishnan's benefit match (in April 1993) at Chepauk, between two teams of veterans. Prasanna was all of 53 then—and Gavaskar 40-plus.

Prasanna was perhaps the most confident bowler I have seen, certainly the most aggressive off-spinner. Short of stature, and generously built, even plump at times, he had a springy run-up to the wicket, whose momentum he used to great effect. At his best, he was perfectly side-on, and brought his right arm down quickly to maximize the spin he imparted to the ball. His variations were subtle—including intelligent use of the crease, changes of grip ranging from fingers loose and far apart to tight and close together to control the amount of turn. He could bowl a flatter, quicker ball with fingers close together or a floater angling away from the bat by rolling his fingers over the seam. All these variations were marked by the invariable magic of the ball dropping short of the length the batsman anticipated.

I was fortunate to play alongside the great spinners of the time. Prasanna may not remember it, but he came over to watch me in action at the State Bank of India nets in Hyderabad (where he had moved for about a year from Bangalore), at the request of my teammate P Krishnamurti. When Murti told me Prasanna had been impressed, it did my morale a world of good, as I was not yet the first choice off-spinner in the bank's team. (Syed Abid Ali was another 'guest' Murti invited to assess my bowling. In a cricketer's life, these are unforgettable gestures of kindness).

My subsequent encounters with Prasanna were as a rival player, and those are not quite the same. Once, when we were playing at the Chinnaswami Stadium, the umpire ruled AV Jayaprakash not out caught behind off my bowling, and Prasanna shouted from the pavilion: “That was off the middle of the bat, not an edge.”

Yes, Prasanna was an outspoken man. He proved it again that day, as I returned to the pavilion at lunchtime, with a couple of wickets in my bag, by telling me I was bowling too fast, I should give the ball more air. I didn’t take too kindly to that unsolicited piece of advice. (Well, you can talk, you have a batting line-up that gives you runs to bowl with, I thought).

It was only in hindsight that I realised he was absolutely right, though there was precious little I could have done, as I was only playing the role my team expected of me.

Naturally, as a competitive sportsman, one tried to be as good as one’s rival, even if he was the world’s best off-spinner, as it happened to be in this case. It was indeed a tall order, as in addition to his formidable bag of tricks, Prasanna had one advantage over taller off-spinners—the extra height to which he could flight the ball.

It was an honour to even to try to compete with him.

VV Kumar

When Sir Garfield Sobers came to Chennai ten years ago to assist former India leg spinner Vaman Kumar at the MAC Spin Academy, he was obviously impressed by the energy and dedication of the veteran who was already well into his sixties. During an informal dinner some of us were privileged to attend at the Madras Cricket Club at the end of the camp, Sobers was therefore not very surprised when we named VV the best orthodox wrist spinner in India after Subhash Gupte in reply to his query if Subhash's younger brother Baloo would have fitted that description.

Like many cricketers of my generation from the south, I have been a life-long admirer of VV Kumar the leg spinner, and an equal fan of his sense of humour and eccentric, unpredictable ways on and off the cricket field.

Long before I saw him in flesh and blood, Kumar had excited my imagination with his heroic deeds in Pakistan as a member of the Indian Starlets team that toured that country circa 1960 under the captaincy of Lala Amarnath, by then retired from Test cricket. It was a great opportunity for young Test hopefuls on both sides of the border to impress the national selectors. On the Indian side, Kumar and fellow Madras cricketer AG Milkha Singh were the undoubted successes of the tour. At my grandfather's Trivandrum residence, I excitedly awaited the arrival of The Hindu around 4 pm everyday from Madras bearing all the cricket news of the day. VV and Milkha rarely belied my expectations that summer.

I first saw VV in action when he made his Test debut not long afterwards at Delhi's Feroz Shah Kotla and my father, then working in the capital, took my brothers and me to the match. I was barely 14 then and my memory of the action is clouded by the passage of time, but I can never forget the thrill I experienced when VV snared his first victim—Imtiaz Ahmed, the Pakistani wicket keeper. Kumar went on to take five in the innings and seven in all in the match.

Unfortunately, Kumar's dreams of prolonged success as a Test bowler were crushed after his second appearance for India. By a strange coincidence, I happened to be one of the spectators at the Brabourne Stadium, Bombay, next season, as my father had by then joined Bank of India there. It was a miserable match for Kumar, as he finished with none for 70 in the first innings, did not bowl in the second and did not distinguish himself in the field. There were murmurs about a hidden finger injury leading to this debacle, and even though only one of the four Indian spinners, Chandu Borde, was among the wickets, VV's failure was highlighted by his critics. One of the other Madras players in the Indian team, left-hand batsman AG Milkha Singh—who had a decent outing at the Kotla versus Pakistan—failed too and was booed by an unsporting crowd, while his elder brother Kripal Singh scored 38 and 13, both not out. Neither VV nor Milkha played for India again despite sterling performances in the Ranji Trophy for several seasons, and Kripal came back into the side under Tiger Pataudi's captaincy. It was all so depressing for the young fan from Madras.

Returning to Madras in 1962, I had several opportunities to watch Kumar bowl in the local league and the Sport & Pastime (later Hindu) Trophy matches and eventually play with and against him—with him in the BS Nets organised by the cricket association, and against him in league games. He was a master bowler who was constantly improving, adding new weapons to his armoury while perfecting those he already possessed. He did not believe in exaggerated flight, but tossed it up in a tantalizing arc, varied his pace, bowled two different types of googlies and bowled an effective flipper, though it was not yet known by that name. He was accuracy personified, as was his younger spin partner in the state team, S Venkataraghavan. Both were workhorses, wheeling away in the nets for three hours every evening. I once made the foolish mistake of charging VV in the nets with some success, and he made my life miserable forever afterwards by switching over to the net I was batting in from wherever he was bowling in the practice complex of half a dozen wickets. He did this day after day for a whole season, even though I was a miserable tailender, not a frontline batsman. He was really intent on testing himself against someone who seemed to master him for a solitary session of practice. It is this competitive streak that made him such a successful bowler against all the top batsmen in the country.

Kumar was some ten years my senior, and was always kindly disposed towards me, as he knew my father as a banking industry colleague. As I left Madras soon after my first full season in the First Division, I did not get to play too often in his company, but vividly remember the few occasions I did. The first instance was a warm-up game for Madras Cricket Club Mr Annadurai of the cricket association arranged against a young eleven of future state prospects to be led by VV in a mentoring role. I bowled a few blistering overs to PK Belliappa, the state captain who seemed all at sea against me. Frustrated by the several near misses, I lost my patience and tossed up a couple of lollipops which the experienced Belli promptly dispatched to the boundary. That is when my captain walked up to me and said, "Don't ever do that. You had the batsman in trouble. You should keep him under a tight leash, never offer him free hits." It was the exact opposite of the advice I received at the Brabourne a few years earlier; and the captain kept me on as well! This is a piece of advice I never forgot in my cricket career, and it also gave me a glimpse of VV's own cricket thinking.

I also witnessed another side of the VV Kumar persona in that game. Once when stand-in umpire CS Dayakar (our own teammate) negatived an lbw appeal by VV, the bowler reprimanded him sharply, and then carried on as if nothing happened. He'd actually snapped "Idiot" at Dayakar but, made of sterner stuff, Dayakar was unmoved. It was one occasion when Kumar's gamesmanship had no effect on the umpire, unlike the occasion when he barked at KB Ramaswamy. He caught the umpire nodding away at the crease and waking up startled by his appeal for leg before. "Told you not to stuff yourself with curdrice at lunch," he admonished. "Come on VV, mind your tongue," the umpire retorted. A couple of balls later, VV rapped the batsman on the pads again, but though the ball was clearly missing the leg stump, he nonchalantly turned to the umpire, and said: "How about this one, I say?" This time, up went the umpire's finger.

No batsman in domestic cricket mastered Kumar, with the solitary exception of V Subramanyam of Karnataka, who in the course of a double century in 1967, punished his bowling severely. In the South Zone, the leading lights of Hyderabad and Karnataka, like Pataudi, Jaisimha, and Viswanath always found him a handful. He had more than 400 Ranji Trophy wickets and 599 first class scalps in all in his long career. He took part in two hard fought Ranji Trophy finals against Bombay in 1967-68 and 1972-73, both of which Madras lost despite Kumar's splendid bowling. Despite all his consistent successes, his return to Test cricket was blocked by the emergence of the unorthodox but match-winning leg spinner BS Chandrasekhar.

I was lucky to win Kumar's approval for my off spin bowling—he even mentioned me as a Test prospect in a newspaper article. He and I were teammates in the SBI side in the Moin-ud-Dowla Gold Cup, when I enjoyed his company on and off the field. To cricketing matters, he always brought an original perspective, as when he said Rakesh Tandon bowled brilliantly in a particular match between Bombay and Hyderabad, though he did not watch the match and two of us who played in that game insisted that Tandon had been extremely lucky to get six wickets in the final innings of the match despite bowling full tosses and long hops galore. VV just dismissed our version of the story as baseless!

EXTRAS

SIR GARRY

"I believe Garry Sobers's innings was probably the best ever seen in Australia. The people who saw Sobers have enjoyed one of the historic events of cricket. They were privileged to have such an experience.

This was Sir Donald Bradman's tribute to cricket's greatest all rounder, after he had made 254 for a Rest of the World XI against Australia at Melbourne in 1971. Sobers was the beleaguered captain of a hastily assembled team of many nationalities, facing criticism for his team's and his own indifferent form. The tour itself had been a last-minute substitute for one by South Africa banned thanks to its practice of apartheid. In the first innings, Sobers had been dismissed for zero and the World XI for 184 by an attack led by a young tear away called Dennis Lillee (5 for 48). Australia had then gained a lead of 101.

Stung by criticism and labelled as Lillee's rabbit, Sobers replied in the only manner he knew - by counter-attack. Entering the scene at 87 for 3 in the second innings, the captain made 254 with 33 fours and three sixes; his team made 514 and they beat Australia by 96 runs. In the words of his biographer Trevor Bailey, the England all-rounder, Sobers played "all the recognised shots (plus a few of his own); the delicate placement, the lofted straight drive against a fast bowler, the square drive off the back foot to both off and leg, the controlled flick off the legs, the imperial hook, and the flowing front foot drive were just some of the delicacies featured in a batting tour de force. From start to finish everything was correct: timing, footwork, judgment and execution."

Sir Garfield Sobers scored 8,032 Test runs at an average of 57.78, figures good enough to place him alongside the batting greats of all time, but his exploits did not stop there. He took 235 Test wickets as well and held 110 catches. And he achieved these extraordinary results by playing the most positive cricket imaginable, enjoying himself and entertaining spectators the world over, never seeking records or averages.

Young readers may know Sobers as the batsman who once hit six sixes in an over, or whose record Test score of 365 not out was broken by Brian Lara, but they may not know what a versatile genius he was. As a batsman, pure and simple, he could have walked into any international side. Just in case proof is needed of his batting ability, let us consult Sir Donald Bradman. He explains: "With his long grip of the bat, his high backlift and free swing, Garry Sobers consistently hits the ball harder than anyone I can remember. This helps to make him such an exciting player to watch because the emphasis is on power and aggression rather than technique - the latter being the servant, not the master. The uncoiling of those strong, steely wrists, as he flicks the ball wide of mid on, is a real joy to watch because it is unique and superbly controlled, whilst the full-blooded square cut is tremendous."

Sobers was three or four bowlers rolled into one. Making his Test debut against England as an orthodox left arm spinner in 1953 , when he was barely 16 , he added several more strings to his bow in his two-decade-long Test career. He could, on occasion, bowl with genuine pace. At other times, he concentrated on movement in the air and off the seam; at yet others, he became a deadly wrist spinner. His fielding was fearless and spectacular, especially close to the wicket, where he pouched catches within handshaking distance of the batsman.

Born in Barbados on July 28, 1936, Garfield St. Aubrun Sobers grew up in a cricket-loving home atmosphere with three other cricketer brothers, and two sisters. Encouraged by doting parents - though his father died when he was barely six - and several father figures in his home town who took him under their wings at every crucial stage of his career, Sobers very quickly graduated from tennis ball cricket to playing for Barbados and the West Indies by the time he was sixteen. One of the earliest to spot his phenomenal talent was India's Vijay Hazare after watching his bowling for Barbados against the touring Indian team in 1953. On his Test debut, Trevor Bailey became his first Test victim. Soon afterwards, in another Test, Australia's Richie Benaud was running to the dressing room to fetch protective gear to field in the slips as the young left hander, opening the innings, slashed repeatedly at the feared pair of Ray Lindwall and Keith Miller, to score a thrilling 43!

Captaincy was the only aspect of Sobers's cricket that did not bring him the highest marks. He was an adventurous and positive captain; he believed in declarations that gave his side - and therefore the opponents as well - a sporting chance to win. One such declaration led to a famous English victory at Port of Spain in 1966-67, Colin Cowdrey and his men making 215 in 165 minutes. Sobers was roundly criticised after that defeat but he has never regretted his decision. On a wicket responsive to spin, he maintains to this day, England should have struggled to save the match rather than canter to a seven-wicket victory as they did. The best fourth innings scores of the series had pointed to such a scenario, and had his bowlers really risen to the occasion, Sobers would have been the toast of the Caribbean. In Richie Benaud's words: "Although, if possible, Garry preferred to be on top, winning or losing is not, and never will be, the beginning or end of the world for him".

No batsman entered a cricket ground with greater nonchalance or elegance, not even fellow West Indian Vivian Richards, whose majestic gait had a gum-chewing, swaggering arrogance about it. If Richards overawed rivals, inducing visions of the imminent decimation of their attacks, I imagined even as a young spectator that Garfield St Aubrun Sobers had a slightly different kind of impact on his opponents - more like inducing a sense of resignation, even reluctant admiration, for so often did he walk into a challenging situation and turn the game on its head almost effortlessly. Not only did his batting leave fielders gasping for breath in admiration, it sometimes elicited spontaneous applause even from the bowler whose deliveries he dismissed from his presence. And he was himself the first to applaud a worthy opponent.

Sobers made a quiet debut on March 30, 1954 in the six-day fifth Test at Sabina Park, Kingston, Jamaica, against the touring MCC, when he made 14 not out and 26 batting at No. 9, and took 4 for 75 in the first innings of a match England won by nine wickets.

Omitted for the first Test versus the touring Australians in the next season, he did nothing dramatic in the next four Tests, until the final Test, in which he scored an unbeaten 35 not out and 64 as a middle-order batsman. His 43-run cameo as stand-in opening batsman in the fourth Test, in his home country, Barbados, had convinced at least two Australian allrounders of his enormous potential - one of them Keith Miller, whom Sobers hit for three boundaries in his first over. Richie Benaud, who like many of his contemporaries considered Sobers the greatest allrounder in cricket, waxed lyrical about the innings. He swore that the 18-year-old left-hander's fierce square cuts and slashes outside the off stump off Ray Lindwall and Miller had him scurrying to the pavilion to fetch the cricketer's "receptacle for cuff links" - a rare instance of a fielder in the slips needing abdominal protection.

The first time I saw Sobers in action, in the fourth Test of the 1958-59 season at the Nehru Stadium, Madras, a huge reputation preceded him, after his world-record 365 not out (followed by a century in each innings in the very next Test) against Pakistan the preceding season, and tons of runs (25 & 142 not out, 4 and 198, and 106 not out) in the first three Tests of the India-West Indies series.

I had already devoured every word written about him and followed his versatile exploits as a batsman who played at almost every position from 1 to 9, medium-fast to fast bowler, orthodox left-arm spinner, chinaman specialist, and brilliant fielder and catcher. Sobers disappointed an eager Madras crowd with the bat, after promising much with his confident entry, shirt-collar up, after the openers Conrad Hunte and Holt were dismissed and he joined Rohan Kanhai with the scoreboard reading 152 for 2.

Sobers was deceived when on 29 by Vinoo Mankad, last-minute appointee to the captaincy and crafty veteran left-arm spinner, who was playing in his last Test as it turned out. Sobers failed again in the second innings, this time falling to legspinner Chandu Borde after making a mere 9. As a consolation, he gave us glimpses of his spin bowling talent with 4 for 26 and 2 for 39; West Indies coasted to a massive victory. His slip catching too was spectacular. What I vividly remember from that game was that despite the lack of runs, the Sobers persona wove a magnetic spell over me (and my friends) nonetheless.

On his next visit to Madras, when Test cricket returned to Chepauk, Sobers, this time captain of West Indies, more than whetted his fans' appetite, with two outstanding innings of 95 and 74 not out. As he had done after misreading a googly from Benaud in the famous tied Test in Brisbane in December 1960, he changed his shot at the last nanosecond to a similar delivery from BS Chandrasekhar to straight-drive him for six. On the earlier occasion, the ball had sped to the boundary for four, almost decapitating the bowler in its path. Sobers' second innings defiance - in the company of Wes Hall and Charlie Griffith - of India's brand-new spin trio of Bedi-Prasanna-Chandrasekhar to draw the Test is now part of the lore surrounding him.

The great allrounder graciously played down his achievements including his Chepauk exploits when he entertained a group of lucky dinner guests at the Madras Cricket Club more than a decade ago with an array of stories real and apocryphal. (One particular anecdote, though hilarious, turned out to be completely fictitious. In it Wes Hall allegedly scored a few runs in a Test in India, helped by non-striker Sobers' hand signals that helped him tell Chandrasekhar's googlies from his legbreaks - only to be dismissed first ball after tea, with his captain deliberately misleading him, after overhearing Hall's boast to Seymour Nurse that he read the ball in the air, unlike Sobers, who failed to do so.) Yet for all his modesty, Sobers confessed he never feared a bowler in his entire career, not even Chandrasekhar, disappointing the Chandra fans in his audience.

To illustrate this point, he recalled how puzzled he had been when Sir Donald Bradman affectionately ruffled his hair as he sat awaiting his turn in the Brisbane Test with his hands cupping his chin, and said, "Don't worry, son, you'll sort him out," referring to Richie Benaud who had dismissed him for nought in a tour game. Though the press had gone to town calling him Benaud's bunny, Sobers approached the Test with great sangfroid, as his 132 in 174 minutes was to prove.

EW Swanton once said of Neville Cardus that the great man was talking through his eminent hat when he claimed Wilfred Rhodes was a greater allrounder than Garfield Sobers. My response to similar comparisons between Sobers and the likes of Jacques Kallis or Imran Khan will be identical, with no disrespect intended to those other great allrounders.

THE LITTLE MASTER

The first time I played for Hyderabad against Karnataka, we yielded a first innings total of 462 for 8 declared after getting through the top half of the batting order for under 150, including the scalps of the great GR Viswanath and the brilliant Brijesh Patel cheaply. It was a proud moment for me to have Vishy caught at short leg by Jyotiprasad a ball after he had extra-cover driven me for four. Tiger Pataudi had run up to me and said, “Stop experimenting and bowl properly.” And as if on cue, the next delivery landed on the perfect spot and fizzed and turned. I was sure it was divine intervention, because I had been upset by Tiger’s remark — it was just a great shot by a great batsman. I was the last bowler to experiment at a time like that — and would have been happy to have Viswanath block that ball quietly, instead of which he gave me the huge bonus of his wicket.

But soon, we found out that God was angry with Hyderabad that day, particularly with me, for some past sin. There was a talented young batsman in the Karnataka XI called Sudhakar Rao who was making his debut that season along with a couple of others like Roger Binny and myself (for Hyderabad). He looked a compact little player with a neat array of strokes, but more important than all that, he had that phenomenal quality called luck in ample measure. In addition to surviving chances and half chances, he was out on five different occasions before he reached 50, only to be reprieved every time by the umpire. I happened to be the bowler each time. The errors were so obvious that the correspondent of *The Hindu*, N Ganesan, actually mentioned each bad decision in his report the next morning. The net result of the gods smiling on Sudhakar Rao and frowning on me was that he made 200 and got selected to tour the West Indies later that season with the Indian team, and I, ending up with figures of 2 for 125, missed getting into the South Zone playing eleven, my other performances that season notwithstanding.

Unfortunately, that is how cricket, and indeed life, pan out often, and you learn to grin and bear it. I came away with my head high and spirits soaring at the end of the first day's play when GRV walked up to me, tapped me on my shoulder and said, "That was a good ball." Sometimes the most lavish praise is delivered with the most modest words. Vishy's appreciative look said it all for me. That compliment and another from him next year when I got him out for 67 brilliant runs, I have treasured all my life.

That second time I dismissed Vishy, he played a gem of an innings. He drove our medium pacers repeatedly through midwicket when they bowled outswingers with three slips and a gully. One by one, the slips kept disappearing into the onside to stop the flow of runs. Unfortunately for us, he started gliding the same deliveries past third man by dropping his wrists in the very last moment, after initially pretending to play them to midwicket. Anyone who has seen GRV at his peak will remember that on such occasions, he would actually give the impression of looking towards midwicket while waving his magic wand of a bat at the ball to send it speeding down the off side. To me, and many of my contemporaries, he was The Little Master.

SUNNY DAYS

Sunil Gavaskar amassed 774 runs in the four Tests he played in the West Indies in 1971. By the end of that tour, he had announced his arrival as prospectively the greatest post-war opening batsman in the world.

India was by then used to being let down by its batsmen. The batting revolved largely around the courage of the captain, MAK Pataudi, and flashes of brilliance from the supporting cast, which included the likes of Ajit Wadekar and the mercurial Salim Durani, with Chandu Borde no longer around to lend it a semblance of stability. Dilip Sardesai had promised much but his best was yet to come.

Happily the first Test of that Caribbean tour at Sabina Park saw Sardesai at his best as he hit a powerful 212, with the next-best score coming from Eknath Solkar, who made 61 in a total of 387. India enforced the follow-on with a first-innings lead of 170 to the complete puzzlement of the rival captain, Garry Sobers. Rain had reduced the match to four days and you only needed a lead of 150 in a game of that duration to put the opposition in a second time. With Rohan Kanhai (158 not out) and Sobers (93) in roaring form, the match was comfortably drawn, but India had gained the confidence that they could challenge this West Indies side in a post-Wes Hall-Charlie Griffith transition period.

Gavaskar, the young prodigy from Bombay University, made his debut in the second Test, in Port-of-Spain, and straight away played a winning hand in India's first Test victory in the Caribbean. West Indies had been bundled out for 214 in the first innings by some superlative spin bowling from Erapalli Prasanna (4 for 54) and Bishan Bedi (3 for 46), with support from medium pacer Syed Abid Ali, who got rid of the dangerous left-handers Roy Fredericks and Clive Lloyd.

Opening the innings with Ashok Mankad (44), Gavaskar made an impressive 65. With Sardesai (112) continuing his great form, and Solkar contributing a valuable 55, India took a lead of 138, and then went on to dismiss the opponents for 261. This time S Venkataraghavan was the star bowler, with 5 for 95, while Durani, who is said to have snatched the ball from the captain, Wadekar, got rid of Lloyd and Sobers, and then nonchalantly returned the ball, as if to say his job was done. Gavaskar made light of the easy target of 124, remaining unbeaten on a fluent 67.

The Little Master made scores of 116 and 64 not out, 1 and 117 not out, and 124 and 220 in the next three Tests, breaking all manner of records in the process. India managed to win the series on the strength of their Trinidad victory in the second Test, as each of the other games ended in a draw. A champion batsman had arrived on the Indian Test horizon, the likes of whom we had never seen before, certainly not since the days of Vijay Hazare, Vinoo Mankad, Rusi Modi, Polly Umrigar and Vijay Manjrekar.

Though his contribution to India's triumph in England the same summer was not significant, Gavaskar impressed the experts with the purity of his technique. Back in India, he did not make too many runs in the series against Tony Lewis' Englishmen, or even in the unofficial Tests in Sri Lanka that followed. On the disastrous tour of England in 1974 (the infamous "Summer of 42") he made a grand start with 101 and 58 in the first Test, but faded away thereafter.

He missed most of the 1974-75 home series under Pataudi against West Indies with an injury he sustained in the first Test in Bangalore. Coming back for the final Test in Bombay, he made a fluent 86. His gradual return to his rightful place in the pantheon of great modern Test openers began during the 1975-76 New Zealand tour and grew to full bloom in the West Indies with his scores of 156 and 102 in the two back-to-back Tests in Port-of-Spain. India's unlikely triumph in the third Test, chasing a target of 403, however, provoked the launch of a four-pronged pace attack by Lloyd, a captain desperate to put West Indies on the top of the cricket world.

GR Viswanath was my favourite batsman, but I had to concede that Gavaskar was the master batsman without equal, for his superb technique, immense powers of concentration, unflappable temperament, and astute cricketing brain. I would go so far as to say that purely as a Test batsman, he was superior to Sachin Tendulkar.

Gavaskar's last Test innings, his 96 at Bangalore in March 1987 against Pakistan on a landmine of a wicket, must rate as one of the greatest exhibitions of batting against spin. He had in the 1974-75 season given hints of his twinkle-toed footwork when he made a delightful 86 against the West Indies at Bombay. For an opening batsman, he was one heck of a player of spin bowling.

ASHOK MANKAD

Kaka, as Ashok Mankad was known to one and all, had been a cricketer I greatly admired for his phenomenal feats as a batsman in domestic cricket and his astute leadership. (I never knew when he was alive that his nickname was because of his fondness for the film actor Rajesh Khanna, also known as Kaka to friends). And for a few years, we enjoyed a great rapport whenever we met as foes on the cricket field or friends off the field, for example, during a conditioning camp for India's Test probables of 1977-78 at Chepauk. That is when we shared a dressing room, and he kept me and the rest of the boys constantly entertained with his mostly apocryphal cricket stories. One particular anecdote involving 'Nana of Poona', PG Joshi, the late Indian wicket keeper, had us convulsed.

Nana Joshi was according to Kaka in the habit of introducing himself with a flourish, as "I'm Nana of Poona." Kaka was telling us the story of a friendly match he played at Poona against the redoubtable leadership of Joshi. It was a celebration of some kind and I don't remember the occasion, but it was Mankad's turn to open the innings after lunch in which a large number of shandies—a cocktail of beer and lemonade for the uninitiated—had figured prominently. Nana, leading the side from behind the stumps perhaps had not imbibed, and was full of enthusiasm in the hot sun. Mankad was so far gone that he was seeing not just two cricket balls but two bowlers altogether. He turned round and saw four slips and a gully eagerly eyeing the outer edge of his bat. Hurriedly looking the other way, he spotted forward short-leg breathing down his neck. The bowler, with a reputation for genuine pace, short-pitched bowling and a short temper, was a distant speck half way to the straight boundary.

Alarmed at this prospect of physical danger, Kaka turned to the wicket-keeper-captain and said to him in his most pleading voice: "*Yeh kya ho raha hai bhai?* This is only a friendly match, and after all those beers, you don't want to kill me on the field, do you?"

Joshi was unmoved. He summoned his best professional manner and said sternly: "Ashok, you do the batting, and I'll do the captaincy. After all, you are a Test batsman. Don't tell me you are scared."

Ashok had no choice but to steel his nerves and try to get out at the earliest and thus escape injury. He literally closed his eyes and flashed at the first delivery. It went screaming past gully for four. Nana, who had an impressive talent for whistling, whistled at the gully fielder and waving his arms furiously and regally, despatched him to deep third man.

Kaka said to himself: That was lucky; now let me try harder to get out this time. Another express delivery, and Kaka followed the same routine. Close eyes. Say prayer. Slash hard. This time the ball went like a bullet to point boundary. Nana whistled again, and waving his arms in a slightly different direction, banished fourth slip to point boundary. The fast bowler was not pleased at Kaka's wild abandon.

The next ball was a vicious bouncer and Mankad's flailing bat sent the ball over fineleg off a top edge for six. Predictably, Nana's whistle-wave-arms routine followed as surely as in a later generation Hawkeye follows the ball.

By now the paceman—I can't swear to it, but I half-remember it to be the express tearaway Pandurang Salgaonkar—was livid with rage. He sent down a vicious toe-crusher and by the sheer power of his self-protection instincts, Mankad dug it out to send it past midwicket for four.

This time around, there was a slight change in the sequence of events. In trying to deport second slip to midwicket, Nana Joshi got the whistling perfectly right but the arm waving, for the fourth successive time, obviously proved a bit of a challenge. "Cramp! Cramp!" he shouted, and turning towards the pavilion, screamed, "*Paani, paani! Jaldi paani aur Electral lao.*"

It was during that camp that I first heard the typically Mumbaiyya expression 'leg n' leg' that Kaka repeatedly used to describe our condition after our coach Darshan Tandon put us through the wringer day after day. The Indian skipper

Bishan Bedi, away playing county cricket in England, joined the camp only for the last three days or so. Kaka's impersonation of how Bishan would come into the stadium for training on his first morning in the camp and find noone there was a brilliant act of mimicry. Imitating the captain, and giving wild vent to his imagination, Mankad went through the whole gamut of emotions—surprise, bewilderment, anxiety, and finally anger—peaking with the dawning of realisation in a sterling show of the adbhuta rasa, when Bishan finds the entire team jogging on the roof of the stadium.

Bishan was part of the audience that stood around Mankad at M L Jaisimha's Marredpally, Secunderabad, residence one evening during Jai's benefit match, in which the Indian team led by Bedi played against an 'international' eleven captained by Jai. Asif Iqbal, Sarfraz Nawaz, Imran Khan, Zaheer Abbas and Mushtaq Mohammed formed the strong Pakistani contingent at the match. Most of them gathered around Kaka, who told story after story, embellishing fact with fiction, slowly building up suspense in each tale, like the master raconteur he was.

Mankad was growing redder and redder in the face as the beer kept flowing after a long day in the sun, and the rest of us were struggling to stay on our feet as he kept us all in rollicking good humour.

That morning, Sunil Gavaskar had pulled a long hop from me straight into Mankad's hands at deep square leg, and one of the guests, a police official, who was generally inflicting his company on the celebrity cricketers at the party, now reminded Kaka about that. “Mr Mankad,” he said, wagging a naughty finger at Kaka, “is there an old rivalry between you and Mr Gavaskar?” Not satisfied with Kaka’s firm reply in the negative, he said, “Then why did he fling his bat in the dressing room after getting out and mutter, ‘Sala, drops catches in Test matches, holds mine in a benefit match’?”

Mankad’s riposte was a classic, but one he was quick to stress was just a joke. He said, “Reddy Saab, catch me dropping Sunil Gavaskar! Wake me up at midnight and I will hold his catches!”

Wondering if he had perhaps gone too far, Kaka immediately tried to play it down. “Reddy saab, you know of course that I am saying all this in good humour.”

It was Bishan’s turn now to bring the roof down. “Kaka says it in good humour all right, but he means it.”

(Disclaimer: Sunil Gavaskar was not amused when he heard this story, failing perhaps to see the humour in it. He vehemently denied there was any rivalry between Kaka and himself. I hope he will see it as no more than a funny story, not meant to cast aspersions on anyone—if he reads this again. Mankad himself thoroughly enjoyed it).

REVERSE SWING

"Do you want to know how we made the old ball swing in Barbados?" The year was 1978, the man talking to us at the Lal Bahadur Stadium, Hyderabad, one sunny afternoon in February or March of that year was one of the inventors of reverse swing, though it was yet to be known by that name. The tall, gangling, tousled-haired, moustachioed, side-whiskered Sarfraz Nawaz then proceeded to rub the fairly new ball on the bare ground just outside the boundary line until it became completely rough. He went on to polish the other side to make it shine like a mirror. The umpires looked the other way, as the match in progress between India XI and an International XI was the ML Jaisimha benefit match, not a first class fixture, though they did need a bit of arm-twisting by Sarfraz before they agreed to let him tamper with the ball.

What followed was a magnificent spell of fast swing bowling by the mad, mad Pakistani seamer, which was made more exciting by the efforts of his colleague from the other end to show everyone who was the quickest bowler around. Imran Khan had just a couple of weeks earlier been declared one of the fastest bowlers in the world by some Australian commentators. "*Bhai, hum dono mein kaun zyaada tez hai?* (Brother, which of us is faster?)," Sarfraz kept asking us. Though all of us knew Imran was yards faster, none of us had any doubt about Sarfraz's skill and wicket-taking ability. Only we did not dare to say that aloud for fear of a boycott by Sarfraz.

In later years, I was to learn that what Sarfraz did that afternoon was give us a demonstration of an innovation that later became world famous as reverse swing, but I did not speak or write about it, worrying that my audience would accuse me of making the whole thing up. I was relieved when Dilip Vengsarkar, who played in that game, gave a detailed account of that incident in his column in the Saturday Sports Special of *The Hindu*.

Three non-Test cricketers—M Narasimha Rao, Shahid Akbar and I—from Hyderabad were part of the International XI led by ML Jaisimha, as were former India captain Tiger Pataudi, Zaheer Abbas, Mushtaq Mohammad, Imran Khan and Sarfraz Nawaz and a couple of Test cricketers who had been part of the Indian Test team that had just returned from a tour of Australia, but were not included in the India XI for this match. The Pakistanis were on their way back from the Kerry Packer World Series cricket. While Zaheer Abbas gave us a foretaste of things to come in the forthcoming Indian tour of Pakistan by hammering our great spinners all around the park, the two quickies gave us a devastating display of fast bowling, the likes of which we had not seen in Hyderabad.

The match started on a slightly damp wicket following an early morning shower. The wicket was certainly not fit for play, with a couple of wet spots threateningly close to the good length area. Chetan Chauhan and Anshuman Gaekwad opened the innings, sportingly agreeing to an on-time start because a large crowd had bought tickets for the benefit game. Unfortunately for the Indian openers, Imran and Sarfraz were intent on outbowling each other unmindful of the physical danger to the batsmen. The ball kept flying from a good length and both Gaekwad and Chauhan had a torrid time negotiating the pace and the bounce. "Come on Jai, what's going on?" Chauhan complained to Jaisimha. "Why don't you tell these guys to take it easy? No sensible batsman would have agreed to bat on this wicket, but these chaps don't seem to care."

The captain looked on helplessly while Pataudi sported a wicked grin as we slip fielders were jumping and leaping, trying to hold on to perfect defensive shots taking off first bounce over our heads.

Jaisimha solved the problem by bringing on the spinners soon after the first two wickets fell, with a grim-faced Chauhan and an equally upset Gaekwad trooping off. Though it should have been a great moment for me, my spirit was somewhat dampened by Mushtaq Mohammad walking in from mid-off every other delivery and saying, "*Runs do, Bhai* (give runs, brother)!" As if the batsmen facing me, Sunil Gavaskar and Dilip Vengsarkar, needed any such help. But the unexpected did happen. While Vengsarkar helped himself to a flurry of boundaries, Gavaskar pulled a long hop straight into the hands of deep square leg Ashok Mankad.

TAMIL NADU'S BEST AND KARNATAKA, MY FAVOURITE TEAM

I shall try to list here some of the finest players I played with or watched in Tamil Nadu. Test batsman CD Gopinath, all rounder MK Balakrishnan, the brothers AG Kripal Singh, AG Milkha Singh and AG Satvinder Singh (Kripal's son Arjan Kripal Singh flattered to deceive with a triple century in the Ranji Trophy), openers K Srikkanth, P Ramesh, Sadagopan Ramesh and M Vijay, middle order batsmen WV Raman (arguably the most gifted of them all), R Madhavan, PC Prakash and S Sharath, medium pacers BR Mohan Rai, U Prabhakar Rao, BR Sekhar, V Rajaram, B Kalyanasundaram, TA Sekar, K Bharath Kumar, S Mahesh, all rounders P Mukund and Robin Singh, and wicket-keeper batsman Dinesh Karthik have been among the most impressive cricketers the state has produced. Many quality spinners could not break in because world—class bowlers VV Kumar and S Venkataraghavan ruled the roost for decades. Left arm spinner MK Murugesh was a match-winner and R Chandrasekharan was one of the finest off spinners of the state, but I have rarely seen a better off-spinner than N Bharathan outside the national level. R Ashwin is of course threatening to smash records galore in his burgeoning career.

We all know the highs and lows of the hugely talented leg spinner L Sivaramakrishnan, who came in at the end of the Venkataraghavan era. It is one of the tragedies of Indian cricket that he did not reach the great heights we expected of him. S Madhavan was another good leg spinner in the 1980s, who did well in a brief first class career for the Railways and Central Zone, but preferred to come back to Chennai, where he could not force his way into the state team. Among the spinners who succeeded that generation, left-arm spinner Sunil Subramaniam was as good as any in the country, but lost out to the likes of SL Venkatapathy Raju, while another talented left arm spinner Murali Karthik, also from a Chennai family, was unlucky not to play more Tests or internationals than he did. One of the most competitive of Tamil Nadu's cricketers, Sunil Subramaniam did splendid duty for the state and deserved to play for India. Another left-hander to miss out was the equally combative D Vasu, who started as a promising tearaway quickie, but switched to effective spin, besides playing many valuable knocks for his state.

As someone who rubbed shoulders with some of the most charismatic personalities in domestic cricket of the 1970s, I loved the Hyderabad cricket team of the period. With abundant talent at our disposal, however, we somehow managed to not win the Ranji Trophy in the two decades Jaisimha led us.

My respect and admiration, therefore, went to another glamorous side in the South Zone, Karnataka, which actually won the title a few times, toppling Bombay from its high perch for the first time a couple of seasons before my first. In March 1974, it prevailed over Bombay in the semifinal by virtue of a 78-run first innings lead. Two master batsmen, the wristy Little Master GR Viswanath (162), and that king of domestic cricket, Brijesh Patel (106), starred in that triumph, while spin twins Prasanna and Chandrasekhar were outstanding while defending a total of 385. Prasanna's floater that removed Gavaskar's off bail was the magical delivery of the match. The victory was no mean achievement, as Bombay's batting line-up included the likes of Ajit Wadekar, run out for 62 and Ashok Mankad, who made 84.

In the final that season, Karnataka beat Rajasthan fairly easily in the end, but not without a few alarms early on. Both Viswanath and Patel failed, but its dashing all rounders came to the fore: VS Vijayakumar who opened both the batting and the bowling, left arm spinner and hard hitting batsman B Vijayakrishna and medium pacer-batsman AV Jayaprakash in the middle order. Each of them was considered Test material at one time or another.

In addition to these splendid youngsters, who formed the nucleus of the team of the seventies, others too came good during the decade. Sudhakar Rao's 200 against Hyderabad in 1975-76 won him a berth on the West Indies tour that season, Roger

Binny soon came into the side, Sanjay Desai became a solid presence as an opening batsman, though kept out of keeping duties by that world class stumper Syed Kirmani, who was also frequently a thorn in the flesh of opponents, just when they thought they had got rid of the cream of Karnataka's batting.

Karnataka was to win the Ranji Trophy once again in that decade in 1977-78, when Viswanath hammered a magnificent double century in the final against Uttar Pradesh, following a hundred in the semifinal against Delhi after a newspaper reporter made the mistake of dubbing him Bishan Bedi's bunny. The state has repeated the feat five times since then.

If the honour of leading the team to its first two title triumphs went to Prasanna, Viswanath was the unfortunate captain to lose two finals—once after Karnataka made 705 in the first innings, only for Delhi to gain a lead. Brijesh Patel was the captain next season in 1982-83, when Karnataka beat Bombay in a gruelling final at Bombay. Significantly, the winning eleven had as many as five players from the champion side of a decade earlier—Viswanath, Patel, Sudhakar Rao, Jayaprakash, Vijayakrishna. Syed Kirmani had been eclipsed by young Sadanand Viswanath—who played a winning hand—only to make a comeback a few years later.

Prasanna and Chandrasekhar of course spun a great web together around batsmen for well over a decade, but amazingly, the team always found a place for at least one other spinner like Vijayakrishna in the playing eleven, besides some excellent seam bowlers like Vijayakumar, Jayaprakash and Binny. Each of them could be counted on to come up with hundreds or five-wicket hauls, especially when the team badly needed them.

Both Prasanna and Patel were astute leaders, and Viswanath a thoughtful one with a softer touch, and the men under them somehow managed to play consistently winning but rarely boring or defensive cricket. With one of the world's finest middle order batsmen in Viswanath, perhaps the most destructive batsman in domestic cricket in Brijesh Patel, a great keeper-batsman in Kirmani, and two members of India's famed spin quartet in Prasanna and Chandrasekhar, Karnataka managed to be an attractive, entertaining outfit throughout the time I watched them at close quarters.

HYDERABAD BLUES

Former England Test cricketer Basil D'Oliveira first showed signs of his class on a tour of the West Indies with Derek Robins's team. Young Kapil Dev impressed senior Indian cricketers with his phenomenal talent on a private tour of East Africa and not long afterwards, he was in the Indian team that toured Pakistan. Teams like Cricket Club of India and Hyderabad Blues have been excellent ambassadors of India, not only in the regular Test playing nations, but in other countries where a small minority pursue the sport with passion. They take young cricketers—and veterans—to some unusual locations of stunning beauty.

I can never forget the experience of playing for Hyderabad Blues (we travelled as Deccan Blues this time) before 35,000 paying spectators at Dhaka, in January 1978, long before any Test nation toured the newly formed Bangladesh. We might have been a loose combination of players from all over India, but as our acting skipper Ajit Wadekar reminded us minutes before the toss, no matter what we were called, we were the Indian team and it was as good as a Test match. The match was played in all seriousness, like the rest of the matches on that tour of Australia, South East Asia and Bangladesh. Our captain ML Jaisimha had gone back to India missing the Dacca game to prepare for his benefit match to be played at Hyderabad.

Today, we have the A team concept and India's young hopefuls gain valuable exposure to international cricket in conditions they do not experience at home. In the 1970s, tours by clubs like the Blues or CCI filled this gap admirably. What they also did was to enable young cricketers to mingle with Test cricketers, past and present, and enrich their cricket education. Equally fortunate were cricketers who knew they had missed the bus and would never otherwise visit these nations and play against their Test and first class cricketers in superb cricketing conditions full of history.

An example of the kind of preparation such tours afforded youngsters was the experience of playing in Australia, where even club grounds have 85-yard boundaries. Anyone who has chased the ball to the fence and thrown it back to the keeper on one of these vast grounds is more likely to go home and strengthen his throwing arm than a stranger to those conditions. You also learnt to bowl and bat on wickets vastly different from Indian pitches. Private tours make for greater interaction with people of the host nation than Test tours do. Very often, the visiting cricketers are billeted with cricketers' families and the resultant friendships are sometimes lifelong.

My own unforgettable memories include playing against and sharing a few beers back in 1978 at a Perth clubhouse with a young Englishman called David Gower, who we thought was not a bad little player! Gower opened the innings for the club Claremont Cottesloe, and treating our medium pacers with scant respect, got away to a flier, making 30 odd in no time. His innings was all too brief, for the wicket yielded some purchase, and the two off spinners of our side, my skipper Jaisimha and I, created serious problems for the young lefthander. To my disappointment, a couple of chances went abegging off my bowling and Gower eventually fell to Jai, though I took five wickets in the innings.

That evening, Gower and the secretary of the club asked me if I would play for the club as a professional the following season, as Gower was not returning. This was not only a huge honour but a tremendous opportunity as well, but I refused the offer, as it would clash with the Indian first class season. I was at the time close to selection to the Indian team and did not want to jeopardise my chances with the long awaited tour of Pakistan round the corner. As it turned out, I did not even make it to the probables list before the tour, despite my record. Thus are once-in-a-lifetime opportunities missed by those who want to play safe.

That innings was one of the high points of my bowling on that tour in which I led the pack with 35 wickets. Another was my performance under gruelling conditions in Penang against an RAF side, when Jai cursed me fluently after I asked to be taken off (the only time in my life), having run out of shirts and trousers, drenched in perspiration as never before or after in my career, and unable to grip the ball, the sweat simply pouring out from every pore in my body. "Stop giving me f-----ing excuses! Can't grip the ball indeed! God save me from bloody sissies!" he said. I had no option but to go on.

My final figures of 30-8-47-8 leading to a thumping win were more than adequate compensation for all the trouble, but even more pleasurable was the praise Jai dished out over a couple of drinks—again for the first time in my life, because cricketers, especially those belonging to the old school, generally don't believe in praising you to your face.

If these were some of the high points, I had a few low ones as well on that tour, starting with our first match—against Kowloon Cricket Club at Kowloon, Hong Kong. Both leg spinner Narasimha Rao (Bobjee) and I bowled badly in that game, nearly losing it for us. Occasional medium pacer K Jayantilal, our opening batsman, came to our rescue, bowling an unplayable spell of swing and seam, and picking up some seven wickets for next to nothing. That night, we received our first dressing down of the tour, with Ajit Wadekar telling us in a team meeting that we were the Indian team, no less. He also confessed how much he had benefited from Jai's wise counsel on the victorious West Indies tour of 1971.

We quickly recovered from that initial shock on the morrow, when we beat the stronger Hong Kong

Cricket Club by a big margin, with my brother Sivaramakrishnan and his fellow left hander P Ramesh scoring hundreds at the top of the order, and me acquiring the only hat trick of my life. Ajit Wadekar took two splendid diving catches at backward short leg, reminding us all what a brilliant close-in fielder he was.

Our experience against Singapore Cricket Club, later on the tour, was even worse. In a near replica of the Kowloon match, we were again rescued from a fate worse than death by Jayantilal, who picked up six wickets after the regular bowlers had proved to be profligate. Jai was never known to be a gracious loser, and this time was no exception. The hospitality in the barroom of the club was long and expansive, but Jai was quite happy to put our hosts firmly in their places for the crowing they had indulged in earlier when the game seemed to be heading their way. Well past closing time, everyone except Jai and the unhappy threesome of Vinod Reddy, Bobjee and I had left, after the hosts had offered in vain to drop us home, failing to persuade our angry skipper to get up from his perch. We finally left after the staff started shutting doors and windows pointedly.

Soon we wandered out, walking extremely carefully with the kind of dignity only the inebriated can muster, but soon realised that all our hosts had gone home. There was no taxi in sight either, and Jai was ranting and raving by now, cursing his extreme bad luck that made it necessary for him to play cricket with such nincompoops. Still unable to locate a cab, we walked on, trying not to pay any attention to the captain's lecture, not realising that we had drifted into a freeway where no vehicle would stop. We saw several taxis fly past us not heeding our desperate pleas and fluent curses in chaste Hyderabadi. All of 90 minutes later, a kindly taxi driver going in the opposite direction, took pity on us, and stopped for us. He of course had to go all the way to where we started before he could take a U turn and drop us at the hotel. It was three in the morning when we reached there!

Coming back to the match at Dhaka, Bobjee and I again went wicketless on a white, gleaming clay wicket, which yielded turn but extremely slow turn. Batting first, we made over 400, with Ajit Wadekar making a hundred and Sivaramakrishnan and Jayantilal playing substantial knocks. The Bangladesh team made a decent reply, some 300 plus for seven or eight, batting out nearly two days. It was slow, excruciating attrition and the Hyderabad bowlers had to be content with containment. Tukaram Surve, our veteran wicket keeper conceded 69 byes and was mercilessly teased by Wadekar, leading the team in the absence of Jaisimha, already back in Hyderabad to finalise the arrangements for his benefit match. "You were in great form, Godfrey,' he said, calling Surve by his nickname on the tour—after the former England great Godfrey Evans. Surve's retort was quick and angry: "How do you expect me to keep to these spinners? One of them bowls off breaks on the leg stump and the other his googlies outside it!"

(Kiran Kumar Reddy, the former Chief Minister of Andhra Pradesh was Surve's teenager understudy on that tour).

Later that evening Wadekar told Surve that both Bobjee and I were deeply hurt by his remarks. A very contrite Surve then sought me out and apologised profusely. "I'm so sorry, Rama. You actually bowled well for the first time on the tour!"

AN ABUNDANCE OF OFF SPIN

Hyderabad has had a tradition of off spinners, sometimes two or three of the tribe fighting for a place in the side. Despite this abundance, there is generally no argument in any discussion among cricketers past and present, about who was the best of them all. The late Ghulam Ahmed has been acknowledged by common consent as by far the greatest exponent of the art and science of off-spin bowling Hyderabad has produced. In fact, Hyderabad's most charismatic captain ML Jaisimha would go so far as to place Ghulam even higher than EAS Prasanna, at least in terms of sheer spinning ability. "You could hear the ball fizz out of his hand as you prepared to face him," he once told me. Jai was a great admirer of Prasanna's bowling and this was therefore the highest compliment, coming from him.

I have heard of, rather than watched, Jairam, the off spinner who followed Ghulam in his footsteps in the Ranji Trophy, except for stray glimpses from afar when I was very young. This dark complexioned, wiry, noticeably plebeian peddler of finger spin, was a game fighter, highly successful during his period, especially on matting wickets. He had a suspect action, something his captains fully exploited like true professionals, for whom all is fair in love and cricket, unless it is the opposition that is indulging in questionable tactics. Jairam's greatest claim to fame was his consistent refusal to wear abdominal protection. He is reputed to have been felled, if that is indeed the correct verb, when hit in that region batting at No.11 for South Zone, by an express delivery from the West Indies fast bowler, Wes Hall.

Noshir Mehta and I played a few games together for Hyderabad, before he faded away from the scene. I was later joined in the eleven by Shivlal Yadav, endowed with shrewd native intelligence. He was a quick learner and a gutsy performer whether bowling, batting or fielding, never running away from a challenge. He had a nice, smooth action and some spinning ability, but lacked the subtleties that separate great from good bowlers. He batted courageously in crisis situations and was a brilliant fielder in the early part of his career.

Arshad Ayub was another off-spinner who made it from Hyderabad to the Indian team, replacing Shivlal, with a run of consistent performances in domestic cricket. At that level, he was a fine all-rounder, his magnificent form a huge factor in Hyderabad's winning the Ranji Trophy under Narasimha Rao. As an off-spinner, Ayub was in the Venkataraghavan mould, very accurate, and delivering the ball from a height rather than flighting it much. He had a deadly faster ball or *wrong 'un,* which came under the microscope sometimes. An excellent team man, Arshad was a champion performer for Hyderabad and enjoyed a decent run in Test cricket too.

The best of them did not ever play for India. Kanwaljit Singh, a few years younger than Arshad Ayub, was a genuine spinner of the ball, despite a slightly contorted action, arms and legs flailing about before he somehow finished in a smooth delivery stride. Kanwal had the misfortune of being a contemporary of both Shivlal and Arshad who kept him out of the state side for years. By the time he became a permanent fixture in the Hyderabad XI, so was Rajesh Chauhan in the Indian team, ironically under the captaincy of Hyderabad's Mohammed Azharuddin. While another Hyderabadi, Venkatapathy Raju, a left arm spinner, broke into the Indian squad, Kanwaljit never did. He served Hyderabad with distinction for over a decade, finishing with more than 300 wickets.

Kanwaljit Singh seems to have been the last of the successful off spinners from Hyderabad, though a certain Noel David did make a brief, undistinguished appearance for India in the West Indies and elsewhere. I am sure there is good off-spin talent aplenty at Hyderabad given its tradition, but no one has so far hit the headlines on the national scene in recent years.

TEST CLASS

When Wisden India Almanack asked me some time ago to pick a team of those I considered good enough to play for India but did not, I tried my best to be inclusive, which meant not only that I had to take into reckoning past greats I had never seen in action, but also players of my own and later generations, whom I had not played with or against or even watched enough. Here, I'll try to do justice to the sterling qualities of players I have watched and admired, but some of whom I had to exclude in the Wisden piece, the prescribed word length being one of my constraints.

First the openers: Saad bin Jung, KR Rajagopal, V Sivaramakrishnan and Carlton Saldanha, are all batsmen who played cricket of a high quality, and might have with some luck, opened the innings for India. I have profiled the first three elsewhere in this book. Saldanha was a mere lad when I first saw him play for Karnataka, but had a mature head on his young shoulders. He seemed to have all the qualities to succeed at the Test level: a straight bat, a cool head and time to spare.

I mentioned in my Wisden article KP Bhaskar of Delhi, Hari Gidwani of Bihar, Amarjit Kaypee of Haryana, and Amol Muzumdar of Mumbai, whose consistent performances in first class cricket for over a decade did not win them the national selectors' nod. I was perhaps unfair to Gidwani in not including him in my final choice. The other three possess better statistics, but Hari, my Rest of India teammate in 1976, seemed to regularly deliver when it really mattered. In addition to a double hundred and at least another hundred each against Karnataka and Bombay, the leading sides in the Ranji Trophy, Hari has an excellent record against touring sides. He was a good captain, too.

Another lovely batsman I missed out on was Michael Dalvi, whom I saw a great deal of when he was playing for Madras CC in the local league and Tamil Nadu in the Ranji Trophy. I bowled to him in the league as well as Ranji cricket, against both Tamil Nadu and Bengal. Solid in defence, Mike played very proper cricket, with the right proportion of aggressive shots, which he played all round the wicket. He was a brilliant fielder patrolling the covers. His distinguished career included impressive innings for Zone teams, one of them a hundred against the touring Englishmen. Distinctly unlucky to miss the bus, he had the consolation of fielding in a Test as a substitute.

Injuries robbed two outstanding middle-order batsmen of Tamil Nadu, AG Satvinder Singh in the 1960s and S Sharath in the 1990s, of any real chance at the highest level. Another TN left hander, Abdul Jabbar, was often overlooked by the selectors, as were Abdul Azeem and MV Sridhar of Hyderabad.

I wonder however if India has ever produced a wicketkeeper more gifted than AAS Asif of Hyderabad, who nearly made it in the late 1960s. With his dashing good looks and cavalier approach to batting at the top of the order, he was an exciting prospect, but migrated to the US, like Gujarat opening batsman Ramesh Nagdev, who partnered Sunil Gavaskar at the university and zone levels.

A Karnataka opener who won many matches for his side was VS Vijaykumar—he did the job with both bat and ball—before Roger Binny replaced him. Bombay veteran Sudhakar Adhikari was a serious contender for the opener's slot for a few years in the 1960s, as was Gopal Bose of Bengal briefly a decade later.

Barun Burman of Bengal, Abdul Ismail of Bombay and Kailash Gattani of Rajasthan were among the best opening bowlers to have missed out, while left-armer Sunil Valson (Delhi), the only member of the squad not to play a single game in India's 1983 World Cup campaign, came pretty close too. Ismail was the quintessential swing bowler who could also wield the long handle effectively, while Gattani was a purveyor of old-fashioned seam, very accurate and miserly. Pandurang Salgaonkar of Maharashtra was a genuine quick who played unofficial Tests against Sri Lanka.

Other fast men of the 1970s like Rajasthan's Pradeep Sunderam and the Railways' unorthodox Sardar Khan, two genuine quicks, and Tamil Nadu's workhorse B Kalyanasundaram, would also come into the reckoning. So would all-rounders P Jyothiprasad (Hyderabad) and AV Jayaprakash (Karnataka), especially in ODIs.

Selecting an off-spinner was the easiest task. The indomitable Sarkar Talwar (Haryana) and the talented Noshir Mehta (Hyderabad) lose out to the one and only Kanwaljit Singh of Hyderabad, with his longevity and match-winning performances year after year. Others of the tribe like Sharad Diwadkar (Bombay) and Uday Joshi (Saurashtra) of an older vintage were also outclassed by Kanwaljit, a genuine spinner of the ball. (My own favourite off-spinner N Bharathan (TN) of the lovely loop played only one first class match).

Among leg-spinners Anand Shukla (UP), B Mahendrakumar (Andhra), Chandrasekhar Joshi (Rajasthan), and Rakesh Tandon (Bombay), it was a tie between the first two, as both were top class leg spinners and both also have double centuries to their credit. With 386 first class wickets, Shukla wins hands down, though the less stable Mahendra Kumar was perhaps more of a class act.

Several left-arm spinners come to mind—and quite a few of them could bat, too. Among the best would be Sunil Subramanian (TN and right at the top), Rajinder Singh Hans (UP), B Vijayakrishna (Karnataka), S Vasudevan (TN), D Vasu of TN (who switched from pace to spin), Mumtaz Hussain of Hyderabad (with his infinite variety of tricks), Ashok Joshi (Gujarat) and Hyder Ali (Railways). Unfortunately, all of them are overshadowed by the two greats in the department who never played for India—Padmakar Shivalkar (Bombay) and Rajinder Goel (Haryana). On good wickets, I would go with the more orthodox Shivalkar, while Goel could be deadly on turning tracks.

Many wonderful cricketers brought colour and excitement or solidity and longevity to cricket in their own way—like J Abhiram, Shahid Akbar, MK Balakrishnan, Sanjay Desai, Jugal Kishore Ghia, Abdul Hai, Ranjit Khanwilkar (who died in a train accident), V Krishnaswamy, R Madhavan, S Mahesh, Anil Mathur, P Mukund, MK Murugesh, Vijay Paul, MN Ravikumar, Sanjiva Rao, M Senthilnathan, Srinivas Prasad, Sudhakar Rao, CS Suresh Kumar, Venkat Sundaram, Vijay Telang, and K Jeshwant—who were expected at one time or other to go on to play for India. Unfair treatment by officialdom, bad luck and/or lack of persistence meant that these brilliant talents were never fully realised. All these were players I played against at some time or other, and it was my pleasure to have rubbed shoulders with them.

CLOSE OF PLAY

CRICKET AS A VETERAN

Going back to my own cricket career, the whole tracksuit episode had been a total defeat, and the prospects of my making it back to first class cricket were dim—at Hyderabad, at any rate. And I saw no future for myself in Andhra Bank, my employer, after my cricketing days. The time had already come for me to think of that. The prospect as a general manager of the bank or thereabouts, without the escape of cricket, was not a particularly alluring one. I started thinking of moving back to Madras. An added incentive was the chance to be of help to my family, with my father shortly due to retire from Bank of India.

Meeting Mr R Ratnam, chairman of Sundaram Industries of the TVS group, was the turning point I was hoping for. My brother Sivaramakrishnan, then working for Lucas TVS, and one of RR's favourite cricketers, had been performing consistently for TVS and Alwarpet Cricket Club.

A few minutes into our meeting, RR told me he was hiring me. Anxious to put the recent Hyderabad experience behind me and fearful of the ordinariness of my career ahead in the bank, I grabbed the chance and straightaway accepted. The decision turned out wrong on more than one count.

To cut a long story short, I soon realised that both Sundaram Industries and I had plunged into this employer-employee relationship without due reflection. With the Chairman rendered *hors de combat* by a major road accident for well over a year, and some seniors of the company resentful of me—and others who joined me there soon to strengthen the cricket team—I was face to face with a king-size mid-life crisis. On the cricket front, too, things were not very cheerful. After a spectacular first league game in which I took ten wickets in the match, I was inexplicably relegated to passenger status in the side for the rest of the season. Selected to represent the TNCA President's XI, the state's second eleven, in the Buchi Babu knockout tournament, I very nearly opted out, feeling insulted as a former South Zone player by what I saw as a demotion.

I would have faded out gracefully had a friend not given me a timely piece of advice. When I griped and grumbled to him about the humiliation of being consigned to the 'B' team along with the next generation of cricketers, he said: "You are not against playing a cricket match, are you? Why don't you go and enjoy this match as any other game?"

The result of my friend's words of wisdom was that I not only played the match in distant Tambaram, but with innings figures of 7 for 65, nearly gained TNCA President's XI the first innings lead over Indian Airlines. In fact, but for a masterly knock of 90 by Ashok Malhotra and his fighting rearguard action with wicket keeper Rajesh Peter, the story might have been different, for IA were perilously placed at some 60 for 7 when the duo came together in reply to our 150-odd score. In the event, they barely managed a ten-run lead, but in the process denied us the chance to progress in the tournament.

That was to be my last match at the first class level—though it was strictly speaking not a first class match as the two innings had over limitation. I was however misled by the state selectors who included me in the official list of 20, which meant that I bowled in the State nets for the next couple of months, with not a sign of my being picked in the squad for the Ranji Trophy. It was only after the first two matches of the season rolled by that I finally decided to return to my own league team's nets to practise. That in effect was the end of my first class career. With 7 for 65 in my last innings, it was not a bad ending!

For several years after that I soldiered on in the local league, deriving perverse pleasure from doing reasonably well—mostly on one good leg—against younger opposition. One particular match in the 1989-90 season gave me great joy. My new team Globe Trotters was on the verge of clinching an innings win against my previous team Alwarpet CC. There was a stiff contest among our bowlers to avoid bowling the last of the mandatory 20 overs in the final hour, with the last ACC pair defying us for over ten of those overs. With two MRF Pace Foundation trainees, Subroto Banerjee and Dinesh Tomar, Robin Singh, Aashish Kapoor and

WV Raman to choose from, the responsibility fell on my old shoulders, and when I somehow willed myself to find the inner edge of the young batsman on the fifth ball of that last over, I was overcome by satisfaction—at a job well done.

The greatest compliment of my cricket career came from Akbar Ebrahim, the captain of the MCC team in a league match a couple of years later. I was now playing for a team in the 2nd division. Before the start of the match, I overheard Akbar tell one of his teammates, "The old bugger will screw us on this wicket." I did precisely that and we went on to win the match.

Such moments were few and far between. Keeping fit enough to play competitive cricket was becoming increasingly difficult, especially with my professional commitments taking a heavy toll on my mental and physical health. I was 49 when I played my last cricket match, and I had already overstayed my welcome by a few years. Given a chance to relive my cricket career, I would have retired at the peak of my fitness and skill level, and never played at a level below my best.

BEYOND CRICKET

My return to Chennai had been a professional disaster, and my misadventures in business post-1988 left me in a bit of a spot in more ways than one, until I reached a point of no return sometime in 1993. My wife and my cousins Balu and Babu advised me to try my hand at writing, as I had always shown that I had some talent in that department. Pessimistic about my chances of making it as a freelance journalist/writer/editor, I willy-nilly plunged into exactly that very occupation. With great help and touching faith in me from *The Hindu, Business Line, the Economic Times,* Mr 'Heritage' S Muthiah, and my present boss N Sankar and his wife Chandra Sankar, I made a gradual comeback to enjoy a wonderful second innings. A number of books as author, co-author and editor have followed, as well as many opportunities as a feature writer and columnist.

Thanks to the open-arms welcome Sashi Kumar extended me sometime in 2006, I have also enjoyed teaching journalism students at the Asian College of Journalism—where I enjoy an unfair advantage over my colleagues or suffer unfair comparisons with them by students, depending on their attitude to sport (or music, my other affiliation).

And when *Cricinfo* founder Badri Seshadri

and his teammate Satya Krishnan launched a translation division in their publishing house New Horizon Media, I joined them as their English editor, having a ball bringing out some 40 titles including many translations of some of the finest works in Tamil, getting to know their superb authors and very nearly bagging national awards for our works.

Since January 2007, I have been editing *Sruti*, a 30-year-old magazine devoted to the performing arts. For a while in between, I worked for the city portal *Chennai Online* as its sports editor. It was during that stint that I met Sir Richard Hadlee, Dayle Hadlee and several talented New Zealand cricketers, some of whom later went on to play for their country. A story from that time follows in the next chapter.

KIWIS GO TO KALAKSHETRA AND VIDYA SAGAR

Sir Richard Hadlee turned to me and asked, "Raam! Does the protocol allow a couple of my boys to take off their shirts?"

The venue was a classroom in Kalakshetra, the iconic arts institution of Chennai, the year 2000. The man posing that question on native sartorial norms was indeed the great New Zealand fast bowler. We had just been witness to a brilliant demonstration of bharata natyam by a couple of girls and a boy, all three students of Kalakshetra.

This story is akin to the apocryphal (non) relationship between Abdul Khader and Amavasya. Back in 2000, I decided that a bunch of cricketing visitors from the antipodes needed to have their education enhanced by a visit to Kalakshetra among other places in Chennai. On a busman's holiday from my day job of sports editor, I had taken a few days off to follow the trail of the New Zealand Cricket Academy team taking part in the Buchi Babu Memorial tournament conducted by the Tamil Nadu Cricket Association. The academy went on to win the championship, though I don't remember if they did it that season or the next.

Many of the players in that side coached by Dayle Hadlee and managed by his brother Sir Richard Hadlee went on to play for New Zealand with the big boys in Test cricket if they had not already done so.

As a regular at the NZCA's matches, I soon got to know the Hadlee brothers and some of the players well. During one of our conversations while watching a game, I asked Dayle Hadlee if he and his team had got round to seeing anything of the city. The answer was in the negative. The boys just went from their hotel rooms to the cricket ground, gym or swimming pool and back, when they were not attending boring parties, formal and prim and proper.

Dayle readily accepted my offer to take the cricketers on a tour of Kalakshetra and Vidya Sagar, formerly Spastic Society of India. I almost regretted my impulsive offer when I considered the logistics and expense of carting 20 New Zealanders all but two of them energetic youngsters whose idea of a day off from cricket would have been slightly different from a visit to such strange places! I struck gold when TA Sekar of the MRF Pace Foundation immediately offered the use of the foundation's bus free of charge to ferry the cricketers that September morning.

My next great piece of luck was the prompt response I received from Kalakshetra Principal S Rajaram. He not only enthusiastically agreed to my request, but also arranged a 20-minute dance recital in one of Kalakshetra's classrooms.

The New Zealand boys were a cheerful lot in the bus, but to my nervous eyes they seemed supremely indifferent to the entertainment I had laid out for them. There were a few moans and groans as some of the youngsters expressed reservations about an alien classical dance, which was sure to be a far cry from the entertainment of their choice.

The Kalakshetra atmosphere was the first brownie point I scored with my visitors. They found it beautiful and remarkably peaceful and quiet in the heart of our urban chaos. The Spartan classrooms and the lovely young ladies only strengthened their positive feelings. The crowning glory was provided by the impressive performance by the young students. The cricketers were totally bowled over, particularly by the dancers' obviously high level of physical fitness.

Then came the climax of the morning. My reply to Richard Hadlee's query about the cricketers' proposed striptease act was that a bare torso was absolutely mandatory for men in Indian classical dance. What followed was an authentic display of the Maori *hakka*, complete with high jumps and war cries. The threesome including the Marshall twins, James and Hamish, received a standing ovation from the small crowd.

More groans and growls of protest prefixed our next stop, but the Hadlee brothers did not offer the cricketers the choice of opting out. The team trooped reluctantly into Vidya Sagar, at Kotturpuram. My friends there were thrilled to receive the cricketers as most of their wards were crazy about cricket. Unfortunately, the air-conditioner did not work, or the hall where we met the kids had none, and a very warm, sweaty session of interaction followed. The children, however, were unfazed by such minor inconveniences and put up quite a riveting show of entertainment. The crowning piece was a bright little speech by a seven-year-old. One-day cricket was very similar to life, he told us. Just as the batsman enjoyed great freedom in the first 15 overs, helped by the field restrictions, in life, too, children enjoyed freedom for the first 15 years, before the cares of life caught up with them, he said. The cricketers gave him a standing ovation and were visibly moved by the spirit and courage of the children. To a man, they came up to me and thanked me for giving them one of the most memorable days of their lives.

'WHAT DO THEY KNOW OF MUSIC?'

As the editor of a leading magazine on the classical performing arts, I lead a life far removed from the excitement of cricket. I find that my cricket experience has been a blessing in this completely new field. As almost every artist is interested in cricket, I am at least occasionally at an advantage. Cricket opens doors!

Carnatic vocalist and film singer P Unnikrishnan is a good sportsman who continues to play recreational tennis but also someone whose cricket is of a very decent standard. Some years ago our paths in these two fields intersected. Unni and I played quite a bit of cricket and less tennis together. He is of course much younger than I, so much younger that I have also played cricket with his father Radhakrishnan, who, besides being a qualified Ayurvedic physician, was a pretty useful batsman in the 1950s and 60s, even into the seventies.

To cut a long story short, Unni's quite promising cricket career started when mine was already over, though I continued to play from memory, to enjoy the perverse pleasure of competing with men half my age. By the time we first played against each other, I for Alwarpet CC and he for Madras CC, I had heard him on the concert platform, starting with a recital at the wedding reception of a fellow cricketer. I still remember the pride with which Radha informed me that the singer of the evening was his son, and the resemblance I noticed in the early Unni voice to that of Yesudas. Later, by some strange quirk, I was invited to first play for and later captain the Parry's Recreation Club when well into my 40s, though I had nothing to do with the Parry group. Unni was by then an executive in the company, and a leading member of the cricket team. During one of our matches, I told Unni how much I had enjoyed listening to "his first film song" (a fairly straightforward rendering of Venkata Kavi's Alai payude in a Malayalam film). Unni's response was quietly modest: "I've sung many film songs already, Ram."

My most memorable Unnikrishnan experience was to follow in about a year's time after this episode. I had organized a chamber concert of his at home (the second or third such occasion) one Sunday, when we came to know that the programme was clashing with a league game for Parry. As captain, I could not relieve Unni from the match, nor did he, as a competitive sportsman, want any such privilege. I toyed with the idea of postponing the concert, but too many people had already accepted our invitation with great anticipation, as Unni was at the very peak of his popularity. Domestic discord was a serious possibility, even a probability, if I did anything so foolish as to call off the performance.

To complicate matters more, it turned out Unni had a wedding concert at Nagercoil the previous night.

The match was at distant Pallavaram, at the English Electric ground, which proved to be a small mercy, as Unni was able to get off the district bus (after travelling all night) very near the ground. I lost the toss, and the good soldier he was, Unni fielded in the hot sun with the rest of the team. He was a dependable no. 3 batsman, perhaps our highest run-getter that year, but I asked him to open the innings—a role to which he was not a complete stranger—so that he could go home early and rest after his batting. Unfortunately, Unni was dismissed for zero or thereabouts, but simply refused to go home, waiting for us to complete the match in the evening. We happened to win the match, so we all went home in a happy frame of mind, but poor Unni had to go all the way to his Royapettah home, shower, change and come to my Kottivakkam home on the East Coast Road. We started the concert half an hour late, but it was a superb performance by Mr. Dependable.

Unni was not quite the first professional classical musician to have played competitive cricket I personally knew. That honour went to the late Ravi Kichlu of the Hindustani vocal duo, the Kichlu Brothers. Ravi often entertained me with snatches of *alap* standing next to me in the slips on the maidan of Calcutta. We were both playing for Rajasthan Club in the 1969-70 league season. But here, I almost forgot wicket keeper Sivakumar my Mylapore Recreation Club teammate, *mridanga vidwan*, son of DK Pattammal and father of well known vocalist Nithyashree Mahadevan.

At the national level, I knew or knew of a few musically inclined cricketers. The great Vijay Manjrekar was a good singer and so is his son Sanjay. Padmakar Shivalkar was another Bombay player who gave vocal performances on stage. The late ML Jaisimha, under whose captaincy I played for Hyderabad in the Ranji Trophy, had an impressive voice with which he belted out popular songs. He brought the roof down at a restaurant at Bangkok back in 1978 when the house orchestra handed him the microphone and he gave a few lusty samples of his Frank Sinatra repertoire and Louis Armstrong's *When the saints go marching in.*

Also seated at the same table was an accomplished vocalist in Shanti Hiranand, disciple and biographer of Begum Akhtar and sister-in-law of former India captain GS Ramchand. Mr and Mrs Ramchand were the gracious hosts that evening and Jaisimha, Murtuza Ali Baig and I the lucky guests during a Hyderabad Blues cricket tour (Thailand has some cricket and on our way back from Australia, we played a game at The Royal Bangkok Sports Club). We even got Ms Hiranand to sing a song for us.

Jai was the life and soul of the party during cocktails after my brother V Sivaramakrishnan's benefit match, which was between two teams of star-studded veteran India players of the past. He completely replaced the band of the evening at the Connemara that night. This was soon after my daughter Akhila had sung some family favourites of Beatles vintage. My own personal highlight was to be part of an improbable trio of MLJ, Sunil Gavaskar and I. Only cacophony resulted, but nobody in the audience seemed to mind.

MAK 'Tiger' Pataudi, whose last season for Hyderabad in the Ranji Trophy was my first, had a keen ear for music, and, according to some of his close associates, could play the tabla. I had this habit of whistling constantly in the dressing room, and Tiger caught me whistling a song from the film *Jahan Ara*—which had some exquisite music by Madan Mohan—and gave a stentorian interpretation of *Phir wohi shaam* in sharp contrast to Talat Mahmood's dulcet tones. Another verse he was fond of bellowing in a voice that threatened to shatter the windows went *Gulshan, gulshan, shola-e-gul ki.* I was intrigued and curious to know the rest of the song, but I had to wait for quite sometime before I solved the mystery. It turned out, of course, to be the opening line of a gentle, romantic Mehdi Hassan ghazal, the first I was to hear from that master of the genre.

The ubiquitous two-in-one dominated the recreational needs of the cricketers of the 1970s, and thanks to the great leg-spinner BS Chandrasekhar, the Hindi film songs of Mukesh were the most popular choice of a whole generation of cricketers. Chandra must have been all of 18 or 19 when he first heard a Mukesh song wafting in out of transistor radios in the crowd during a match. *Dil jalta hai* I believe was the song to cast a spell on him, and he actually mistook Mukesh's voice for KL Saigal's. That Chandra became a diehard fan and later a close friend of Mukesh is part of the cricket lore of the period.

After more than thirty years of competitive cricket, I have been writing on music and editing a magazine on the performing arts during the last decade or so. People ask me to explain how a cricketer like me took to writing on the arts, and I tell them that I was dropped on my head as a child—which sometimes causes startled, incredulous responses. The real answer is that if you were born in the Madras of the 1940s in a middle-class brahmin family (even if you are a bad brahmin like me), chances are that you grew up in the midst of much music and much cricket. This is probably still true of most households that come from similar backgrounds. Add to that a love of language and you can end up writing on both music and cricket, as I did after failing at several other vocations!

There have been a few—though all too few—great writers through history whose gaze focused on these two great arts and sciences. You may raise an eyebrow or two at my inclusion of cricket in the category of art and science, but you would then be indirectly doing that to possibly the first writer to excel at both—Sir Neville Cardus, who described the batting of Sir Garfield Sobers thus: *His immense power is lightened by a rhythm which has in it as little obvious propulsion as a movement of music by Mozart.*

According to writer, broadcaster and biographer Robin Daniels, Cardus believed in the power of great art to change lives from within. “Genius is a miracle to be revered whether in fashion or not,” Cardus said, and he did revere genius in cricket as well as music. Daniels also said that Cardus fought the good fight for Gustav Mahler when the composer was largely unknown. He rated him as a great critic “because he combines deep feeling and imagination with an eye that saw symbolically”.

Cardus was known to exaggerate, was even accused of writing on matches and concerts he did not attend, but he brought literature to cricket writing as much as to music criticism. “To go to a cricket match for nothing but cricket is as though a man were to go into an inn for nothing but drink,” he said

He described CB Fry, the great English all rounder, as “a national gallery and a theatre and a forum”. Of the inimitable KS Ranjitsinhji, the Jam Saheb of Nawanagar, he said “he never played a Christian stroke in his life”, in praise of his delightfully unorthodox ways.

One of the most remarkable personalities of English cricket was the radio commentator John Arlott, the man responsible for Cape Coloured cricketer Basil D’Oliveira’s entry into English cricket and eventual ascent to world fame. Arlott had an unconventional voice for BBC, “a sound like Uncle Tom Cobleigh reading Neville Cardus to faraway natives”, according to Welsh poet Dylan Thomas, his drinking buddy.

Arlott was a most unusual all rounder whose career included stints as a policeman, in a mental hospital, as a wine-taster, poet and hymnist, and above all a humanist of the best kind. He was the epitome of the ultimate cricket person whose breadth of vision extended far beyond the boundary. Did not CLR James, the West Indian author of Beyond a Boundary say, "What do they know of cricket, who only cricket know?"

And indeed may we ask, "What do they know of music, who only music know?"

IN CONCLUSION

"Mr Ramnarayan must have his coffee." So began the first lines of the first draft of this book, when I began to put pen to paper—literally—over 30 years ago, after a long cricket conversation at the Besant Nagar residence of my friends Parimala and Joe, with Joe and his guest Pradeep of Orient Longman. At the end of it, Pradeep insisted that I write my cricket stories. Within a week or so, I filled some 30 pages of a ruled notebook in one continuous burst of spontaneous writing, but life interrupted that, my maiden, literary endeavour—by a mere couple of decades. Even this final fling has taken nearly ten years of intermittent writing, mainly because I really did not believe I had a worthwhile story to tell. Now that it is done, it is up to you to judge.

Many circumstances conspired to make me the strange animal I am, starting with the early influences of my father's cricket-crazy family. In parallel, I was also exposed to Carnatic or south Indian classical music. My mother Rukmini is a trained vocalist, whose young voice as I was growing up was as impressive as that of any performing musician. Vacations at my grandfather's home in Trivandrum were occasions for much family community singing, and some of it brushed off on my siblings and me.

There was never any shortage of music at home, and I actually joined my sister and cousin in a class taught by a teacher who came home most evenings. Though I was interested in the lessons, I found them very annoying as the teacher arrived at exactly the same time as our evening cricket game. The result was the premature death of Project Carnatic Music, though I maintained a lively interest in Hindi film music, thanks to the lead my cousins showed, *Binaca Geetmala* and *Vividh Bharati.* One of my cousins ran a circulating library, a collection of second-hand novels, illustrated classics and comics as well as thrillers in Tamil (of the Tamilvanan kind) and English, and that started me on my reading career.

My uncle Pattabhi's cricket scrapbook was a gold mine. He had left his treasures behind when migrating to the USA as a student—he later became a UNDP official, and did not return to India for decades. His collection included old editions of the Wisden almanac and daily reports in The Hindu of several Test series in India and abroad. For the ardent young cricket fan I was, summer vacations were heaven on earth as I curled up with this secret cache of unforgettable cricket reports and photographs. Every Test match nation figured in the collection, as did trivia of every description. A rare photograph for instance was of no. 10 Chandu Sarwate (124 not out) and no. 11 Shute Banerjee (121) posing in front of the giant scoreboard at Surrey reading India all out 454, and last wicket fell at 205. I remember a wrong report of Mohammad

Nissar's death in the Quetta earthquake, followed by a correction a few days later, admitting a case of mistaken identity.

In addition to my parents' encouragement of all our extracurricular interests which included films, books, music and theatre, I came under the influence of some interesting cousins, friends and teachers during my teen years. Hero worship played an important part in my ever-growing range of interests. I simply read every book my heroes of the day read. From George Bernard Shaw to Bertrand Russell, Terence Rattigan to Eugene O'Neill, the Beatles to Ravi Shankar, Naushad to Madan Mohan, Stephen Leacock to PG Wodehouse, not to mention cricket literature of every kind, I grew to love a wonderful assortment of authors, and some of the most delightful film music of all time, with of course disastrous consequences for my academic reading.

Through it all, love of music was a constant, if not often advertised part of my life, nourished by the atmosphere at home and in the extended family. Marriage in 1970 to Gowri, a granddaughter of Kalki, the celebrated novelist-music-and-dance critic-political commentator-freedom fighter, and grandniece of MS Subbulakshmi and trained musician herself (Gowri is today a playwright and her mother Anandhi was a dancer and dance teacher, too), meant a deepening of interest in the performing arts, and several opportunities to listen to great music and watch the Kalakshetra art festival annually. My uncle Dr N Pattabhi

Raman—the same uncle Pattabhi of scrapbook fame—came back to Madras and launched Sruti magazine in October 1983, with Gowri and I his chief helpers in the early days of the magazine, I as a part-time resource after hours from my day job at the TVS group.

It was in 1992 that I first met Mr S Muthiah. It was the major turning point in my life beyond cricket, after my attempts to be an entrepreneur ran into heavy weather. In addition to editing the fortnightly *Madras Musings,* Muthiah was busy writing several books of city and corporate history, besides editing many more books for numerous publishers. Starting with proofreading *Athletic Gold*, a remarkable blueprint for Indian athletics by the late Olympian Eric Prabhakar, I went on to assist Muthiah in editing and writing books for the next few years. I also helped him with *Madras Musings* on a regular basis. Followed a stint in the corporate communications function in The Sanmar Group, where I gained experience in bringing out the house magazine, managing the group's website, publishing brochures, booklets, annual reports and the like, as well as making corporate films. When I retired from the group, I took up three jobs at the same time: editing *Sruti*, which Sanmar took over four years after Pattabhi Raman's death, editing the English imprints of the publishing house New Horizon Media, including Indian writing in translation, and teaching Language and Style at the Asian College of Journalism.

I have tried to explain how I ended up writing on both cricket and the performing arts. Perhaps my earlier explanation—that I was dropped on my head as a child—was a more convincing one. Whatever the truth, I am not complaining. How many people can claim the friendship of some of the greatest cricketers and most accomplished musicians of India as I can? How can I ever forget the evening I spent listening to the fantastic anecdotes of Sir Garfield Sobers at Madras Cricket Club, or the other, entirely different, experience of listening at close quarters to MS Subbulakshmi and Semmangudi Srinivasa Iyer together?

With my whole family—my wife Gowri, daughter Akhila, son Abhinav and I—involved in writing, teaching, theatre, music and dance, it has been a blessed life. And if and when I feel I have had a surfeit of it all, I can switch to watching, reading, talking cricket. Lucky me.

ACKNOWLEDGEMENTS

Many friends, my captive audience from time to time for my cricket stories real and fictional, encouraged me over the decades to put this book together.

These include my students at the Asian College of Journalism, my willing guinea pigs, probably because they preferred listening to anecdotes to my old-fashioned lectures on writing.

My cousins G Balachandran and S Subramaniam, as well as my wife Gowri, daughter Akhila, and son Abhinav, have been strong pillars of support, besides planting the idea in my head in the first place that I could be a writer.

My mother Rukmini Venkatraman blesses all I do.

My author-illustrator friend Krishna Shastri Devulapalli constantly egged me on to write this book.

Another catalyst, my brother Sivaramakrishnan, has also provided corrective feedback whenever I have tended to stray from facts owing to an occasionally faulty memory.

Senior journalist 'Charukesi' Viswanathan has read the text at various stages and made helpful suggestions.

My former teammate MN Ravikumar has been

of invaluable support, especially in sourcing photographs. So has senior photographer D Krishnan. The cover photograph was shot by the late KN Chari of *The Hindu* in November 1976.

The appreciation and critical inputs I have received from such friends as Nasar Azam, Madras Chandrasekar, Krishna Shastri Devulapalli, Prakash Dharmarajan, Subbarayudu G Kameswara, Ashok Kaushik, Khurshid, Prasanna Kumar, Gita Nair, Sudha Prakash, Raja Ramanathan, Anbu Selvan, Nikhil Sivaramakrishnan, Venkat Subramaniam, Arun Venugopal and others for several blog posts directly or indirectly connecting to this book have helped me clear my thoughts on what should go into it.

The profiles of spin bowlers in this book were expansions or adaptations of some of my blog posts that appeared in Cricinfo and those of my former Hyderabad teammates were based on my column in the city portal Chennai Online.

My employers *The Sanmar Group*—and in particular, Mr N Sankar, Mr N Kumar and Mr Vijay Sankar, genuine sports lovers all—have always taken an active interest in my cricket writing.

Sambit Bal and his young team at Cricinfo who brought me back to cricket writing have been great motivators. Dileep Premachandran and Anand Vasu of Wisden India have been equally good for my morale.

Publishing consultant N Madhavan and my journalistic senior S Muthiah pointed me in the direction of Westland at a time when I was unsure in my search for a publisher.

Veteran cricket commentators Harsha Bhogle and Suresh Menon have done me proud with their affectionate forewords. They bring credit to their tribe by recognising honest toilers like me just as they extol the stars.

E Ravikumar has provided consistent office support throughout the writing of the book.

Finally, my incredible siblings—Nagan, Sarada, Sivaramakrishnan, Vijayalakshmi, and Sarojini—and their loved ones, and my superb cousins have supported me in all my activities, even the more foolish ones.

This book would have been impossible without all those I have mentioned here and some I must have inadvertently omitted. Many, many thanks to all of them.

This book has become reality thanks to its ready acceptance by Gautam Padmanabhan and Westland, though I wish I had approached them when Gautam's father KS Padmanabhan was still alive. I know he would have approved the project. I must also thank Gautam for entrusting Karthik Venkatesh with the task of editing it. Karthik is an author's best friend, helpful, unobtrusive, reliable. It's been a pleasure to work with Westland.